SUNNYLANDS

SUNNYLANDS

Art and Architecture of the Annenberg Estate

in Rancho Mirage, California

Edited by DAVID G. DE LONG

Foreword by KATHLEEN HALL JAMIESON

Afterword by ANNE D'HARNONCOURT

PENN

UNIVERSITY OF PENNSYLVANIA PRESS

Philadelphia

Copyright © 2010 The Annenberg Foundation Trust at Sunnylands.
All rights reserved. Except for brief quotations used for purposes of review or
scholarly citation, none of this book may be reproduced in any form by any means
without written permission from the publisher.

Published by
University of Pennsylvania Press
Philadelphia, Pennsylvania 19104-4112

Book design by JUDITH STAGNITTO ABBATE / WWW.ABBATEDESIGN.COM

Printed in Spain on acid-free paper
10 9 8 7 6 5 4 3 2 1

Library of Congress Cataloging-in-Publication Data

Sunnylands : art and architecture of the Annenberg estate in Rancho Mirage, California
/ edited by David G. De Long ; foreword by Kathleen Hall Jamieson ; afterword by
Anne d'Harnoncourt.
       p. cm.
   Includes bibliographical references and index.
   ISBN 978-0-8122-4161-7 (alk. paper)
   1. Annenberg, Walter H., 1908–2002—Art collections. 2. Annenberg, Lee—Art
collections. 3. Art—Private collections—California—Rancho Mirage. 4. Annenberg,
Walter H., 1908–2002—Homes and haunts—California—Rancho Mirage. 5. Annenberg,
Lee—Homes and haunts—California—Rancho Mirage. 6. Jones, A. Quincy (Archie
Quincy), 1913–1979. 7. Sunnylands (Rancho Mirage, Calif.) 8. Rancho Mirage
(Calif.)—Buildings, structures, etc. I. De Long, David Gilson, 1939– II. Title: Art and
architecture of the Annenberg estate in Rancho Mirage, California.
   N5220.A64S86 2009
   728.809794`97—dc22
                                        2009005894

CONTENTS

FOREWORD | *Kathleen Hall Jamieson*   ix

THE DESIGN OF SUNNYLANDS | *David G. De Long*   1

THE MODERN SCULPTURE | *Suzanne Glover Lindsay*   67

SELECTED PAINTINGS AND WORKS ON PAPER | *Gwendolyn DuBois Shaw*   83

THE STEUBEN GLASS COLLECTION | *M. J. Madigan*   93

DECORATIVE ARTS | *Donna Corbin*   105

A MAYA FIGURINE IN JAINA STYLE | *Jeremy A. Sabloff*   121

TWO HINDU TEMPLE DOOR PANELS WITH SILVER REPOUSSÉ | *Michael W. Meister*   125

CHINESE ART | *Virginia Bower*   129

AFTERWORD | *Anne d'Harnoncourt*   157

NOTES   160

LIST OF CONTRIBUTORS   177

INDEX   179

ACKNOWLEDGMENTS   184

Walter and Leonore Annenberg, September 1993, at The Regent Beverly Wilshire, Beverly Hills, California (Photograph by Charles Bush Studio, www.CharlesBush.com)

FOREWORD

Named Sunnylands after the summer retreat of Walter Annenberg's father, Moses, the Annenberg estate is situated in the Coachella Valley of the Colorado Desert in Rancho Mirage, California. Long before emigrants from the East put down roots in the area, the native people of the desert considered this serene region to be holy. Sacred hot springs of the Cahuilla people, for example, were located nearby.

The recorded history of the area dates to 1542 when Carlos V, King of Spain, claimed the territory that now includes Sunnylands. A number of countries oversaw the land during the intervening centuries. When Mexico seceded from Spain in 1821, the area, then known as Alta California, became part of Mexico. Two and a half decades later, the 1848 Treaty of Guadalupe Hidalgo transferred it to California. That state officially entered the union in 1850.

Just over a century later, in 1963, the publisher, diplomat, and philanthropist Walter Annenberg (1908–2002) purchased the bare expanse on which he and his wife, Leonore (1918–2009), built Sunnylands. Set between the San Jacinto and Santa Rosa Mountains, Sunnylands today includes eleven man-made lakes, a golf course, and hundreds of olive trees.

The house and its connected rooms, designed by the Los Angeles architect A. Quincy Jones and furnished by William Haines and Ted Graber, is nearly 30,000 square feet in size. It took three years to build the elegant, two-hundred-acre estate that is the subject of this book.

Walter and Lee Annenberg created Sunnylands as a sanctuary. After the couple transformed acres of sand into a place that their friends likened to Eden, Lee Annenberg commented that, "The design of Sunnylands was intended to bring in the light and the view and the gardens."[1] Walter Annenberg noted, "The ancient Chinese philosophers believed that reverence for the landscape was the highest ideal of life. . . . Sunnylands has come to represent that in our lives."[2]

Part of what gives Sunnylands its singular aesthetic is the striking way in which the California modernist architecture of A. Quincy Jones embraces art from dissimilar and sometimes distant periods. Sensitively situated within the open expanse of the house and its terraces and bathed in desert light are bronzes by Auguste Rodin, sculptures and optical art by Jean Arp, Alberto Giacometti, and Yaacov Agam, paintings by Pablo Picasso, Rembrandt Peale, and Andrew Wyeth, Mayan tomb statuary, Ming dynasty *cloisonné* enamels, and exquisitely crafted Steuben glass. Against the backdrop of soaring windows, coffered ceilings, and fluid spaces, Ted Graber and William Haines set sofas, chairs, and tables that are pieces of art in their own right. In a palette rich in shades of pink and green, the beauty of the house is continuous as it streams from the interior to the exterior, drawing in the oasis of lawns and lakes designed by Quincy Jones with Dick Wilson and Rolla Wilhite. In this book the reader will find photographs of the house and its artwork, and accounts by scholars designed to heighten one's appreciation of the Sunnylands experience.

Sunnylands conveys a strong reminder that a home is an expression of the people who conceive it, build it, love it, celebrate holidays, birthdays, and anniversaries in it, and relish the other important moments in their lives within its walls. For more than forty years, Sunnylands was the West Coast home of the Annenbergs. During part of that time, from 1969 to 1974, Walter Annenberg served his country as ambassador to the Court of St. James's. Lee Annenberg was also called to public service and represented the country as U.S. chief of protocol during the first year of Ronald Reagan's presidency. They are among a handful of couples in American history who have both held the rank of ambassador. Mementos of their service are preserved at Sunnylands in what the family calls the Room of Memories.

The Sunnylands estate is also rich in historical significance. Shortly after his election in 1968, Richard Nixon stayed at Sunnylands as he assembled his cabinet. And he drafted his 1974 State of the Union address there as well.

In 1979 when the sister and mother of the exiled Shah of Iran were being tormented by hostile demonstrators, the Annenbergs invited them to stay at Sunnylands. As a gesture of thanks the Shah gave the Annenbergs a silver box now on view in the main house.

President-elect and Mrs. Reagan and many members of their newly appointed cabinet rang in the first New Year's after his 1980 election at a black-tie dinner at the Annenberg estate (see fig. 64). It was at Sunnylands that President Reagan signed the draft of the North American Free Trade Agreement (NAFTA).

Standing on a poolside patio, in 1990 Walter and Lee Annenberg announced their historic $50 million gift to the United Negro College Fund. At that time, the gift was the largest single contribution ever made to benefit historically black colleges and universities.

That same year, the Annenbergs hosted an official dinner given by United States President George H. W. Bush in honor of the Prime Minister of Japan, Toshiki Kaifu. To commemorate the dinner, the city of Rancho Mirage named Sunnylands a historic site.

In early 2004, 2007, and again in early 2009, Supreme Court justices Sandra Day O'Connor, Stephen Breyer, and Anthony Kennedy met with Lee Annenberg at the estate. During these sojourns at Sunnylands, they helped shape the programming for high school students on the Constitution that is sponsored by the Annenberg Foundation Trust at Sunnylands.

Shortly after Arnold Schwarzenegger was elected governor of California in December 2003, he and thirty California members of the U.S. House of Representatives and both of the state's U.S. senators met in Rancho Mirage at a Sunnylands Trust-sponsored retreat on California's future.

The Annenbergs' beautiful desert home also has been the site of many memorable social occasions, including New Year's celebrations with family and friends and the weddings of Lee's daughter Elizabeth and grandson Howard. The marriage ceremony of the Annenberg friend and neighbor Frank Sinatra took place in the atrium at Sunnylands. Witnesses to that July 1976 celebration included then-presidential hopeful Ronald Reagan and his wife, Nancy, Mr. and Mrs. Gregory Peck, and Rosalind Russell.

The Sunnylands guest books constitute a registry of the individuals who shaped the culture, arts, and politics of the second half of the twentieth century. The consensus telegraphed by their remarks is noteworthy. On February 14, 1995, for example, one entry contains the signature of President Bill

Clinton. "Thanks for your hospitality to me and my family. Valentine's Day 1995," wrote the Democratic incumbent. The capitalized word "AMEN!" jumps from the adjoining page. Seconding Clinton's sentiments was the immediate past president, George H. W. Bush.

Preserved in the guest books are the signatures of other presidents, including Eisenhower, Nixon, Ford, Reagan, and George W. Bush; and first ladies from Mamie Dowd Eisenhower and Pat Nixon to Betty Ford, Rosalynn Carter, Nancy Reagan, Hillary Clinton, and Laura Bush. Royalty is represented, from Queen Elizabeth and Princes Charles, Andrew, and Edward to Princess Grace of Monaco and Prince Bernhard of the Netherlands. Represented, too, are heads of government such as British prime ministers John Major and Margaret Thatcher, and Israeli Prime Minister Benjamin Netanyahu, as well as U.S. secretaries of state Henry Kissinger and George Shultz, Federal Reserve Chairman Alan Greenspan, and generals from Al Haig and William Westmoreland to Colin Powell. Signatories also include senators Paul Laxalt, Howard Baker, Elizabeth Dole, John Danforth, and John Kerry (accompanied by his wife, Teresa Heinz); and governors Pete Wilson and Arnold Schwarzenegger.

The guest books are rich in ambassadors' names, including Robin Renwick and David Manning, of Great Britain, and U.S. ambassadors William Luers (Czechoslovakia, 1983–1986, and Venezuela, 1978–1982), William Wilson (The Vatican, 1981–1986), Leonard Firestone (Belgium, 1974–1977), Charles Price (Belgium, 1981–1983, and the Court of St. James's, 1983–1989), and John Gavin (Mexico, 1981–1986). And cabinet members Alexander Haig, John Connally, Caspar Weinberger, and William Cohen are represented, in addition to political leaders of both parties, from Democrat Bob Strauss to Republican Anne Armstrong. Here, too, are greetings from business leaders such as David Rockefeller, Justin Dart, John Whitehead, Steve Forbes, and Sam Walton; and philanthropists from Brooke Astor and Sharon Rockefeller to Bill and Melinda Gates.

Entertainment and cultural icons convey warm thanks, including James Stewart, Kirk Douglas, Dinah Shore, Merv Griffin, Frank Sinatra, Rosalind Russell, Helen Hayes, Red Skelton, Bob Hope, Kitty Carlisle Hart, Mary Martin, Hal Wallis, Mike Nichols, Andrew Lloyd Webber, Art Linkletter, Truman Capote, Eppie Lederer (Ann Landers), and Oscar de la Renta. The directors of the nation's great museums and libraries who lavish praise on the Annenberg art include Vartan Gregorian, of the New York Public Library, J. Carter Brown and Earl Powell III, of the National Gallery of Art, Anne d'Harnoncourt, of the Philadelphia Museum of Art, Philippe de Montebello and Thomas Hoving, of the Metropolitan Museum of Art, and John Walsh, of the Getty Museum. In addition, world-renowned conductors Zubin Mehta and Christoph Eschenbach express their appreciation and thanks.

The guest books also reflect the world of communications, with the signatures of publishers such as Norman Chandler, of the *Los Angeles Times*, and Donald Graham, of the *Washington Post*; journalists from NBC's Andrea Mitchell to ABC's Barbara Walters, Diane Sawyer, and Peter Jennings; and government officials including former FCC chairman Newton Minow (who helped Walter Annenberg found the Annenberg CPB education project), and Charles Wick, former director of the United States Information Agency.

The letters preserved in the Sunnylands Room of Memories brim with expressions of gratitude for the Annenbergs' hospitality, exclamations about the beauty of the landscape, and evidence that time spent at Sunnylands created lasting memories. "Yours is without doubt one of the world's most magnificent houses," noted President Richard Nixon. "But what is more important, it is without doubt one of the world's greatest homes." "Nancy and I are sorry we can't be with you," wrote President Ronald Reagan in birthday greetings to Walter Annenberg on February 25, 1983. "Sorry, h—l, we're desolate and it doesn't do any good to say we're with you in spirit. Washington isn't Sunnylands." On New Year's Eve weekend in January 1988, first lady Nancy Reagan reported in the Annenberg guest book, "Home Again!"

Her feelings were similar to those of her husband's successor. "Well, here I am in the Oval Office. I should be thinking about the budget resolution, how to help Nicaragua's democracy, or the anti-drug fight," wrote President George H. W. Bush in a letter of March 1990. "But no. I'm thinking about our time with you—from that opening dinner for [Japanese Prime Minister] Kaifu all the way til that lucky 4-iron to the pin on 18. Some classic great time!" After another visit in 1990, President Bush wrote, "Thank you for hosting that special important dinner." The Bushes returned regularly to Sunnylands after leaving the White House. "You make the Bushes feel like family," noted the former president in March 2004. "Love George Bush old #41." "I love Sunnylands almost as much as you do," Prime Minister Margaret Thatcher wrote to Walter and Lee Annenberg in 1998. "It is so lovely and unique."

To share the joy that they and their guests took in its scenic beauty, architecture, and art, the Annenbergs specified that when both of them had died (he passed away in 2002, she in 2009), they would leave the estate to the nation by placing it under the protection of the Annenberg Foundation Trust at Sunnylands. Their gift specifies that at the estate, the Trust will convene:

leaders of the United States to focus on ways to improve the functioning of the three branches of government, the press, and public schools;

educators to determine how to better teach about the Constitution and the fundamental principles of democracy;

leaders of major social institutions including learned societies to determine how these institutions can better serve the public and the public good;

scholars to address ways to improve the well-being of the nation in such areas as media, education, and philanthropy; and

conduct tours for the public to inform them about the educational and historical significance of Sunnylands, its architecture and art.

Sunnylands is not only an exemplar of California midcentury modernism and the home of a remarkable collection of art and memories, but also one of Walter and Leonore Annenberg's many gifts to the nation.

KATHLEEN HALL JAMIESON, PH.D.
Program Director, Annenberg
Foundation Trust at Sunnylands

Trellis outside living area, main house (Photograph by Graydon Wood, April 2006).

1 | *Night view from arrival court to main house entrance (Photograph by Graydon Wood, December 2006).*

THE DESIGN OF SUNNYLANDS

David G. De Long

Great houses teach us about architecture and design. They show us how buildings can relate to gardens and impart a stronger sense of place to even the most expansive of planned landscapes. They hold collections that capture our interest, collections displayed in ways that enable us to see art in new ways. They present backdrops for notable events and provide retreats for renowned guests. Most important, they portray their occupants in ways no other media can, enhancing admired lives through their special settings (fig. 1).

Sunnylands was built as a winter retreat near Palm Springs by Walter and Leonore Annenberg, yet in the years since its completion in 1966 it has become something grander than its initial mandate might suggest (fig. 2). When designs were begun in 1963, the Annenbergs were already regarded as leaders of one of America's most prominent families, and in the years that followed, their stature, too, grew greater, so that for many Sunnylands has come to symbolize the ultimate American dream.

The lives and many accomplishments of the extended Annenberg family have been detailed in several biographical accounts.[1] Walter Annenberg's father had immigrated to the United States from Germany in 1885 and moved to Milwaukee, Wisconsin, in 1907. By 1908, when Walter Annenberg was born, his father had begun to prosper, and by 1920, when the family relocated to Great Neck, Long Island, he had begun to accumulate great wealth. He held major positions with William Randolph Hearst's publications, but also began to acquire newspapers of his own, including, in 1936, the *Philadelphia Inquirer*, which became a major focus for his son's own work. By the mid-1960s, when Sunnylands was completed, Walter Annenberg had become the owner of a vast media empire.

Leonore Cohn was born in New York in 1918, but her mother died when she was only seven years old, and four years later her father arranged for her to live with his younger brother in Los Angeles. There she could enjoy the benefits of a more settled life. The uncle with whom she stayed was Harry Cohn, the head

2 | *Aerial view of Sunnylands, 1979 (Photograph by Bruce Dale/ National Geographic Image Collection).*

of Columbia Pictures, and the atmosphere must have been stimulating. Harry Cohn's wife, Rose, took an active role in raising the girl, and Leonore (known to her friends as Lee) remained in California for college, graduating from Stanford University in 1940.[2]

She met Walter Annenberg in 1950, while visiting a close friend in Palm Beach, and the two were married the following year, both with children from previous marriages.[3] They moved into Inwood, a large, elegant house in the Philadelphia suburb of Wynnewood, a home that Annenberg had acquired in 1941. Its comforts were many, and in those early years they began what became a renowned art collection. Yet Lee missed the mild climate of Southern California, and the Annenbergs began to spend extended periods of time in Palm Springs.

Palm Springs was—and remains—no ordinary place. Members of the Hollywood movie industry had discovered the small desert town in the 1920s, attracted by its salubrious climate and by dramatic views to surrounding mountains: Mount San Jacinto to the west, Mount San Gorgonio to the northwest, and the Santa Rosa Mountains to the southwest. Early visitors were also drawn by its location—only two hours by car from Los Angeles. People of business from more distant locations soon followed, but Hollywood stars remained the most visible residents. At first the palatial winter homes they built for themselves drew from images of Spanish colonial architecture, a favorite mode of design in California in the years between the two world wars. But after World War II such romanticism gave way to modernism, and gradually Palm Springs became a showcase of mid-century modern architecture.[4]

By the time the Annenbergs began their winter sojourns in Palm Springs, well-known architects had established flourishing practices in the area. Among them were Albert Frey (1903–1998), who had worked for Le Corbusier in France, and E. Stewart Williams (1909–2005), who designed large houses with particular responsiveness to the desert setting. Famous architects from outside the area were also given commissions, such as Richard Neutra (1892–1970), whose winter

retreat of 1946 for department store owner Edgar Kaufmann has become a modernist icon. Even more alluring in the 1950s were the residents themselves, including, at one time or another, Lucille Ball, Jack Benny, Bing Crosby, Kirk Douglas, Clark Gable, Cary Grant, William Holden, Bob Hope, Harpo Marx, William Powell, Randolph Scott, Dinah Shore, Red Skelton, Frank Sinatra, and Jack Warner, among others.[5]

The Annenbergs moved easily in these circles. Walter Annenberg had, in fact, begun to visit Palm Springs in the 1930s during outings from Los Angeles, where for a while he represented one of his father's newer acquisitions, *Screen Guide*.[6] His involvement with a movie-oriented publication facilitated his entry into Hollywood circles. Through her uncle, Leonore Annenberg had also come to know leading figures in Hollywood, so that for both of them Palm Springs was welcoming for its social connections.

At first the Annenbergs stayed in resorts such as La Quinta Hotel, located outside Palm Springs. Golf was a favorite pastime in the area, and they played at the Tamarisk Country Club. From its course they could see undeveloped land nearby; it held special appeal because of its views, and they soon decided to build their own home in that agreeable location.[7] What they would achieve embodies the elegant informality that characterizes the best of Palm Springs architecture.

Sensing the area's enormous potential for development, Walter Annenberg began acquiring land in the area as an investment. Then early in 1963 he bought land for their house, later adding to that purchase with more tracts. Philadelphia's *Sunday Bulletin* reported that he first acquired 197 acres for $899,500, a further 69 acres in 1967 for $238,000, and 658 more in 1968 for $1,661,500, thus amassing over 900 acres of what was then undeveloped desert.[8] This expansive site is located several miles southeast of the historic center of Palm Springs, at the intersection of what was known at the time as Rio del Sol and Wonder Palms Road, in an area identified then as Cathedral City. The streets have since been renamed as Bob Hope and Frank Sinatra drives, and the community is now known as Rancho Mirage.

THE DESIGNERS

The Annenbergs moved quickly to realize their project for a home, meeting with architects and designers early in 1963 to outline their ideas. Leonore Annenberg had no hesitation in identifying that team. She had seen the large, luxuriously appointed house of the investor Sidney Brody and his wife, Frances, in the Holmby Hills section of Los Angeles and wanted the same people to design hers. That home had been a collaboration between the architect Archibald Quincy Jones (1913–1979) and the interior designers William Haines (1900-1973) and Ted Graber (1920–2000). Haines and Graber, whom she had first met at the Brodys', had also done work for her friends Alfred and Betsy Bloomingdale, of the department store family, and they had remodeled the interiors of a new house for the film producer Armand Deutsch; his wife Harriet Simon was a college friend with whom she remained close and the one she was visiting in Palm Beach when she met Walter Annenberg in 1950.

The Annenbergs had attended the Deutsches' first dinner party in their newly transformed house in 1960, and it was at the Deutsches', in January 1963, even before their first purchase of land for the house was finalized, that they met with Haines to initiate their project. He, in turn, asked Quincy Jones to a later meeting with the Annenbergs; as he wrote to them, "I discussed with Quincy your desire of building a home of distinction and excitement and his interest was completely captured by the idea as is mine."[9] Thus the team that Leonore Annenberg favored was reassembled, with Haines in a key position.[10] The following month, Walter Annenberg contacted Jones himself, writing, "Although I have not had the pleasure of talking to you, I have been impressed with the work you have done, and, accordingly, if and when I acquire the Palm Springs area acreage, I should like to consider retaining you as an architect for the purpose of building a home on this property."[11]

Problems with clearing the title to the land were soon resolved, and the team met with their clients for the first time on April 11, 1963.[12] A few days later, Jones sent the Annenbergs a formal letter of agreement to provide his architectural services, adding cordially, "It was certainly a pleasure to have the meeting . . . with both of you and Mr. William Haines."[13] By then Haines and Jones had made their first visit to the site, on April 14.[14]

Although born in Kansas City, A. Quincy Jones, like Leonore Annenberg, had spent much of his childhood in Southern California, where he was reared by maternal grandparents following his own parents' divorce.[15] He studied architecture at the University of Washington and following graduation in 1936 returned to California, where he began working for architectural firms in Los Angeles. After serving with the U.S. Navy in World War II, he opened his own office in Los Angeles and in 1951 entered into partnership with Frederick Earl Emmons (1907–1998). Among those working for Jones was Harry Saunders, who had received his architecture degree from Texas A&M in 1948 and entered Jones's firm that same year. Saunders was made an associate of the firm in 1956 and later assumed much of the responsibility for design details at Sunnylands, assisting Jones in developing his ideas (as typical in architectural offices) and making frequent trips to the site to supervise work.[16] Saunders continued to be involved with work at Sunnylands even after he left the firm to open his own practice in 1966. The office itself continued as A. Quincy Jones and Associates after Emmons retired in 1969.

Although Jones had designed several large homes before receiving the Annenberg commission—for example, the Omar Fareed house of 1949 in Los Angeles—he had designed nothing that would compare with Sunnylands. Indeed, few had. Except for Sunnylands, he is better known for small, affordable houses that were uncompromisingly modern. Beginning in 1951, he and Emmons designed a series of prototypes for Eichler Homes, and by 1964 some 5,000 of these had been realized in new suburban developments, mostly in California and all financed by Joseph Eichler.[17] They are notable for their sleek detailing and open, informal plans, their generous walls of glass, their internal courtyards, and their integration of related gardens. The rising popularity of these houses in recent years attests to their appealing design.[18] In 1961, a commission to contribute to the prestigious Case Study House series further enhanced Jones's reputation as one of the nation's leading architects. This series, intended to promote modern design, comprised more than twenty proposals for single-family dwellings. The designs were meant to serve as prototypes for postwar America, and each architect was selected (and commissioned) by John Entenza, known for his ability to identify outstanding talent. He featured them in the pioneering magazine he founded and edited, *Arts & Architecture*, where they attracted much favorable attention. Jones's design, officially Case Study House No. 24, was the only one proposed for the Case Study program as part of a planned community, with 260 houses to have been built on 148 acres in semi-arid terrain.[19] Although unrealized, it incorporated elements that were to figure in Sunnylands: the use of earth berms, interior courts, and interior planting beds to effect close links with the surrounding landscape, as well as open interiors and a steel frame. Steel construction was relatively uncommon in affordable houses, which at the time were routinely framed in wood. Jones was also known for his academic appointments: he taught architectural design at the University of Southern California and later served as Dean of their School of Architecture from 1975 to 1978.

Unlike Jones, William S. Haines (1900–1973) had no professional training either as an architect or a designer, but he had considerable personal flair.[20] Betsy Bloomingdale, one of several influential clients and friends, reminisced when a biography of him, *Class Act*, was published, "We adored him and went to his home for small dinners with interesting people."[21] Looking back some forty years after the completion of Sunnylands, Leonore Annenberg recalled with animation that Haines was "fun to work with."[22]

Born in Virginia, Haines won a stage talent contest in 1922 and promptly moved to Los Angeles to begin his first career as an actor. By 1926 he was rated among the top ten Hollywood stars, and in 1930 he rose to the top of that list.[23] That same year he began to deal in antiques, sometimes advising clients how to use them in decorating their homes. He was soon so successful in his new enterprise that in 1933 he left acting to turn his full attention to it. Ted Graber, who had professional training as a designer, joined his firm in 1945, and it became known as William Haines Inc. In the years that followed, Haines shifted from a traditional to a modern vocabulary, which elicited positive response from his growing list of clients. By the time of the Annenberg commission, his patrons included a large number of Hollywood luminaries, among them Joan Crawford, Joan and Constance Bennett, Claudette Colbert, George Cukor, Jack Warner (head of Warner Brothers), and William and Edie Mayer Goetz (she was the daughter of Louis B. Mayer and her husband the studio chief of Twentieth Century-Fox).[24]

Critical to Haines's success was his belief in collaboration. He and Graber both recognized the importance of working from the beginning of a commission with a team including architects and landscape architects, and this they assembled at the very start for the Annenbergs. The Brody house, which had captivated Leonore Annenberg, was Haines's first collaboration with Jones; several more would follow. Jean Hayden Mathison, who held important positions within the Haines office from 1955 to 1985, also contributed to Sunnylands, as did a former employee, Michael Morrison.[25]

Haines's style has been characterized as Hollywood Regency, "having a glamour that required seemingly effortless balancing between the formal and the casual."[26] Peter Schifando, who took over the firm when Graber retired in 1989, wrote, "Haines redefined the way movie stars lived. He gave their residences a new look that was lighter, fresher, and more cosmopolitan than the heavy, dark rooms that were then the norm in the movie community. This grand style is now called Hollywood Regency because the look was inspired by early-nineteenth-century England."[27] His style has also been described as "at once grand and contemporary, opulent and easy."[28] Summarizing his accomplishments, one writer noted, "Haines was a brilliant designer and his contributions to the field are significant. . . . The anomaly of Haines's career, paired with his aesthetic ability, truly makes him synonymous with the region and its culture. . . . His highly personal, pedigreed aesthetic gave the industry and its moguls a style that is inseparable from Hollywood royalty."[29]

At their first meeting with Jones and Haines in April 1963, Leonore Annenberg suggested that a Maya theme be incorporated into the design, a theme that she felt would relate the house more sympathetically to its desert site.[30] For many at the time, Maya, or Mayan as it was then more usually called,

ANNENBERG RESIDENCE

A. QUINCY JONES, FAIA FREDERICK E. EMMONS, AIA

3 | *Perspective view of main house and guest pavilion, August 1963 (Department of Special Collections, Charles E. Young Research Library, UCLA).*

ANNENBERG RESIDENCE

A. QUINCY JONES · FREDERICK E. EMMONS

4 | *Elevation of main house and guest pavilion, August 1963 (Department of Special Collections, Charles E. Young Research Library, UCLA).*

was a term rather loosely applied to diverse sources of Pre-Columbian architecture without expectation of archaeological accuracy.[31] Frank Lloyd Wright had been similarly inspired in the 1920s when designing a series of houses for undeveloped areas of Los Angeles, believing Pre-Columbian architecture to be a natural, indigenous expression of the California locale.[32] Like Wright, Jones would abstract this source to reflect the feeling of Maya architecture without literal quotation. Leonore Annenberg also suggested that the roofs reflect the pink of the mountains in the late afternoon, and accordingly Jones used pink not only for the roofs but for portions of the walls as well.

In early August, Haines wrote to Walter Annenberg that "Jones has done his first great preliminaries and he is now restudying his creation."[33] Presentation drawings of this first scheme are dated August 11, 1963; they feature a perspective and elevation showing three low, pyramidal roofs that in shape distantly recall Pre-Columbian pyramids, but with a lightness reflective of mid-century modernism (figs. 3, 4). Each pyramidal roof articulates a major space within the otherwise flat-roofed and expansive structure. Along the outer walls near the largest of the three, a single row of freestanding

columns recalls similar Maya compositions, as at Chichén Itzá, but here they support a cantilevered concrete trellis. This trellis continues beyond the two smaller pyramidal roofs at each corner, unifying the composition. Below, the masonry walls of the house are battered (thus sloping, or angled, inward), as are the walls of the broad platform on which they rest, recalling the inward-sloping profiles of Maya architecture.

As seen in the plan (fig. 5), the largest pyramidal roof was to shelter a central atrium within the main living area, while the smaller pyramids were to roof a combined billiard and game room at one corner and the master bedroom at the other, each seen projecting from the central block in the perspective view. The evocative composition of the roofs accords with Jones's attention to such devices; as the architecture writer Esther McCoy wrote, "He liked a serious roof."[34]

Jones located staff bedrooms and guest accommodations in a long, flat-roofed pavilion overlooking a swimming pool; this wing is shown in the perspective drawing on the left of the main house. Out of view on the opposite side of the house, a covered parking court was to extend out from the main entrance and to terminate in a large aviary. The site plan (fig. 6) shows a driveway winding through extensive gardens that

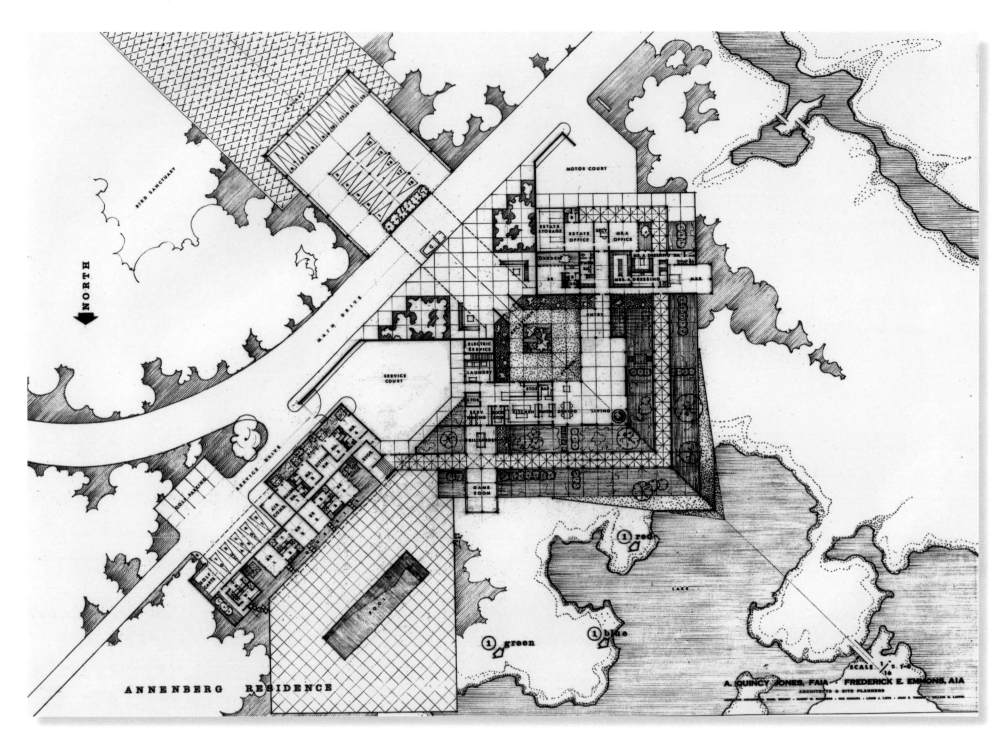

5 | *Plan of main house and guest pavilion, August 1963 (Department of Special Collections, Charles E. Young Research Library, UCLA).*

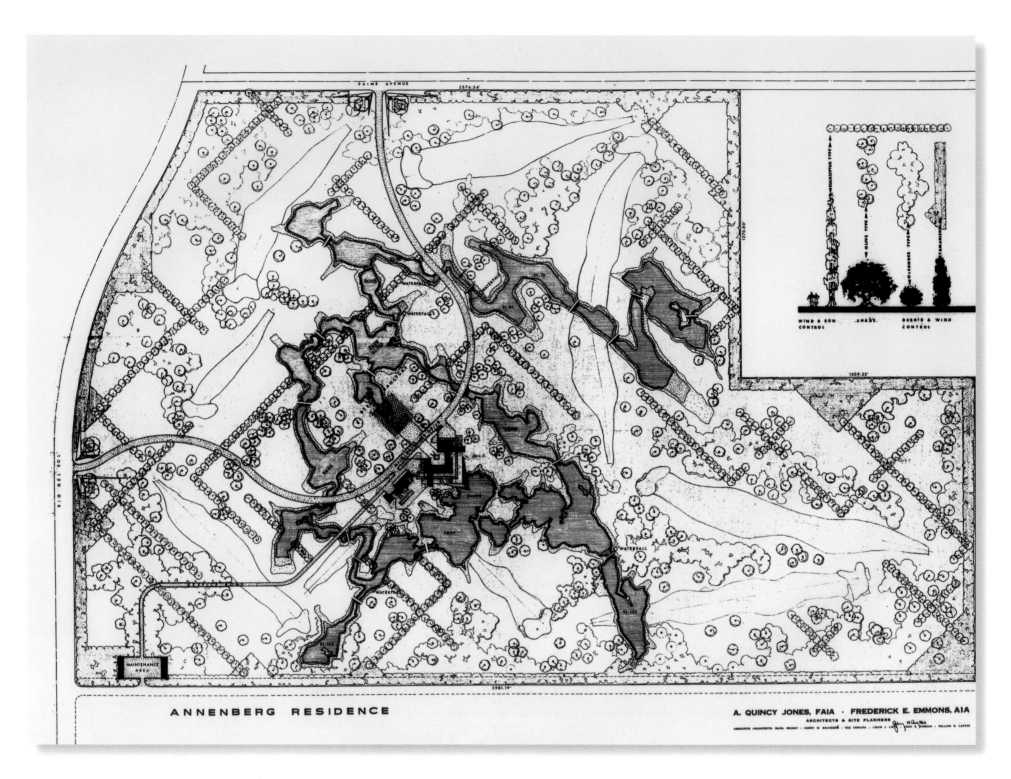

6 | *Site plan, August 1963 (Department of Special Collections,*
Charles E. Young Research Library, UCLA).

incorporate interconnecting lakes within a golf course; long rows of trees, schematically diagrammed, reinforce the lines of the central pavilion. A section at the upper right of the plan diagrams how eucalyptus, olive, oleander, and tamarisk trees would provide shade as well as sun and wind controls.

Completed drawings were mailed to Annenberg's office in Philadelphia, and on September 6, 1963, Jones traveled there to meet with the Annenbergs and discuss his scheme.[35] At that time Jones estimated the cost of his design at $700,000, acknowledging that such a figure was arbitrary but would assist in the calculation of his fee. Annenberg asked him to revise the guest rooms and game room, to restudy general house relationships, and to eliminate the aviary. Jones acknowledged these requests in a letter shortly after the meeting, also mentioning his coordination of the landscaping with Dick Wilson, who was to design the golf course, and the development of the interiors, which were to be jointly designed with Haines.[36] A revised Letter of Agreement was enclosed; Jones now estimated the house would cost $40 per square foot (not unusually expensive for the time), except for roofed but unenclosed areas such as terraces and carports, which were to cost $10 per square foot. He also agreed to consult on landscape questions in addition to his architectural work.

Annenberg seemed taken with the Maya theme. For an upcoming meeting of his with Jones and Haines, he arranged for a private showing of a newly released film on Maya civilization, and to an editor of *National Geographic* he wrote, "I am contemplating the construction and development of a home in the desert area of southern California and am planning this project in terms of the Mayan influence," asking that articles illustrating Maya culture be sent to Haines.[37] He evidently wanted them to suggest elements that Haines might incorporate into his designs.

Haines was not receptive to this idea. He wrote to Annenberg, "You asked what the period of the house was, I said it was suggestive of the Mayan architecture in Chichen-Itza in its retaining walls. Actually, this remark was not intended to identify or associate the architecture of your house with any particular style or period. I feel that it was Quincy's intent, and I most surely know it is mine that your house should definitely be as timeless as it can be, or as much as Jones can make it, and I can furnish it."[38]

Haines must have discussed Jones's design for the house on at least two earlier occasions: in late August, when he entertained the Annenbergs at his home in Los Angeles, and on September 18, 1963, when he was a guest at Inwood, their Colonial revival estate near Philadelphia.[39] Annenberg had complimented Haines on his taste after the August dinner, and perhaps partly in light of that, Haines, in the just quoted letter of October 1963 in which he had distanced himself from literal Maya references, continued,

There are two kinds of taste—good and bad. There is no integration here. Most people do not have taste, never know they don't have it, thus being extremely happy like all people who have not been exposed to beauty beyond the point of their noses. Then there are the exquisite few who do have taste. They can't explain why, but they know it; they can feel it, but can't touch it. It's like intangible fog you can see and feel it, but can't touch it. . . . I don't know what brought that on! I suppose I was trying to say that your house first should reflect yours and Lee's taste and interests which I can easily see are very inquisitive and catholic. . . . I have never seen nor heard of any Mayan furniture extant, but who knows.[40]

Annenberg replied, "When I suggested editorial material on the Mayan civilization, I had no such thought as pictures of furniture, but rather the general spirit and character of materials used therein. It was my thought that you, Bill, with your creative talent could pick up some expressions that might be translated into the furnishings."[41]

As shown in this and other correspondence, Haines and Walter Annenberg developed close ties during the design and construction of Sunnylands, often joking informally and some-

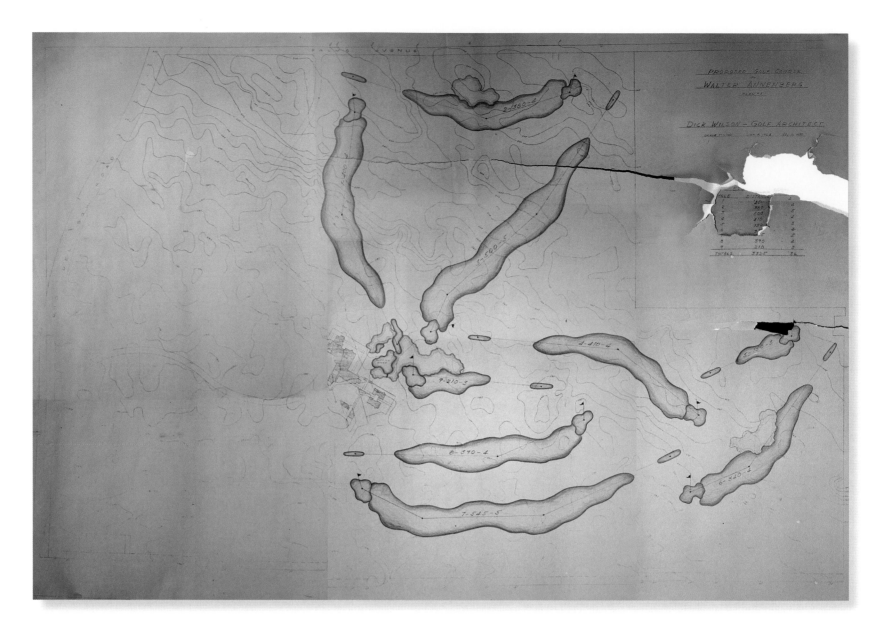

7 | *Golf course layout (Department of Special Collections, Charles E. Young Research Library, UCLA).*

times even exchanging recipes. Haines emerged as a strong presence, a man not easily intimidated. In lighthearted moments he sometimes referred to Leonore Annenberg in the third person as "madame," and on one rare occasion when they disagreed on a minor detail (she suggested green for an upholstered piece, he wanted white), he wrote, "However, if you really want these changes made, I will concur sadly, but I will concur."[42]

Correspondence further documents the Annenbergs' close

attention to details of the design. In late September 1963, they reminded Jones of the need for flower arranging and pressing rooms, a second route of access to dressing areas so maids could leave the master bedroom undisturbed, and windows that would light Mrs. Annenberg's otherwise dark dressing room. Jones gave full attention to details of the design as well, and indicated concern in coordinating his work with that of Dick Wilson, who had been hired by Annenberg to design the golf course. Jones wrote to Annenberg to confirm that plans and elevations had been sent to Wilson, adding: "I hope you will hear from him in the near future concerning his work on the golf course in relation to the house. . . . I surely would appreciate knowing what transpires between the two

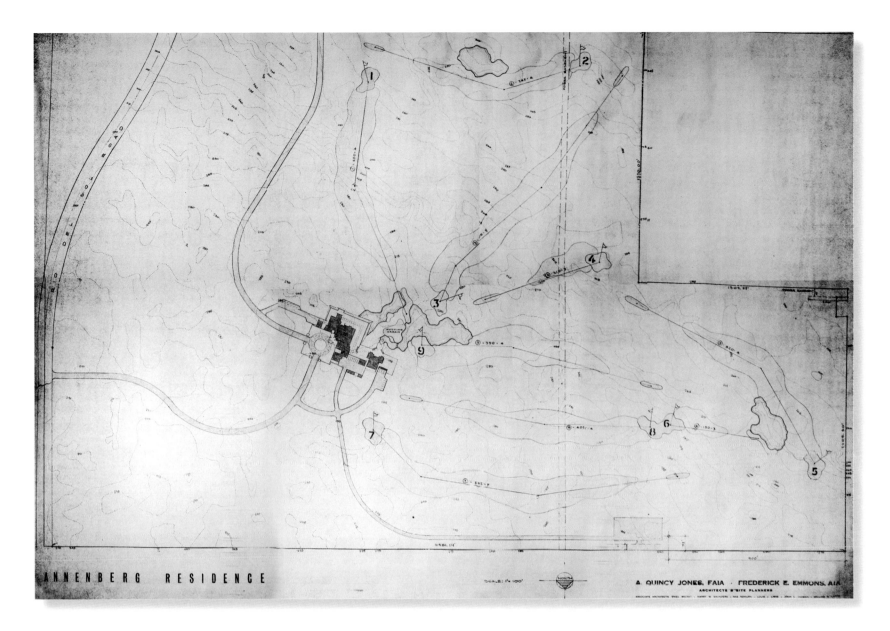

ANNENBERG RESIDENCE

A. QUINCY JONES, FAIA · FREDERICK E. EMMONS, AIA
ARCHITECTS & SITE PLANNERS

8 | *Revised site plan (Department of Special Collections, Charles E. Young Research Library, UCLA).*

of you."[43] More forcibly, he reminded Wilson that Annenberg had "suggested . . . that you and I coordinate the landscape scheme and work with his estate manager."[44] Wilson's layouts that followed were soon incorporated into Jones's site plan for the estate (figs. 7, 8).

The following month, while in Mexico City to attend a meeting of architects, Jones visited Pre-Columbian ruins and sought out buildings that incorporated lava stone (a dark, porous substance), a material he and Annenberg had discussed.[45] According to Harry Saunders, of the Haines firm, Annenberg had first suggested using the stone in the house to reinforce its Maya theme, and it came to be a featured component of the finished building.[46]

During the fall of 1963, other experts were brought into the job. A site manager—David Anderson—was hired to stay at the estate as the Annenbergs' representative, and Jones suggested a full-time clerk-of-the-works to supervise construction.[47] Locations for wells were identified, and drawings showing revisions to the main house were sent to Haines.[48]

In his August 1963 site plan, Jones had outlined his basic concept for landscaping the site and suggested specific variet-

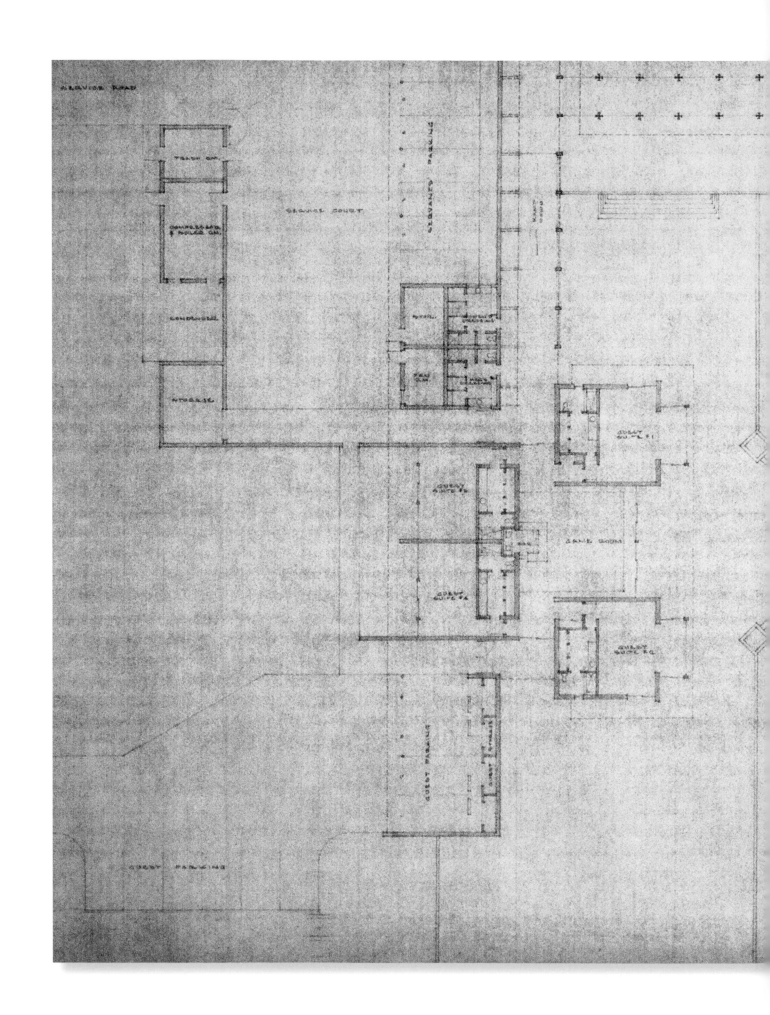

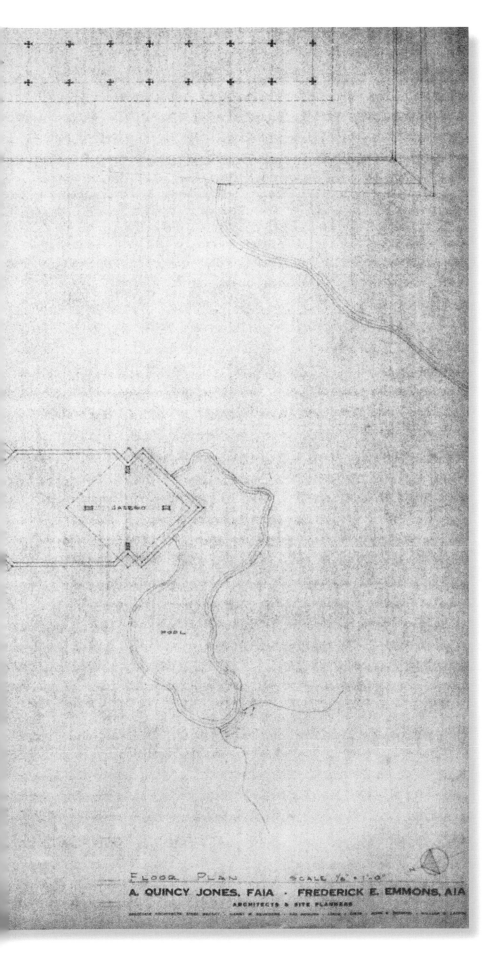

FLOOR PLAN   SCALE ⅛"·1'-0"

A. QUINCY JONES, FAIA · FREDERICK E. EMMONS, AIA
ARCHITECTS & SITE PLANNERS

ies of trees that might be planted. As to what charge his client gave him in this regard, Walter Annenberg is quoted as saying only, "I don't want to see one grain of sand except in the sand traps." For her part, Leonore Annenberg later recalled, "We didn't want to have a lot of palm trees."[49]

As Haines had known from the beginning, a landscape architect would be a necessary addition to the team to help realize Wilson's design of the golf course and develop Jones's basic concepts for other planted areas of the estate. At first, drawings identify Emmet Wemple as this landscape architect, with a plant contractor—Rolla J. Wilhite, ASLA—named to supervise the actual work of planting. As work progressed, Wilhite assumed both roles. He explained that Wemple—who taught with Jones at the University of Southern California—had been Jones's first choice to produce detailed plans, but he lacked practical experience for a job of such scope. When interviewed by Jones and Haines, Wilhite—who had received his master's degree in Horticulture from the University of California in Los Angeles—recalls that he accepted the assignment without hesitation, although at the time he was not fully aware of the project's size.[50] But he had the extensive experience required for planting in such harsh climates, he knew what plant materials would survive, and he knew where to find them. One of his first demands, for example, was to order a soil test. Others had thought this unnecessary.

Jones presented his revised plans to Annenberg at a meeting in New York on January 17, 1964. Except for minor revisions, the design of the house was now essentially set, and on January 24 Annenberg called Jones to request that a model be made.[51] Further details were discussed with David Anderson in February in preparation for an upcoming visit to the site by the Annenbergs that next month.[52]

In changes to his August 1963 scheme, Jones complied

9 | *Revised plan (in two parts), guest pavilion (left) and main house (following page) (Department of Special Collections, Charles E. Young Research Library, UCLA).*

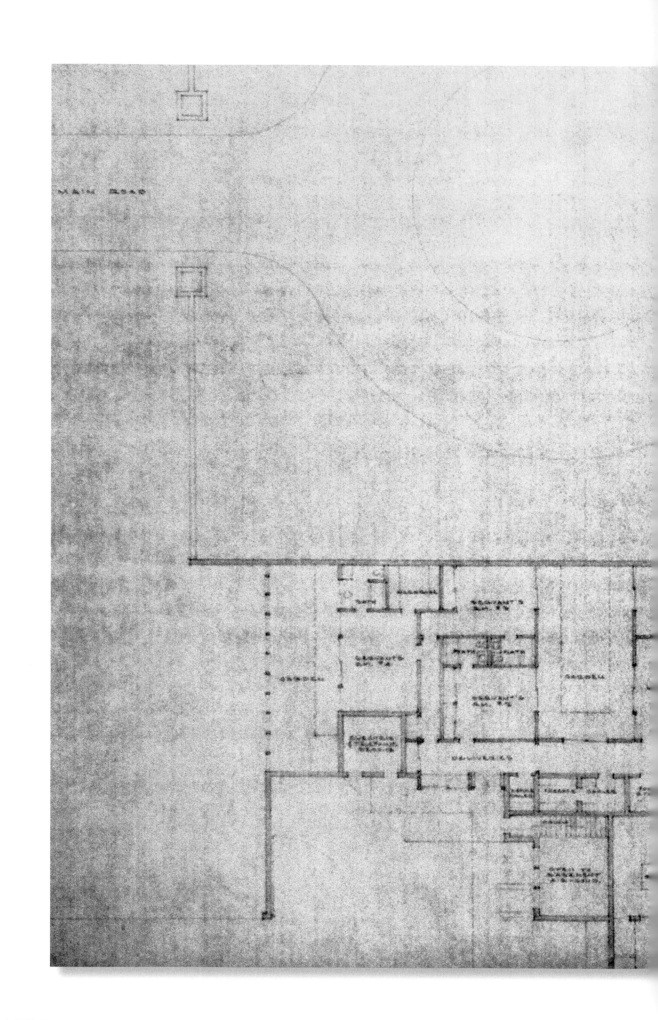

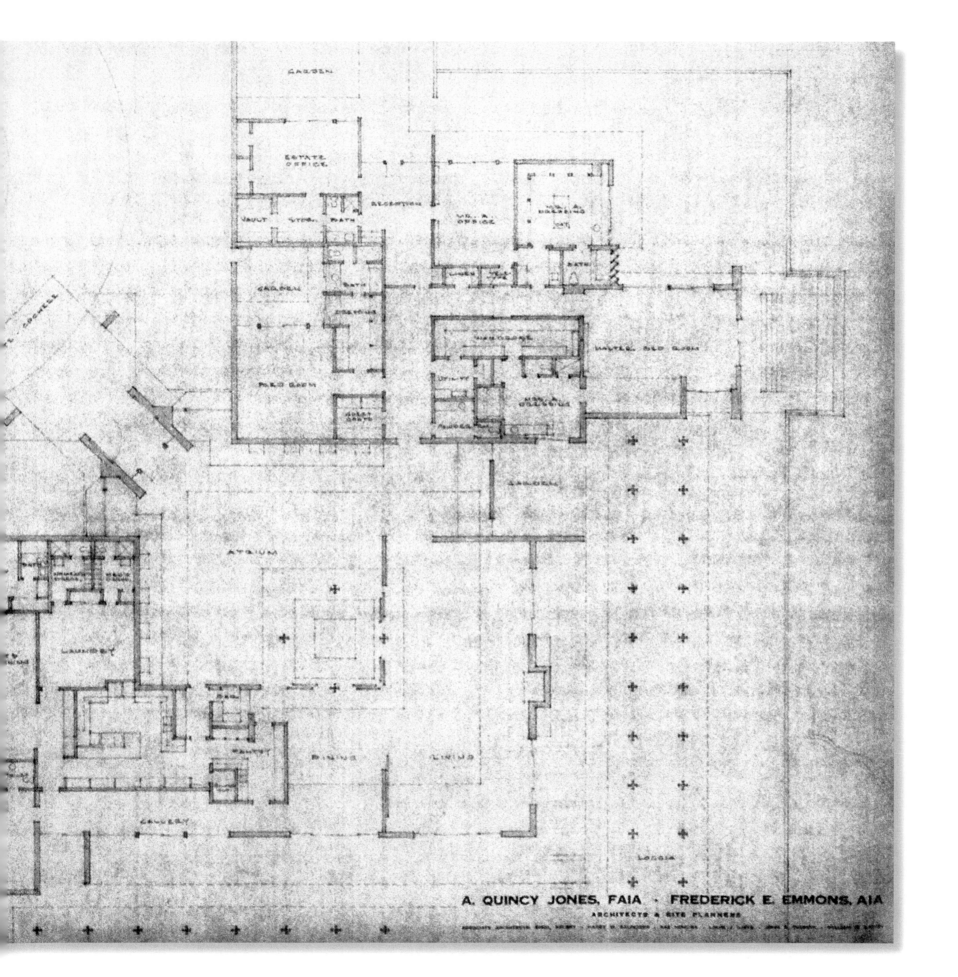

A. QUINCY JONES, FAIA · FREDERICK E. EMMONS, AIA
ARCHITECTS & SITE PLANNERS

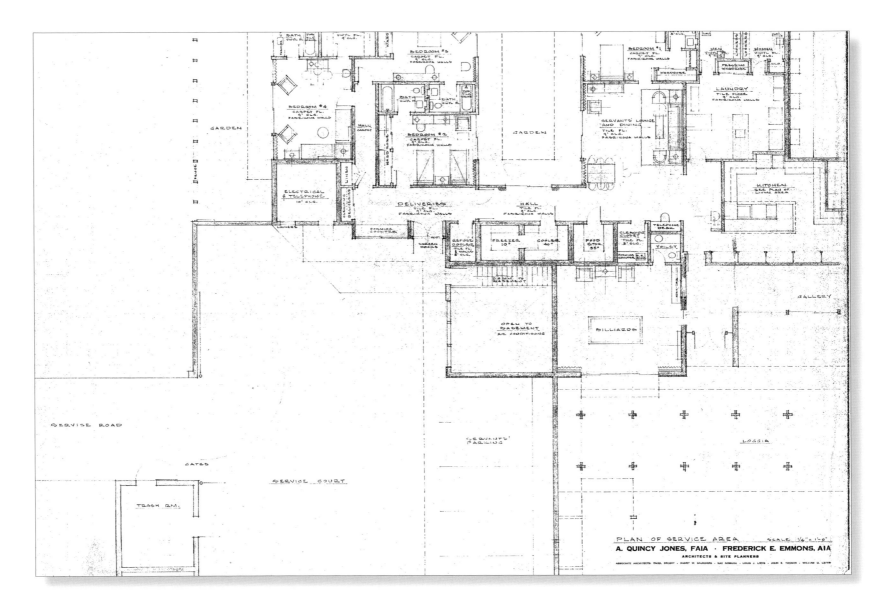

10 | *Furnishing plan of revised service area, main house (Department of Special Collections, Charles E. Young Research Library, UCLA).*

with the Annenbergs' requests regarding the plan (fig. 9). He altered the semi-detached pavilion housing guest and staff accommodations, relocating the staff quarters into an expanded service area within the main house (fig. 10) and reconfiguring the guest rooms so they more effectively enclosed a central game room (fig. 11). Dressing rooms to serve the golf course and swimming pool were given a separate pavilion, located between the main house and the new guest pavilion, where it would help screen the expansive service courts behind. The guest pavilion's shape was made more compact, with the game

room now located at its center, where it related more directly to the projected swimming pool in front. Jones also altered his site plan for Sunnylands, simplifying the entrance drive so that only one main gate was needed and relocating guest parking to a new parking area behind the guest pavilion.

The exterior of the house changed as well. The two smaller pyramidal elements were eliminated in favor of flat roofs, and the battered walls of the first scheme were made vertical (fig. 12). The trellis was given a lighter profile with the substitution of steel for concrete; reportedly Leonore Annenberg had found the first version to be unattractively heavy.[53] The central atrium assumed more prominence under the single pyramidal shape that remained: this was clearly central to Jones's concept (fig. 13). It accorded with earlier work by Haines as

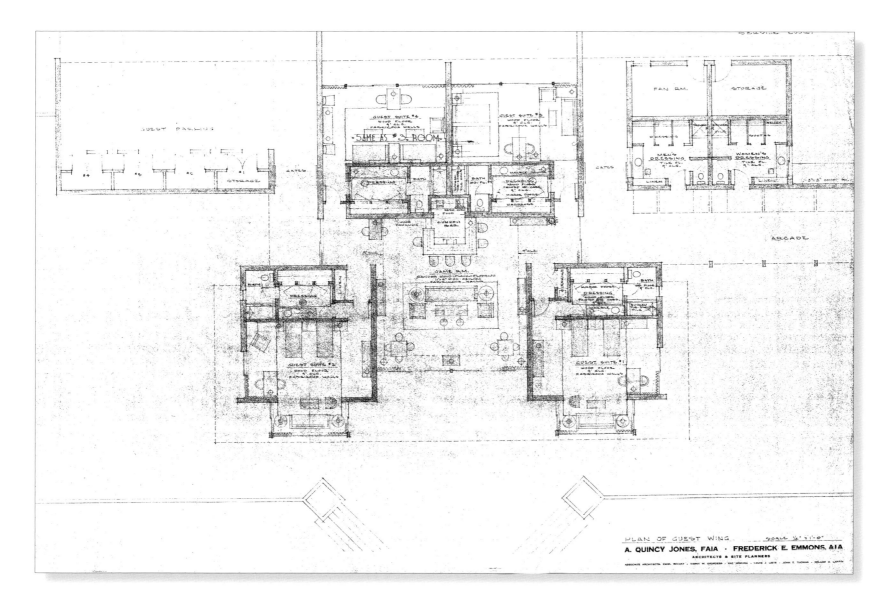

PLAN OF GUEST WING.

A. QUINCY JONES, FAIA · FREDERICK E. EMMONS, AIA
ARCHITECTS & SITE PLANNERS

11 | *Furnishing plan of revised guest pavilion (Department of Special Collections, Charles E. Young Research Library, UCLA).*

well, for he had incorporated a similar atrium (though one that was smaller and less dramatically roofed) in his remodeling of the Bloomingdale house.[54]

At that same February meeting between Jones and Anderson, new components of the estate were discussed. There were to be three staff cottages located near the western edge of the property, two with two bedrooms (later increased to three bedrooms in each) and the third—designated for unmarried staff—with eight bedrooms (reduced to four a few days later).[55] A maintenance building was also to be designed, with a shop, office space, locker facilities, and extensive storage.

When the Annenbergs met with Jones at the site on March 14, 1964, critical issues arose. They had earlier questioned Jones's siting of the house, and it was now staked out for their

approval. Leonore Annenberg recalls that with sticks and a length of rope she and her husband realigned the proposed location of the house themselves to effect what they regarded as a better relationship with its setting.[56] Within a matter of days plans show the house as they suggested it should be.[57]

Knowing that extensive grading would be required for the golf course as well as surrounding gardens, Jones also proposed elevating the main house some twelve or more feet on an artificial mound so as to obtain better views, and a twenty-five foot wooden tower was erected so the Annenbergs could bet-

ANNENBERG RESIDENCE

ANNENBERG RESIDENCE

12 | *Revised elevation of main house and guest pavilion, January 1964 (Department of Special Collections, Charles E. Young Research Library, UCLA).*

13 | *Section through atrium of main house, January 1964 (Department of Special Collections, Charles E. Young Research Library, UCLA).*

ter evaluate this proposal. They rejected the idea of a raised mound (which would have added significant costs), preferring instead a less dominant position, and the house remained at the lower, more natural elevation.[58]

BUILDING THE ESTATE

By late March 1964, the model that Annenberg had requested was finished (fig. 14).[59] It shows how the flat roofs were to connect the separate guest and locker room pavilions, and also how they would extend out from the private bedroom wing of the main house partly to define a walled parking area. Joseph Harvey was hired as clerk-of-the-works that same month, and

14 | *Model of main house and guest pavilion (Department of Special Collections, Charles E. Young Research Library, UCLA).*

in April construction began on the golf course, maintenance building, and three staff cottages.[60] Installation of an elaborate irrigation system was under way by July: water pumped from wells was to fill a main reservoir lake supplying this system as well as eleven additional lakes and connecting streams that were to weave throughout the property.[61]

When the Annenbergs visited the property in July 1964, there was still little to be seen, especially near the site of the house itself. An aerial photograph that same month confirms Leonore Annenberg's emphatic description: "Nothing was here. . . . There was nothing."[62] But at least a primitive construction road had been scratched into the sandy desert, allowing a whole flotilla of vehicles to assemble near the place where the house was to rise, and vestiges of the temporary tower can be glimpsed (fig. 15).

By the end of July the maintenance building was complete, and by September 1964, the staff cottages were essentially completed as well (fig. 16), with Haines finishing his work on their interiors.[63] The simple cubic forms of these houses, constructed of block walls with flat roofs (figs. 17, 18), echo the modern prototypes Jones had designed for the Case Study House program and for the Eichler Homes.

Bids for the main house—opened on September 8, 1964—proved to be much higher than expected. The low bid was $1,850,000, Harry Saunders recalls, a considerable sum at the time. It fell to him to propose whatever changes would be necessary to bring the cost down to $1,500,000. His most significant cut was to eliminate two of the four guest rooms, resulting in a narrower configuration for their pavilion.[64] R. J. Daum, a respected builder known for his large-scale projects, was hired as general contractor and began grading for the house in October. Saunders recalls that construction proceeded without problems—unusual in work of such complexity.[65] Late in October, the golf course was described as nearly completed and the newly installed irrigation system was put into operation (fig. 19).[66] By early December work had begun on foundations for the house itself (fig. 20). In the months that

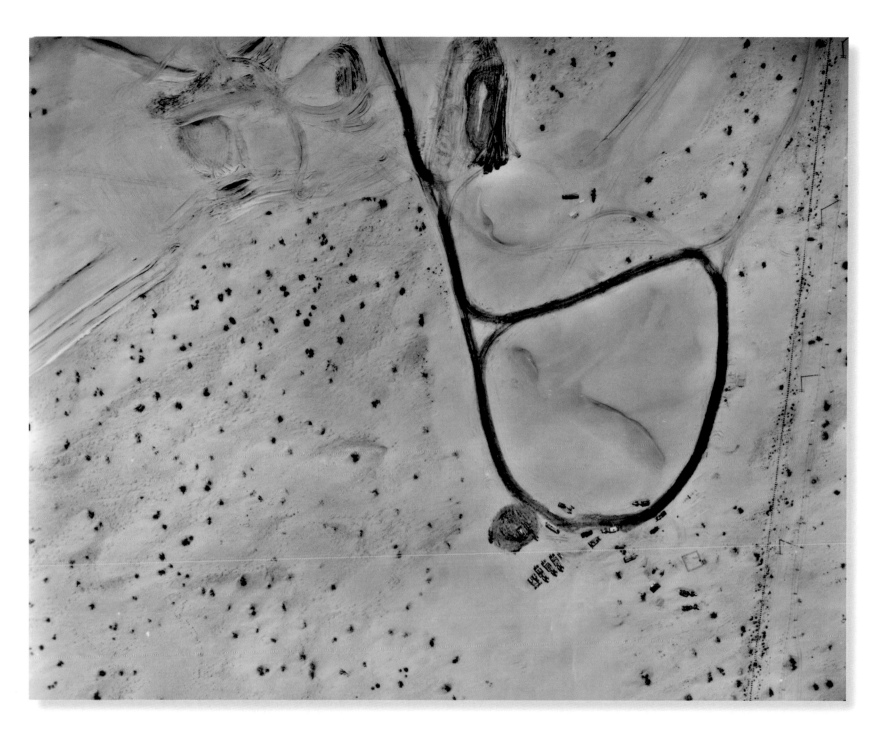

15 | *Aerial view of site, July 1964 (Department of Special Collections, Charles E. Young Research Library, UCLA).*

16 | *Staff cottages, November 1964 (Department of Special Collections, Charles E. Young Research Library, UCLA).*

followed, the steel frame began to rise above concrete block walls (fig. 21), and gradually the central atrium and main living area took shape (fig. 22). By May 1965, the rough enclosure of the house was completed (fig. 23); by late September the house appears nearly finished, except for the glazing of the window walls (fig. 24). For those windows, Jones chose clear rather than tinted glass, arguing that he planned wide overhangs to shade its surfaces and that he feared tinted glass would distort interior colors.[67]

17 | *Former staff cottage (Photograph by Graydon Wood, December 2006).*

18 | *Former staff cottage (Photograph by Graydon Wood, December 2006).*

19 | *View looking at golf course from house site, November 1964 (Department of Special Collections, Charles E. Young Research Library, UCLA).*

20 | *Main house foundation under construction, December 1964 (Department of Special Collections, Charles E. Young Research Library, UCLA).*

21 | *Main house framing (Department of Special Collections, Charles E. Young Research Library, UCLA).*

22 | *Main house under construction (Department of Special Collections, Charles E. Young Research Library, UCLA).*

23 | *Main house and guest pavilion under construction, May 1965 (Department of Special Collections, Charles E. Young Research Library, UCLA).*

24 | *Main house under construction, September 1965 (Department of Special Collections, Charles E. Young Research Library, UCLA).*

LANDSCAPING

Landscaping the property proved to be a monumental task. Jones had designed the general layout of the gardens, and detailed drawings were done in his office showing the lakes and their connecting streams, bridges, and even the locations of each of the rocks that were to be brought to the site. Other details fell to Dick Wilson, who designed the golf course, and to Rolla J. Wilhite, who detailed the extensive gardens and selected the actual plantings. In addition to coordinating their efforts, Jones informed the Annenbergs of progress through drawings and written reports, supplementing the more official progress reports prepared first by David Anderson and later by Joseph Harvey.[68] Annenberg himself devised the way in which the golf course of nine greens, with two ways to tee off, could be arranged to provide eighteen tees, and the course was changed accordingly to expand playing options without using additional acreage.[69] Jones designed the naturalistic swimming pool located outside the guest pavilion so that it blended with the twelve interconnected lakes in a seamless manner (fig. 25), and tennis courts later added at the northeast corner of the property were screened with dense plantings.

Rows of oleanders and tamarisks were placed at the perimeter of the property to provide privacy, their lines softened by extensive groupings of other trees and shrubs. The numbers are impressive: 7,114 oleanders, 915 tamarisks, 2,060 eucalyptus, and 850 olive trees, many already twelve to fifteen feet high when brought to the site.[70] Wilhite relates how a team of some thirty people worked on the job at the peak of this effort; they stayed in a rented house nearby together with a hired cook.[71] In addition to graders needed to reshape the terrain, cranes were used to plant the larger trees, with work sometimes interrupted by violent sandstorms.

Wilhite made frequent inspection trips to the site, driving down for the day from his Los Angeles office and sometimes taking Walter Annenberg on trips to nearby sites so that he might see firsthand how some of the plants he suggested to Wilhite would require special protection in the harsh climate. Wilhite liked working with Jones and recalled no problems in coordinating his work with Wilson. He also grew to have great respect for Annenberg, who often telephoned with questions at a late hour. He recalled only one incident in which a potential problem arose: for his own office, Wilhite had purchased two rare Beaucarnea trees from the estate of Edward L. Doheny (1856–1935), one of Los Angeles's most conspicuous citizens, whose great wealth had derived from oil. Annenberg wanted one of Doheny's Beaucarnea trees for himself, and Wilhite, although not wanting to part with either, ultimately acceded to Annenberg's wishes. It then fell to Wilhite to transport the large specimen, a task requiring several days of driving over a circuitous route of back roads (overhead barriers would have restricted his movement along major highways). Successfully transplanted, the tree stood majestically near the swimming pool until its death in 2008 (fig. 26).

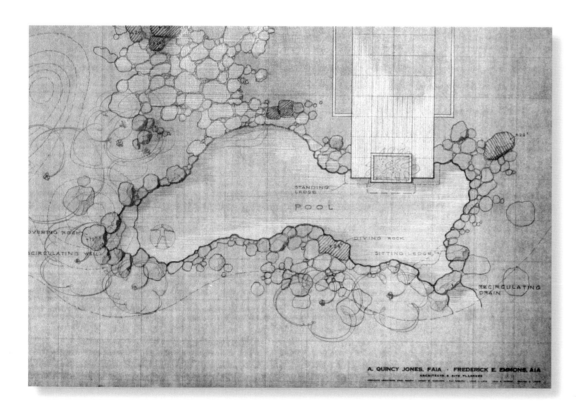

25 | *Plan of swimming pool* *(Department of Special Collections, Charles E. Young Research Library, UCLA).*

26 | *Beaucarnea tree (Photograph by Graydon Wood, April 2006).*

As the house neared completion, detailed plans were made for landscaping smaller areas nearby. Wilhite's drawings for these are dated 1965 and early 1966; they indicate a succulent garden adjacent to the private wing of the house, plantings of dwarf Meyer lemon and evergreen pear trees enclosing dressing areas of the master bedroom, and a formal rose garden behind the guest pavilion. On only one point did he and Jones briefly disagree: Jones believed the Virginia oaks that Wilhite wanted to plant along the trellis on the garden side of the house, overlooking the swimming pool in the distance, would not survive. Wilhite prevailed, as have the trees.

INTERIORS

Work on the interiors of the house continued for several months after construction of the house itself was completed. Leonore Annenberg remembers this as an agreeable time, with one exception. On an early visit, she was horrified by the appearance of the columns that held up the hipped roof of the atrium: they were exposed steel, painted bright red and embellished with seemingly arbitrary round holes. "We stood there aghast . . . we said we have a monster on our hands . . . it's the worst thing I'd ever seen."[72] They worked with Jones to rectify the problem, leaving the steel exposed, as Jones wished, but painted in a more pleasing color—a pale celadon green—and with round pegs inserted in the holes to refine their appearance.

On other details of the interiors, the Annenbergs worked mainly with Haines and Graber, who specified all interior finishes (in consultation with Jones), designed all of the furniture, selected objects (including several antiques), and arranged everything according to carefully detailed plans. Every element was shown to the Annenbergs in advance, including fabric samples and sometimes the objects themselves, and everything was integrated into a single, unified composition. For Leonore Annenberg, such thoroughly detailed procedure seemed a twentieth-century parallel with the interior design method of the eighteenth-century British architect Robert Adam (1728–1792), who had also designed all components of beautifully coordinated interiors. She also recalled how amenable Haines was to any changes they suggested and how easily he incorporated objects that they chose themselves.

Among the objects that Haines and Graber fabricated for Sunnylands were lamps made from Chinese antiques, something that had become almost a trademark of the firm, for they were known for their Chinoiserie, which extended to furniture and cabinet details as well as to other objects selected for their clients, such as Chinese screens.[73] For example, for conversion to lamps for the main living area of Sunnylands (see Virginia Bower's essay in this volume), they selected a pair of matched Chinese foo dogs, dated ca. 1622–1722, and for the atrium, a large hawk dated ca. 1662–1722.[74] Their pieces of custom-designed furniture were essentially modern but sometimes incorporated various historic motifs, as indicated by drawings they prepared to study its details (for example, figs. 27, 28, 29). Sometimes they embellished their pieces with Chinese-themed touches that recalled a similar joining of classical and oriental elements during the English Regency period of the early nineteenth century, a similarity underlying the term Hollywood Regency as a characterization of Haines's and Graber's work (see Donna Corbin's essay in this volume). Also typical of Haines's design, arrangements were informal, establishing a relaxed, comfortable setting for entertaining (fig. 30).[75]

According to Jean Mathison (one of Haines's biographers), for the custom furniture at Sunnylands, Haines adapted earlier designs that Michael Morrison had developed as part of his work for the firm, where he was employed from 1950 to 1960.[76] The designer was generous in later crediting Morrison, leading some to assume that Morrison alone was responsible for the furniture, although this seems not to have been the case.[77]

Jones's design for Sunnylands also included interior planting beds, an element incorporated into many of his California houses. In this case it was not Wilhite who selected the actual plants, but Jones together with Haines and Graber, and it was Leonore Annenberg rather than her husband who became involved in supervision.[78]

27 | *Plan, elevation, and details of hexagonal table for Sunnylands (Undated drawing, courtesy of The Peter Schifando Archives).*

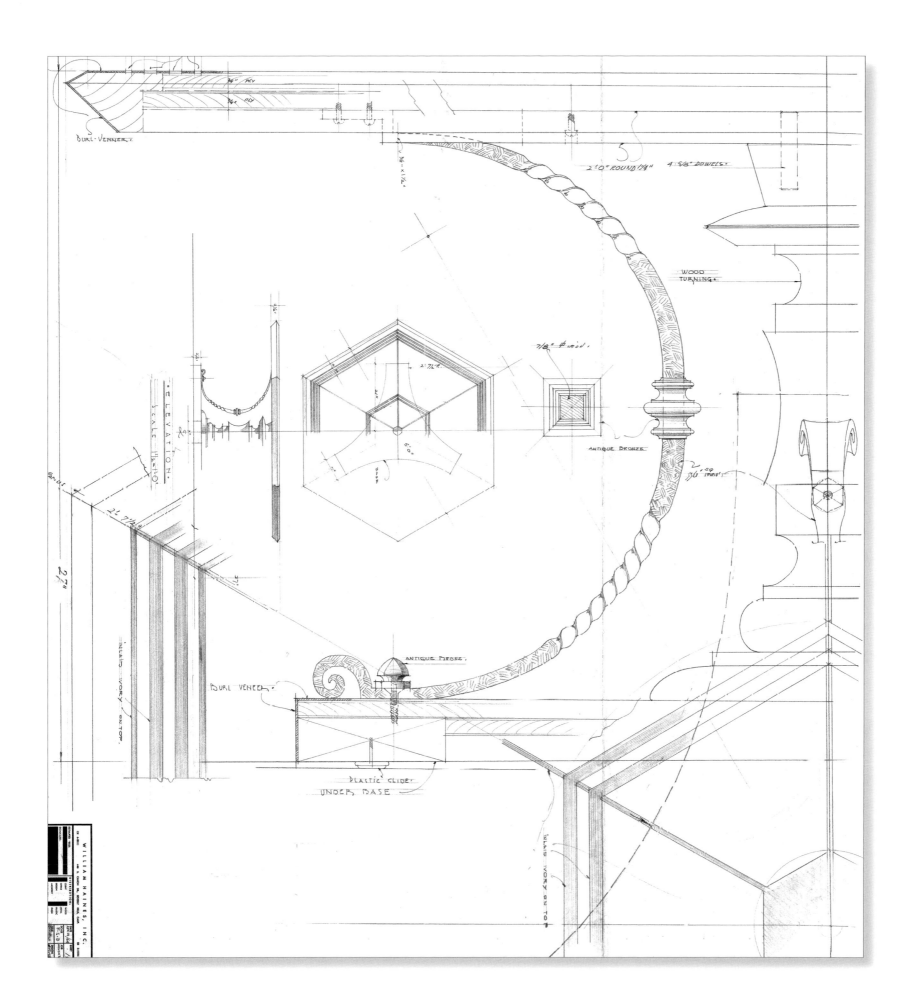

BURL VENEER

¾" PLY

¾" PLY

2'-0" ROUND 1⅜"

4 ⅝" DOWELS

WOOD
TURNING

⅞" # ROD.

ANTIQUE BRONZE

ELEVATION
SCALE ¾"=1'-0"

ANTIQUE BRONZE

BURL VENEER

PLASTIC GLIDER
UNDER BASE

WILLIAM HAINES, INC.

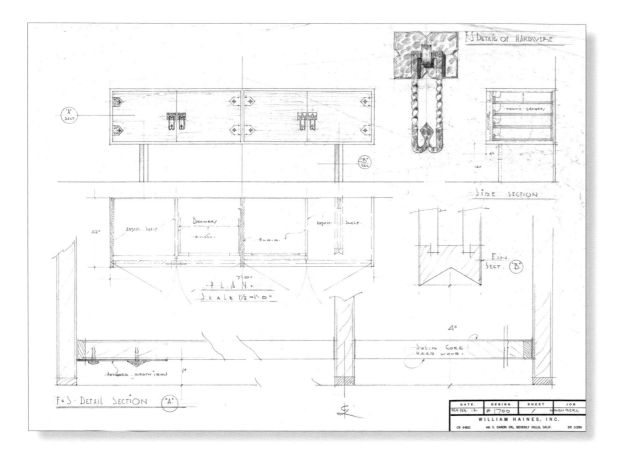

28 | *Plan, elevation, and details of cabinet for Sunnylands (Undated drawing, courtesy of The Peter Schifando Archives).*

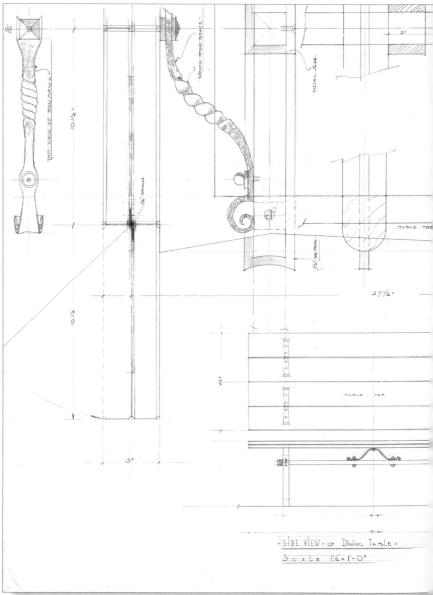

29 | *Plan, elevation, and details of dining table for Sunnylands (Undated drawing, courtesy of The Peter Schifando Archives).*

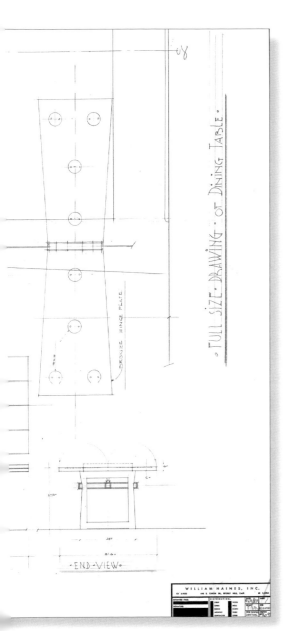

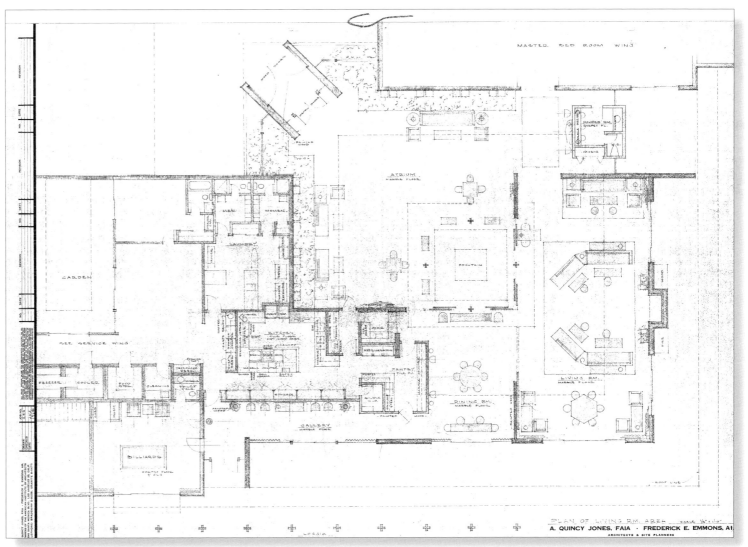

30 | *Furnishing plan of living room area (Department of Special Collections, Charles E. Young Research Library, UCLA).*

COMPLETING SUNNYLANDS, 1966

Sunnylands was finished at last in 1966, and March 6 was set as the official date of the Annenbergs' occupancy (figs. 31, 32, 33).[79] Amplifying the Maya theme, Louis I. (Bud) Liets, an architect in Jones's office, adapted a Maya image of a sun god as an emblem for the estate (see page v).[80] Emblazoned on a white flag to be flown when the Annenbergs were in residence, it can be seen in the arrival court at the main entrance to the house. The sun god image proved adaptable to other applications as well, for it came to be an identifying feature inscribed on stationery, golf cards, and related items.[81]

Both Jones and Haines had offered suggestions for nam-

31 | *Main house from southeast (Photograph by Graydon Wood, April 2006).*

ing the house, but the Annenbergs themselves chose to call it Sunnylands after the country retreat in the Poconos that Walter's father had bought in 1936 and sold in the 1940s.[82] The name, thus revived in Rancho Mirage, has remained constant, and in its general appearance the exterior of the house remains today much the same as when it was first completed. Yet inside and on the grounds, ongoing changes have transformed that original appearance. For Sunnylands has continued to evolve, as most houses do. Reflecting on this, Leonore Annenberg asked, "Does any house ever stay the same?"[83] Yet changes at Sunnylands have remained sympathetic to the original design, thus sustaining the underlying concepts of Jones and of Haines.

32 | *Plan of main house and guest pavilion as completed in 1966 (Drawing by and courtesy of Harry W. Saunders, AIA, 2007).*

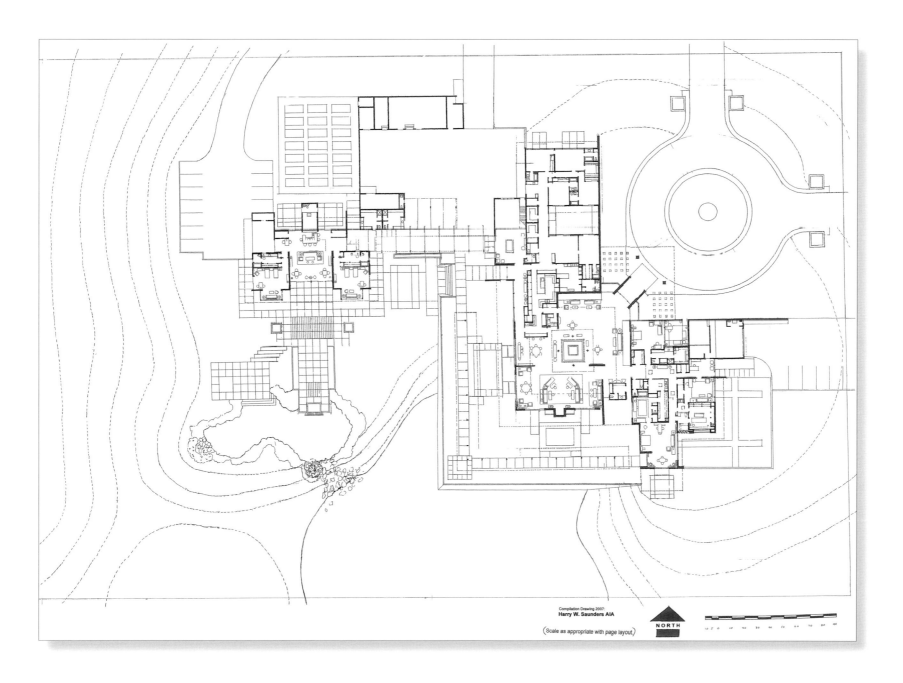

Compilation Drawing 2007:
Harry W. Saunders AIA

(Scale as appropriate with page layout.)

NORTH

33 | *Main house from southwest (Photograph by Graydon Wood, April 2006).*

CHANGES TO SUNNYLANDS AFTER 1966

Some changes at Sunnylands resulted from routine maintenance, like the periodic re-upholstery of furniture. Patterns of stitching as well as the profiles of the pieces have been maintained, but fabric colors were sometimes altered to relate more effectively to changing surroundings; thus several pieces in the main living area went from pink to a soft, celadon green more sympathetic to colors in newly acquired paintings. A few of the original pieces of furniture, such as low triangular tables and one-armed sofas, were exchanged in later years for alternates that Haines and Graber also designed, but changes to the arrangements themselves remained minor. Other changes were simpler still: following a visit to an elegant house in Venezuela—a house with richly colored marble floors but unadorned with carpets—the Annenbergs decided to remove their carpets, too, feeling the marble alone was a more suitable finish.[84]

More observable changes occurred with the interior plantings, which Jones conceived in part to integrate the spaces of the house with their surrounding gardens. The central atrium received his main attention: tall plants there were meant to create a screen between the entrance area and the main living area beyond. The Annenbergs decided a less interrupted view would be preferable, however, and they chose low, flowering bromeliads to replace the taller plants.[85] These needed to be grown indoors in preparation for transplanting, as did the orchids they wanted for interior arrangements, so three greenhouses were eventually added to the maintenance area of the property.

Other changes affected landscaped areas immediately adjacent to the house. Plantings in the circular entrance court were altered in 1968, when the original fountain was replaced by a thirty-foot-tall replica of the famous Maya column displayed in the National Museum of Anthropology in Mexico City (fig. 34; see also page vi). As Annenberg wrote to Jones, "we have completed the column in the courtyard, as a replacement for the fountain, and it is fantastically superb."[86] It, too, serves as a fountain, with water cascading from its top into a dry bed below, and it reinforces the Maya theme of the house as few objects could. An interior swimming pool added next to the master bedroom replaced the secluded garden that had once been there; the Palm Springs firm of Williams and Williams were architects for its enclosure.[87] Windows to an adjacent dressing room were consequently lost, but the original skylight in the dressing room was retained, positioned over a planting bed that gained emphasis as a result. Plans of 2007 by Peter Schifando allowed the interior pool to be removed and its enclosure converted to a sitting area to enhance the master bedroom suite. It would be known as the Inwood Room in recognition of its collection of antique furnishings brought from the Annenbergs' Philadelphia home.

Over the years, the Annenbergs continued to add to their numerous collections, and sometimes these acquisitions led to other changes. In some instances this involved the objects themselves, as in 1972, when living-room pieces were being rearranged under Haines's direction. On another occasion he persuaded them to purchase a rare pair of Ming dynasty cloisonné stools as important additions to the room, describing them as "fantastic, and like nothing we have ever seen" (see fig. 133).[88] About that same time, an executive from Corning Glass offered them a unique Asian-themed collection of Steuben glass, which they purchased (see M. J. Madigan's essay in this volume). They knew immediately where they wanted it displayed: in the long gallery leading from the main living area to what was then the billiard room. Graber and Saunders designed special cases to display the collection, where it enlivens what had been, according to Leonore Annenberg, "just a wall with some trees, bushes, and jars."[89] In early 1974, the Annenbergs purchased a pair of silver doors of Indian origin; in his letter to Ted Graber asking him to "work them into Sunnylands," Walter Annenberg described them as "allegedly . . . from a Maharaja's palace from the North of India."[90] Mounted

34 | *View from main house entrance to arrival court (Photograph by Graydon Wood, December 2006).*

on a wall at the end of a corridor leading into the private wing of the house (see fig. 43, far right), they, too, enliven their space (see Michael Meister's essay in this volume).

More significant changes occurred later in 1974, when the Annenbergs returned to Sunnylands after a prolonged stay in London, where Walter Annenberg had served as the United States Ambassador to the Court of Saint James's, a defining moment for him and an achievement of which he remained justly proud for the remainder of his life. They began to entertain more often and wanted a better-situated dining room.

Jones had located the original dining area in one corner of the living room, as typical in modern houses (although less often in houses of such great scale). Leonore Annenberg had questioned this from the beginning, preferring a more conventional arrangement where the staff could work unseen before and after the meal itself. Her wishes were now accommodated. Harry Saunders, who had been deeply involved with Sunnylands while an associate of Jones and who assumed the role of architect for later changes, reconfigured the original billiard room to create a separate, clearly defined room. The west wall overlooking the guest pavilion was pushed out to enlarge the space, and to correct what was perceived as an awkwardly low height, the roof linking the newly configured dining room to the game and guest suite pavilion was raised. As part of this alteration, Saunders suggested locations where a work of sculpture from the Annenbergs' collection might be advantageously placed.[91] Harry Bertoia's *Peacock* was selected, placed where it enhances the view from inside. Other changes to the space included new lighting fixtures and a wood parquet floor that replaced the original tile. The kitchen and service areas were also altered at this time to better serve the new space, and the original dining area was converted into a seating alcove, fitted out with new shelves and partially screened within its corner of the main living area.[92]

The Annenbergs had taken their collection of Impressionist and Post-Impressionist paintings with them to London. Now, in 1974, they decided to return these paintings to Sunnylands rather than to Inwood, where they were originally on view. The main living area at Sunnylands provided an ideal setting for them, and Leonore Annenberg remembers with great fondness the experience of arranging them on its walls. But as with most collections, this one also grew, most notably upon their purchase of fifteen more paintings from Walter Annenberg's sister Enid A. Haupt in 1983. By 1991, when they gave their collection to The Metropolitan Museum of Art in New York, the collection had grown to more than fifty superb paintings.[93]

As the Annenbergs added to their collection of paintings through the 1970s and 1980s, it became necessary to alter the main living area for their display. Original planting areas along the two long walls were removed and paved over with marble matching that of the original floor, and the skylights above were closed, thus making the walls more suitable for hanging; the dark brown, richly textured lava stone proved to be a perfect foil for the canvases. Haines, who had incorporated collections of paintings into other houses he designed, had anticipated that the Annenbergs might one day want more exhibition surfaces, so he had already provided concealed electric outlets which were now available for supplemental lighting.[94] Other works of art were added after 1974 as well, including paintings from different periods (see Gwendolyn Shaw's essay in this volume) and sculpture by Jean Arp and

Harry Bertoia, among others (see Suzanne Lindsay's essay in this volume). At first the house had contained few such pieces, being more of an unembellished desert retreat; now it assumed a different character.[95]

As originally built, the main house included two enclosed courtyards: one adjacent to the staff dining room in the service wing, and the second next to a guest bedroom in the private wing. This bedroom was planned for Walter Annenberg's mother—thus its special location. She died in 1965, while the house was still under construction, and the room and its courtyard languished. In 1977 Saunders planned their conversion to a library. The courtyard was roofed over to gain more space, and a large skylight was added to provide natural light in what was now a windowless room.[96] Shelves and cabinets were installed, and the bath and dressing areas were modified to provide additional closets that were then needed. It came to be known as the Room of Memories, and it still is, for in addition to books it is densely filled with memorabilia that include signed photographs of distinguished friends, guest books inscribed by prominent visitors, and other personal effects. Also in 1977, three additional guest rooms were added to the guest pavilion, extending it to the west. Saunders was again the architect for this alteration.[97]

Additions were made within more distant landscaped areas as well. In 1976, to create a sheltered spot for picnics midway in the golf course, Saunders designed a Chinese-themed pavilion where picnic lunches could be served (fig. 35).[98] Later, following a trip to the Greek islands, Walter Annenberg requested a semicircular stone seat that would recall one he had seen on Delos; this Saunders designed in 1979 (fig. 36). Annenberg had it flown in by helicopter, saying that he "did not want any trucks making tracks across his fairway."[99]

The borders of the property were also altered. As part of Jones's original commission, Saunders had designed a formal entrance gate anchored by low wing walls and elegant lighting fixtures. Elsewhere the estate was walled with chain link fence, screened by the rows of oleanders and fast-growing tamarisks that were part of the original planting scheme.

35 | *Chinese pavilion on golf course (Photograph by Graydon Wood, December 2006).*

36 | *"Delos" bench on golf course (Photograph by Graydon Wood, December 2006).*

But in the early 1990s the oleanders died as a result of a widespread blight, and the fence was unattractively exposed. To remedy this situation, a concrete block wall—painted the same color as the battered retaining walls at the back of the main house—was added in its place.[100]

SUNNYLANDS TODAY

Today, with additions made since 1966, the main house alone is 19,115 square feet, and with the basement, adjacent guest pavilion, locker room, and service facilities it encompasses 29,380 square feet (fig. 37)—many times the size of an average American house, and most of it on a single level. The three staff cottages (later primarily used for guests) add another 8,394 and service buildings add 9,000 more, for a grand total of 41,886 square feet. In the main house, the living area alone is 5,022 square feet (including the open spaces of the atrium, reception area, and adjoining alcoves)—an enormous room by any standard.[101] Yet none of this is immediately visible, for the Annenbergs preferred to maintain a more casual image even with so huge a house. They could have built another Biltmore, or even another San Simeon, William Randolph Hearst's house also known as Hearst Castle, where both Walter Annenberg and William Haines had been guests.[102] Yet such was clearly not their wish. They chose instead to build a house that in its basic parts draws from the same modernist elements that underlie the affordable ideal of the Case Study House program and the Eichler Homes. Quincy Jones was the right architect to undertake this task, for he had earlier designed just such prototypes, and he understood how to make a modern house that was truly livable, one responsive to the personal wishes of occupants in ways that more abstract examples of orthodox modernism were not.

When Queen Elizabeth II visited Sunnylands in 1983, Walter Annenberg is said to have told reporters, "I just want-

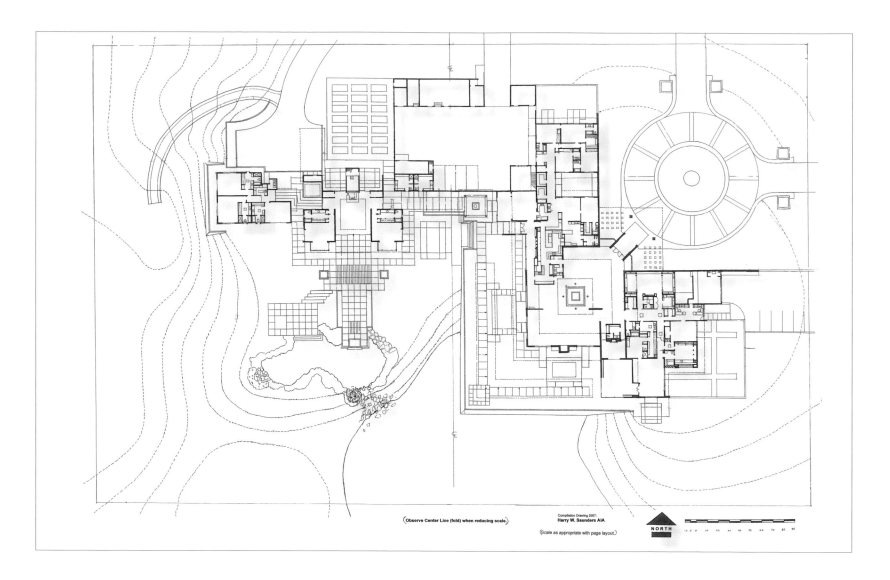

Observe Center Line (fold) when reducing scale.

Completion Drawing 2007:
Harry W. Saunders AIA

(Scale as appropriate with page layout.)

NORTH

37 | *Plan of main house and guest pavilion in 2007 showing future Inwood Room in place of interior swimming pool (Drawing by and courtesy of Harry W. Saunders, AIA, 2007).*

ed to show Her Majesty how the average American lived."[103] Clearly this was in jest, but perhaps not totally so. Obviously Sunnylands is not the model of how most Americans live, but even at its vast scale the estate honors rather than diminishes the values of more ordinary houses, thus celebrating those values while elevating them through a grandeur of scale and an elegance of finish. It accords with Walter Annenberg's wish to have a house "that was not too formal" but "had the majesty of being formal."[104]

Details of Sunnylands emphasize its informality and its accessibility. With all its opulent furnishings, enviable collections, and conveniences of every description, it still impresses one with a relaxed style unexpected in so grand an estate, a style without exact parallel. A long, freely winding drive of more than half a mile establishes this theme as it leads from the entrance gates through informally landscaped gardens. The house itself, low for its size, emerges gradually on a distant horizon, seeming to grow naturally out of its terrain (fig. 38). Any sense of a bombastic, intimidating allée leading to a formal façade—something so typical of imperial European estates—has been avoided.

The drive leads to a circular arrival court, marked dramatically by the Maya column at its center, which heralds the

38 | *Approach to main house (Photograph by Graydon Wood, April 2006).*

39 | *Arrival court (Photograph by Graydon Wood, December 2006).*

underlying Maya theme of the design (fig. 39). Two sides of this court are enclosed by long, windowless walls faced with lava stone; they screen the private wing on one side and the service wing on the other. At the corner of the court where they intersect at right angles, double doors—placed at an oblique angle to suggest informality—lead into the house itself (see fig. 1). From the open reception area just inside, diagonal views extend across the atrium to the open, casual living areas beyond, an extended line of more than one hundred feet (fig. 40). Views continue through walls largely of glass to landscaped gardens beyond (fig. 41), with distant mountains visible above the trees that encircle the property. This arrival sequence amplifies a sense of the estate's splendid isolation, of a place elegantly detached from its more immediate, and more ordinary, surroundings.

At the center of the grand living area is the atrium itself, nearly a thousand square feet housed beneath the pyramidal roof. Within this central space, borders of flowering bromeliads surround a central pool, providing a special setting for *Eve*,

40 | *Night view of entrance to main house (Photograph by Graydon Wood, December 2006).*

41 | *View across atrium from entrance to living area (Photograph by Graydon Wood, April 2006).*

42 | *View across atrium from living area to entrance (Photograph by Graydon Wood, April 2006).*

43 | *View to private wing from living area (Photograph by Graydon Wood, April 2006).*

the Rodin sculpture that had been chosen for that location by 1965 (fig. 42). Jones designed its base to pivot so that it might face in different directions, and wrote to Annenberg that "All of us at this end are tickled to death with the thought of seeing 'Eve' in the atrium."[105] Exposed steel columns support the hipped roof, which rises some twenty-six feet above the atrium, where it terminates in a skylight shaded by a smaller pyramidal element above. The columns are not located at the corners of the atrium, as would be expected, but instead along its sides, rendering its definition less formal.

The initial sequence of interior spaces, leading around the skylit atrium from the vestibule and reception area to the living areas beyond, recalls that in an ancient Roman domus, or townhouse. Yet the diagonal line of the Sunnylands axis dissolves any Roman formality, as do the open links to lateral areas of the main living space. For rather than a single, rigid route of movement, as was routinely dictated by the ancient Roman domus, the design presents no fixed line of movement, but rather a series of choices to be explored. To the left upon entering (fig.43) are informal seating areas that lead first past a doorway to the private wing of the house, then to guest cloakrooms beyond. To the right (fig. 44), similarly informal seating areas lead first to a partially screened seating area, then to the Steuben gallery with the dining room at its terminus. The main living area opposite the atrium, distinguished by its broad fireplace (fig. 45), can be approached from either direction. There is no rigid allée either within or without.

In accord with principles underlying modern architecture, walls are treated more as freestanding screens than boxlike enclosures, and they sometimes terminate below the ceilings, promoting a sense of openness. Doors and windows are detailed more as unframed openings between those screenlike elements, further amplifying spatial continuity. Ceiling planes are varied, too. Suspended in the atrium, a floating grid of coffered openings links visually with the plane of lithe trellises outside, diminishing any sense of rigid enclosure.

Dark, richly textured lava stone clads the two walls of the living area nearest the vestibule, establishing visual continuity

44 | *View to seating alcove from entrance (Photograph by Graydon Wood, April 2006).*

45 | *Fireplace in living area (Photograph by Graydon Wood, December 2006).*

46 | *Seating alcove seen from atrium (Photograph by Graydon Wood, December 2006).*

47 | *View from terrace to Steuben collection in gallery leading to dining room at left (Photograph by Graydon Wood, December 2006).*

with the walls of the arrival court just outside and thus reinforcing visual continuity between interior and exterior spaces. Vertical boards of sandblasted redwood, painted a light celadon green, line other walls of the space. Inlaid bands of black and brown stone border the rose aurora marble floor, which, as Leonore Annenberg saw early on, provides an elegant, expansive surface that needs no added element of carpets.

The informal groupings of low sofas, chairs, and tables that furnish the main living area reinforce a sense of free, informal choice. There is no rigid hierarchy in the design of these pieces, or in their arrangement—a remarkably adept approach by Haines and one appropriate to California settings. As another of his clients once remarked, "He designed all of my pieces low to the floor. That way the people were grander, not the furniture."[106]

The Annenbergs' extraordinary Impressionist and Post-Impressionist paintings were hung primarily in the main living areas, most densely on the lava stone walls where they gave unparalleled presence to the spaces. Reproductions now hang in their place, but other paintings remain, both here and throughout the house, as do sculptures by Jean Arp, Auguste Rodin, and others. Their placement enhances rather than intimidates.

The distant alcove to the right of the entrance contains two long, refectory-like dining tables holding a collection of Chinese antiques (see fig. 42). The shelves added along one side of the alcove display framed photographs of members of the English royal family—visitors to Sunnylands over the years (fig. 46). Through this alcove one proceeds to the long gallery bordered on one side by the remarkable collection of Steuben glass (fig. 47), a more formal space leading to the most formal area of the house: the main dining room. Yet even here formality is muted, for in place of the grand baronial table that might be expected are two tables that can be arranged more spontaneously (fig. 48). As in the main living area, the wall surfaces of wood are painted a pale celadon green, but here the floor is wood parquet rather than marble.

48 | *Night view from terrace looking into dining room*
(Photograph by Graydon Wood, December 2006).

49 | *View from dining room to terrace (Photograph by Graydon Wood, December 2006).*

A single skylight with an antique chandelier below provides centralized focus.

Through walls of glass that enclose one side of the dining room are views to the guest pavilion beyond, with Harry Bertoia's *Peacock* placed just outside in a way that defines that axis (fig. 49). A roofed terrace links the main house with this pavilion, bordered on its outer side by neutral walls enclosing

50 | *View from dining-room terrace to guest pavilion; Bertoia sculpture at right (©2008 Estate of Harry Bertoia/ Artists Rights Society [ARS], New York; Photograph by Graydon Wood, April 2006).*

51 | *Terrace adjacent to living area (Photograph by Graydon Wood, April 2006).*

52 | *Game room (Photograph by Graydon Wood, December 2006).*

53 | *Game room; swimming pool visible through windows at left (Photograph by Graydon Wood, December 2006).*

the changing rooms and service courts that lie beyond (fig. 50). A door from the Steuben gallery leads to this terrace and to the broader, more open terrace that extends back around two sides of the main living area. There the trellis is placed several feet from the house itself (see page xiii), adding to the sense of a layered, screenlike enclosure (fig. 51).

The game room, with views across an adjoining terrace to the swimming pool, lies at the center of the guest pavilion (figs. 52–54). Two original guest rooms border this more open space, with the three added rooms located on the far side, in a

54 | *Swimming pool with game room at left (Photograph by Graydon Wood, April 2006).*

55 | *Blue guest room (Photograph by Ned Redway, March 2007).*

wing extending away from the main house. Each is essentially identical in size, but decorated in a different color, providing a ready means of identification: yellow, pink, peach, blue, and green (fig. 55).

Balancing the sequence of spaces that leads from the main living area to the guest pavilion, a second sequence of spaces leads from the living area through the private wing of Sunnylands. A corridor opens along the wall to the left as one enters from the circular arrival court, a corridor terminated not by a major room, as on the opposite side, but instead by the pair of

56 | *View toward desk in Room of Memories (Photograph by Graydon Wood, December 2006).*

57 | *Wall of inscribed photographs in Room of Memories (Photograph by Graydon Wood, December 2006).*

silver Indian doors, mounted prominently on the wall so they are readily visible from the living area itself (see fig. 43).

The corridor leads first to what the family calls the Room of Memories, a space like no other in the house. It is the only major room to have no windows at all. Instead, it is illuminated by the large skylight added over the center of the room (fig. 56). Walls are paneled in lightly stained wood, with cabinets located at each narrow end. Above the cabinets, niche-like enclosures are lined with a warm-toned white fabric. The resulting atmosphere of protective enclosure suits the room's contents: the cabinets include guest books and framed photographs inscribed by some of the world's most famous people, including most of the recent American presidents beginning with Dwight D. Eisenhower (fig. 57). On the wall of one of the two vestibules leading into the room are framed, personally signed photographs of the Queen Mother, a special friend of the Annenbergs' (fig. 58). She sent these at Christmas each year, from 1972 to 2001, and together they form a remarkable portrait. The famous Andrew Wyeth portrait of Walter Annenberg hangs at the far end of the room, where the courtyard used to be (fig. 59). Leonore Annenberg placed a photograph of Annenberg below as a suggested correction to features she feels are too sternly rendered in the portrait itself (see fig. 85). Books line shelves at the opposite end of the room; a desk just in front contains additional shelves for large volumes that include photograph albums of the house and of the events held there.

A suite of offices beyond the Room of Memories includes Walter Annenberg's private study, where a portrait of his mother hangs above his desk. A small room adjoining the study once held the teletype he used to conduct business while at Sunnylands, a machine rarely found in private homes, but essential here before advances in electronic communication made less cumbersome connections possible.

The master bedroom lies at the far end of the private wing. The predominant tones of the room are yellow—a pale yellow carpet and upholstery, with floor-to-ceiling draperies in a brighter shade. The pale ivory color of the wood panel-

58 | *Wall of inscribed photographs from the Queen Mother in Room of Memories vestibule (Photograph by Graydon Wood, December 2006).*

59 | *View toward alcove with Wyeth portrait in Room of Memories (Photograph by Graydon Wood, December 2006).*

ing balances these elements. Windows on two sides overlook gardens beyond (fig. 60). Two suites of dressing rooms adjoin this space.

A service wing, concealed behind walls to the right as one enters from the circular arrival court, remains unnoticed by most visitors. The wing's generous, well-planned spaces include a restaurant-sized kitchen, pantries, wine and bar storage rooms, silver and china vaults, and a laundry. On the far side, behind the wall of the arrival court, four staff bedrooms and a staff dining room are grouped around the interior court. Discreetly located points of access to the adjoining dining room and living areas allow service to come from seemingly invisible sources. These thoughtfully designed facilities allow for entertaining on a grand scale.

With its long, low, horizontal lines, open interiors, and screenlike enclosures, Sunnylands draws from underlying principles of modern architecture that were first explored by Frank Lloyd Wright (1867–1959) in the first years of the twentieth century. A later generation of European architects—influenced by Wright and led primarily by Walter Gropius (1883–1969), Ludwig Mies van der Rohe (1888–1969), and Le Corbusier (1887–1965; the name he assumed in place of Charles Edouard Jeanneret-Gris)—began to expand upon these attributes in the mid-1910s and early 1920s, but with an emphasis on plain, untextured materials and with stricter, less varied geometries. The increasingly abstract buildings that resulted, with boxy shapes, walls usually devoid of texture and windows often cut like holes into unadorned surfaces, came to be categorized as the International Style (now more generally termed orthodox modernism). They were at odds with Wright's warmer, more varied approach. Quincy Jones's work, as seen at Sunnylands, is closer in spirit to Wright's, yet he achieved this tie without direct emulation of Wright's highly

60 | *View to gardens from master bedroom (Photograph by Graydon Wood, December 2006).*

personal details. Instead the more general attributes of color, texture, and varied geometries combine with low lines, informally defined interiors, and varied wall planes to form a major example of mid-twentieth-century architecture specific to America, a modern architecture responsive to its occupants as individuals and reflective of place as a determinant of design.

Most descriptions of Sunnylands overlook these traits, tending instead to sensationalize other qualities of the estate. It has been described as a "modern Xanadu," "like a Persian carpet dropped on a moonscape," and "not so much a residence as a small, elegantly appointed principality."[107] Because of the pyramidal roof over the living area, it has been likened to a tent, one writer even claiming that "the concept behind the house was a 'great tent,'" and imagining "Annenberg as an Arabian Sheikh holding court in the desert."[108] The Annenbergs never had this thought, although Saunders reports that some of the people in Jones's office discussed the design in this manner.[109] More simply, Annenberg wrote of himself "as a California visitor with a resort home in the Desert."[110] And with insight, Thomas Hoving, the former director of New York's Metropolitan Museum of Art, described Sunnylands as the one United States home of recent date comparable to the "stately homes" of England.[111]

VISITING THE ESTATE

As at England's "stately homes," running Sunnylands required a large staff. During the Annenbergs' time at their California home, more than fifty were employed full-time, including, in addition to an estate manager and a manager of the grounds, four butlers, a chef and two assistant chefs, parlor and guest room maids, a maid for the staff, a laundress, nearly thirty gardeners, at least three maintenance personnel, and two assistants for the office of the estate manager. In addition, the head butler and one personal maid traveled with Leonore Annenberg.[112] Security personnel further expanded the count.[113]

This meant that the guests, cosseted within a secluded and secure location, well served by an ample and professional staff, could relax in a manner virtually impossible anywhere else.

Dwight and Mamie Eisenhower were among the first guests, in March 1966.[114] Leonore Annenberg recalls that on this and later visits, the former president "was a good chef. . . . He would put on an apron . . . and do delicious barbecued steaks."[115] Palm trees that President Eisenhower suggested be planted as a hazard on the golf course came to be known as the Eisenhower Palms, and they still adorn the property (fig. 61). Richard and Patricia Nixon were frequent visitors; it was at Sunnylands, in December 1968, that Nixon asked Walter Annenberg to serve as Ambassador to the Court of Saint James's,[116] and it was to Sunnylands, in September 1974, that he returned after resigning as president. Nixon was clearly moved by the Annenbergs' act of compassion, writing in the guest book, "When you're down you find out who your real friends are."[117]

Gerald and Betty Ford visited Sunnylands many times, as did Ronald and Nancy Reagan. For Nancy Reagan, Sunnylands was "Heaven, as always!" and on one of his visits the President wrote, "Why, as we leave, do I feel I'm playing 'Paradise Lost'?"[118] George H. W. Bush wrote, "Happiness is a visit with the Annenbergs at Sunnylands," and for Barbara Bush staying there was "Paradise!"[119] Lady Bird Johnson visited in 1977, and Bill and Hillary Clinton on separate occasions in 1995. Rosalynn Carter, a guest in 2003, remembered Sunnylands as a "Beautiful, peaceful home."[120]

Entertaining weekend guests who could often include the president and more than one former president as well as British royalty proved Leonore Annenberg's skill at protocol, a gift that was recognized by her appointment as Chief of Protocol for the United States in 1981. This position carries the rank of ambassador, although she preferred not to be so addressed, saying that "one ambassador in the family is enough."[121] At Sunnylands she took exacting care with every detail, as with seating plans for dinner parties which she alone determined.

Records were kept by the head butler, one of whose tasks at such events involved the selection of carefully coordinated and sometimes elaborate table settings (fig. 62).[122] One of the grandest of such affairs was the lunch for Queen Elizabeth II in 1983, as suggested by both the seating plan and menu (fig. 63). After her visit, the Queen is reported to have noted that the Annenbergs had the same china pattern as she did (Flora Danica)—but more of it.[123]

Leonore Annenberg often arranged for creative and sometimes unexpected juxtapositions of guests. Once she said, "I just mixed everybody up and we had fun."[124] Thus, when Prince Charles stayed at Sunnylands in 1974, other guests included Bob Hope and Frank Sinatra (Palm Springs neighbors) as well as then-Governor Ronald Reagan.[125] The royals must have enjoyed themselves: Prince Charles visited again in 1986, and both Prince Edward and Prince Andrew on several later occasions. Sustaining British ties, Margaret and Denis Thatcher visited in 1991, 1995, and 1997.

These brief mentions give only a suggestion of those who have been guests at Sunnylands. A single-spaced listing of them up to 2005 fills thirty-five pages in the estate's guest books, with names that include leaders of business, philanthropy, and the arts; and they, too, are mixed with the politically powerful. Truman Capote, visiting in 1968, described Sunnylands as "a desert dream."[126] Anne d'Harnoncourt, director of the Philadelphia Museum of Art, and her husband, the curator Joseph J. Rishel, have often been guests. Many have noted the beauty of the art collection, such as Philippe de Montebello, then director of New York's Metropolitan Museum of Art, who wrote on the occasion of Walter Annenberg's eightieth birthday, "the pictures at Sunnylands are very much in your image, intense, strong, colorful, expressive."[127]

Among events held at Sunnylands, the annual New Year's Eve party must have been the most festive.[128] This tradition began in 1966 and continued through 2007. For these occasions, the main living area was transformed into a grand ballroom, with furniture rearranged and an orchestra brought in. At one such gala in 1981, Walter Annenberg danced with

61 | *"Eisenhower palms" (Photograph by Graydon Wood, December 2006).*

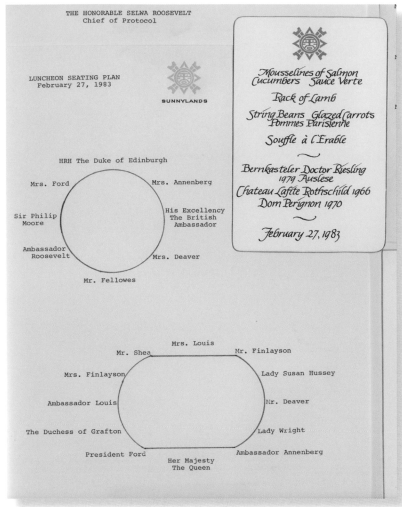

62 | *Table setting in dining room (By permission of Royal Copenhagen; Photograph by Michael Comerford, March 1990).*

63 | *Seating plan and menu for luncheon for Queen Elizabeth II (Photograph by Michael Comerford, February 1983).*

Nancy Reagan and Ronald Reagan with Leonore Annenberg (fig. 64). Family gatherings on holidays remained an important part of Sunnylands as well, accommodating many of the Annenbergs' grandchildren, nieces, and nephews, uniting the different generations of their family.

Those who designed Sunnylands remained connected to the Annenbergs in the years that followed its opening in 1966. William Haines and Ted Graber were both guests there on several occasions; retaining his sense of humor, Haines wrote in the guest book, "It was almost worth it!" On a later occasion, Graber, more sedately, wrote, "You have made it even more beautiful."[129] In 1969, the Annenbergs selected Haines and Graber to restore Winfield House, the United States Ambassador's residence in London. Highly praised by discern-

ing British critics, this restoration was mostly financed by the Annenbergs as a gift to the United States.[130] Looking back, Walter Annenberg wrote to Haines, "I know it is not necessary for me to point out the fun and good fellowship we have had together over the years, and it is indeed my hope that it will continue for many more years to come."[131] The work of Haines and Graber has grown in stature over the years, with furniture designed by their office now much sought by collectors.[132]

Quincy Jones was also involved with later commissions sponsored by the Annenbergs, such as the Annenberg School for Communication of the University of Southern California, which he designed in 1976.[133] After his death, his widow, Elaine K. Jones, wrote to Walter Annenberg, "As you know, Quincy enjoyed every moment of his relationship with you and

64 | *At New Year's Eve party, left to right: Leonore Annenberg, Ronald Reagan, Nancy Reagan, Walter Annenberg (Courtesy of the Ronald Reagan Library, December 1981).*

65 | *Golf course (Photograph by Graydon Wood, April 2006).*

Mrs. Annenberg and held you both in the highest regard at all times."[134] Rolla Wilhite later worked for Walter Annenberg's sister, Enid Annenberg Haupt, in Beverly Hills.[135] As for Dick Wilson, his golf course by 1982 was reportedly one of only two private courses then maintained in the United States (the other was at the Rockefeller estate in Pocantico Hills). It was probably the country's "best-maintained golf course," wrote that same reporter, "over which the least number of rounds are played anywhere" (fig. 65).[136]

A LASTING TRIBUTE

One last tradition of longstanding importance is upheld at Sunnylands: the moving commemoration of place through burial. This tradition extends back to the very beginnings of civilization, as seen in the urban settlement of Çatal Hüyük, in Anatolia, ca. 6500–5500 B.C.E., where ritualistic burial occurred within the houses themselves. During the late Roman Empire, some private citizens of prominence built mausolea on their country estates, such as the mausoleum identified by the name Tor de Schiavi, near Rome, ca. 300–310 C.E. The celebrated British architects John Vanbrugh (1664–1726) and Nicholas Hawksmoor (1661–1735) designed one of the most notable of such edifices at Castle Howard, in Yorkshire: their great, temple-like structure, built during the first quarter of the eighteenth century, dominates the castle's landscape. More recently, the family of Edgar Kaufmann built a secluded crypt at Fallingwater, their famous country retreat designed by Frank Lloyd Wright in 1935.

The Annenbergs sought a different form for this purpose. Rather than a massive monument or underground crypt, they chose instead to build an open pavilion that celebrates light, a structure responsive to its landscaped setting and one that sustains the architectural themes and humane modernity of the main house. Harry Saunders first designed an open, hexagonal enclosure; a simpler version, rectangular in plan, was built instead following drawings prepared by a Palm Springs architect, Allen Cook. Following the deaths of Walter Annenberg in 2002 and Leonore Annenberg in 2009, this last, deeply affecting part of Sunnylands achieved the special meaning that was intended and positions this great house for the expanded, more public role that it now assumes.

66 | *View to main house entrance from arrival court (Photograph*
by Graydon Wood, December 2006).

THE MODERN SCULPTURE

Suzanne Glover Lindsay

Sculpture is displayed everywhere at Sunnylands—often prominently—and represents a wide array of cultures, periods, and moods. Just inside the gate, by the Canadian Art Price (1918–2008), *Birds of Welcome* stands on the lawn (see page 156) as a visual link to the house on the horizon, an emblem of hospitality whose buoyant, simplified forms recall the lyrical birds of Henri Matisse (1869–1954). On the golf course looms a Northwest Coast totem pole, while the reproduction Maya column-fountain in front of the house announces the house's architectural theme, as David De Long notes in this volume, through its elaborate reliefs as well as its form. Framed within the windows at the entrance, two bronzes by Jean Arp (1887–1966) flank the double doors into the atrium, which highlights a monumental bronze *Eve* by Auguste Rodin (1840–1917) (fig. 66). More bronzes by Arp and his generation cluster around selections from the celebrated Annenberg collection of paintings and works on paper (fig. 67).[1] *Peacock* by Harry Bertoia (1915–1978) dominates the covered passage from the dining room to the guest pavilion (see fig. 50). The terrace around the house featured, at one end, Rodin's marble *Eternal Spring* in an intimate corner garden setting (fig. 68) and, at the other, *Square Wave* by Yaacov Agam (b. 1928) on the pool's edge (fig. 69). Small works animate tabletops throughout.

As with the paintings, this eclectic collection of sculpture reflects the Annenbergs' highly personal choices; above all, as they affirmed in published interviews, they chose works that they "genuinely loved and respected and wanted to live with"—over any predetermined program.[2] Yet several aesthetic strands emerge. The collection offers a century of modern sculpture beginning with Rodin, from the period represented by many of the Annenbergs' paintings—the 1880s–1890s—and ending around 1980. Its strongest emphasis, however, coinciding with the years that the house was designed and built, is on twentieth-century sculpture, featuring aspects of late European modernism: the portraiture of Alberto Giacometti (1901–1966) and the natural forms of Arp, Émile Gilioli (1911–1977), and Étienne Hajdu (1907–1996). Such holdings especially recall

67 | *Left: Jean Arp*, Sculpture Classique, *model ca. 1960, bronze reportedly a lifetime cast, ht. 50 in. (127 cm) (©2008 Artists Rights Society [ARS], New York/ VG Bild-Kunst, Bonn). Center: Émile Gilioli*, Le Coq, *model 1949, date of cast unknown, bronze, ht. 13.5 in. (34.29 cm), ed. 1/6 (©2008 Artists Rights Society [ARS], New York/ ADAGP, Paris). Right, background: Jean Arp*, Leaf on Crystal, *model 1954, bronze reportedly a lifetime cast, ht. 24 in. (60.96 cm) (©2008 Artists Rights Society [ARS], New York/ VG Bild-Kunst, Bonn). (Photograph by Graydon Wood, December 2006).*

the collection of an American contemporary, the industrialist Joseph Hirshhorn (now seen at the Hirshhorn Museum and Sculpture Garden, Smithsonian Institution, Washington, D.C.). In art-historical terms, the modernist sculptors of Sunnylands are often linked, in a filial if contentious line, with Rodin through his erstwhile assistant Constantin Brancusi (1876–1957), forming a generation that rethought Rodin's example for their own work. Some of the latest and most diverse sculpture in the collection is by Americans, notably Bertoia and Paul Rossi (b. 1929).

Rossi's *All This You Must Imitate* (fig. 70), in the game room of the guest pavilion, depicts a historical American sub-

ject that complements those evoked in the so-called Room of Memories. It presents a legend of the Cheyenne, the best known of the tribes of the Great Plains: wolves give hunting lessons to Owl Friend, founder of the Wolf Soldier Band, the finest warriors of a powerful clan identified with this animal for its superior intelligence, hunting prowess, and strong family ties. This small but dramatic bronze, the second in an edition of twenty-five casts,[3] also reinforces the Native American presence at Sunnylands introduced outside, by the totem pole and reproduction Maya column-fountain. It was not the first work by Rossi, a noted Western artist and historian, that had attracted the Annenbergs, for his sculpture especially suited

69 | *Yaacov Agam*, Square Wave, *1976, polished aluminum, 73 × 73 in. (185.43 × 185.43 cm) (©2008 Artists Rights Society [ARS], New York/ ADAGP, Paris; Photograph by Graydon Wood, December 2006).*

68 | *Auguste Rodin*, Eternal Spring, *plaster ca. 1881, marble executed 1905, ht. 28 in. (71.12 cm) (Photograph by Graydon Wood, December 2006).*

70 | *Paul Rossi*, All This You Must Imitate, *The Beginning of the Cheyenne Indian Wolf Soldier Band. Bronze, 14 × 22 × 12 in. (35 × 55 × 30 cm), sculpted in 1979, casting number 2 (1982) in edition of 25 (Photograph by Graydon Wood, December 2006).*

their vision of America. Walter Annenberg bought the first cast of Rossi's set of twelve miniature bronze saddles as a symbolic history of the United States (starting with a sixteenth-century Spanish saddle and ending with a 1910 American Western saddle), and lent the series to Ronald Reagan, who kept it in the Oval Office throughout his presidency. It is currently at the Reagan Presidential Library in Simi Valley, California.[4]

The modern sculpture at Sunnylands presents several famous "schools," beginning in the late nineteenth century, that challenged inherited definitions of mediums. The selection has sensuous appeal, without the jarring impact of certain avant-garde art: it offers Giacometti's haunting portraiture, for example, but not his Surrealist work. And humor and playfulness run through it, as in the work of Arp, Bertoia, and Agam. References to nature—especially Leonore Annenberg's beloved flowers (Hajdu) and Walter Annenberg's cherished birds (Price, Bertoia, Gilioli)—marry the Sunnylands sculpture with its live surroundings.

Above all, and epitomized by the Rodin *Eve*, the selection highlights Woman. More than the paintings, Sunnylands' sculpture explores her many facets and impact. This theme may embody Walter Annenberg's often-mentioned admiration for women, beginning with his wife, Leonore, and his mother, Sadie, and including his seven sisters.[5] He claimed as much for *The Album* by Édouard Vuillard (1868–1940), a large canvas of 1895. Because this image of an interior with seven women reminded him of his sisters, it presides over the dining room.[6]

The Annenbergs began to buy sculpture at the same time as painting, soon after they married in 1951, yet this collection took a manifestly different direction: while they pursued Impressionist and Post-Impressionist paintings, they acquired twentieth-century sculpture. Early purchases went to Inwood, their former home near Philadelphia, and certain small works first resided at their summer homes in the Rockies.[7] But major pieces were woven into the Sunnylands design from the beginning: As David De Long reveals, the base for the Rodin *Eve* appears among the architect Quincy Jones's early drawings for the house. A surge of activity followed the Annenbergs' return from their ambassadorial duties in London in 1974, as De Long also observes: the Arps and Bertoia's *Peacock* were moved to Sunnylands and the latter was installed in its present site, outside the newly configured dining room.[8] The Annenbergs continued to buy sculpture for Sunnylands into the early 1980s but they focused on painting during their final acquisitions campaign over that decade.[9] After selling their last summer home in the Rockies, they moved its sculpture to Rancho Mirage,[10] widening the collection's range to its current state.

Throughout the decades, the couple also made direct contact with the living artists whose art they bought. Arp dedicated one of their earliest purchases, *Souvenir d'Athènes* cast ca. 1955 (fig. 71), to Walter Annenberg; Paul Rossi's wife warmly remembers Mr. Annenberg from his visits to see and buy her husband's bronzes. And *Again* came to Sunnylands repeatedly in the late 1970s, when the Annenbergs, after buying *Square Wave* for Sunnylands, commissioned works for their homes and offices.[11]

Moving about the house and grounds, visitors easily sense the importance of sculpture to daily life at Sunnylands. In the following discussions, I briefly consider the history of select works in their own time and their impact within its surroundings today.

71 | *Left (foreground): Jean Arp,* Leaf on Crystal, *model 1954, bronze reportedly a lifetime cast, ht. 24 in. (60.96 cm). Right, on floor: Jean Arp,* Souvenir d'Athènes, *reportedly cast 1955, bronze, ht. 30.5 in. (77.47 cm), ed. 2/3 (©2008 Artists Rights Society [ARS], New York/ VG Bild-Kunst, Bonn; Photograph by Graydon Wood, December 2006).*

RODIN'S *EVE* AND *ETERNAL SPRING*

The two works at Sunnylands by Rodin, the most famous and controversial sculptor of his day, brought him new acclaim as the preeminent "poetic" sculptor of the turn of the century.

The Annenbergs' powerful statue of *Eve* (fig. 72) grew out of Rodin's plans for an *Adam* and *Eve* in the 1870s, sculptures that evolved into the projected jamb figures for his colossal *Gates of Hell*, doors commissioned in 1880 for a proposed museum of decorative arts in Paris but never finished. That teeming relief is a compelling sculptural meditation on human nature based on Dante's *Inferno*.[12] The biblical Eve had gained new symbolic force in late nineteenth-century France. Long familiar in Christian art as the human agent of the Fall, Eve appeared often in the Paris Salons of Rodin's lifetime, in nonreligious sculpture that explored humanity's moral complexity, an issue that haunted a France in turmoil since the Revolution.[13] Certain works also interpreted her as the root of all human bonds, some of them tragic: Louis-Ernest Barrias (1841–1905) portrayed her as the First Mother, mourning the first murder (of her son Abel killed by his brother Cain) and, in another group with her husband Adam, conducting his funeral.[14] Rodin built upon these guises with a stunning new chosen moment, the expectant Eve's anguish over her moral legacy. Rodin claimed the subject grew out of the revealed pregnancy of his model, an unnamed favorite whom he admired for her earthy power.[15] Because she quit modeling sessions before the figure was finished, the sculptor purportedly abandoned the project for a smaller, more conventionally handled variant, but he returned to this first conception amid controversy over his monuments to Balzac and Victor Hugo in the late 1880s and 1890s. Rodin commissioned two casts of this large version from the master bronze founder François Rudier (completed 1897); according to new evidence, he exhibited the cast that is now at Sunnylands, the second

72 | *Auguste Rodin, Eve (grande modèle), plaster model ca. 1881, bronze cast by François Rudier, July 1897, ht. 68 in. (172.72 cm) (Photograph by Graydon Wood, December 2006).*

(marked "Deuxième Épreuve," second proof) (fig. 73), in two pivotal Paris exhibitions: the annual Salon of the progressive Société Nationale des Beaux-Arts in 1899 and his own independent exhibition that coincided with the Centennial World's Fair of 1900.[16]

At both shows, the massive statue drew wide critical and

73 | *Detail of* Eve, *founder's inscription (Photograph by Graydon Wood, December 2006).*

public attention. For some, it was the most admirable entry of 1899, redeeming the beleaguered Rodin.[17] Certain critics felt that its dark power, lack of conventional beauty, finish, and pose recalled Michelangelo's epic statues.[18] Unlike most of Rodin's figures and the portrayal of the Fallen Eve by other sculptors, this *Eve*, they claimed, neither grimaced nor gestured emphatically yet personified a "grief unspeakable" that seemed almost too painful to behold.[19] Some observers connected her pose and subtly rendered pregnancy as signs of the First Woman's pain not just for herself, but for the consequences of her transgression upon future generations.[20] Many felt Rodin made new poetry from a traditional art form and its environment. Critic Arsène Alexandre saw this monumental *Eve* as a "caryatid that supports the weight of the sins that she brought upon humanity."[21] Most writers pointed to the bronze's unprecedented placement, in the middle of the main gallery, on a low mound of sand on the floor—*without a base*—an unnerving choice that caused the First Mother to rub elbows with her living successors as light from the high gallery windows washed over them, joining them symbolically.[22]

New research reveals that this bronze was purchased during the 1899 Salon by painter-critic Henri Duhem (1860–

1941/42) of Douai in northern France—apparently among his first acquisitions for a much-admired collection of modern art—who placed it in his garden, a new Garden of Eden.[23] There, just over a decade later, *Eve* gained the limelight again. During World War I, Duhem hid beside it the arms and uniforms of French soldiers he helped to escape from the invading Germans; the bronze was then buried during the ensuing Occupation to prevent its being looted or melted down. At war's end, a major Paris newspaper published a photograph of French troops "exhuming" the statue from its garden tomb. It was a poignant sign of France's revival and of Eve's ongoing legacy of a fractious progeny.[24]

The plant-filled atrium at Sunnylands again suggests the Garden of Eden. *Eve*'s central placement there lends dark drama and conceptual depth to the idyllic core of a cultured domestic interior. Her epic grief becomes approachable, perhaps, if we concentrate instead on the monumental figure's surging contours, Rodin's most often-mentioned aesthetic concern in his sculpture. *Eve*'s lighting even invites us to look closely. During the day, its volumes are accentuated by natural light falling from the overhead skylight, in a more focused "spotlight" than the light that pooled around it from the high windows of its first exhibition spaces mentioned above; Rodin generally called for high lateral light to counterbalance overhead sources in public exhibitions of his sculpture.[25] Though the architect for Sunnylands provided the statue with a rotating base, similar to some of Rodin's work produced on a low modeling stand, the Annenbergs preferred that *Eve* stand compellingly still, with us moving around it, like its viewers when first publicly exhibited.

Contrasting markedly in its luminous material and intimate scale, *Eternal Spring* (see fig. 68) also grew out of Rodin's work of the 1870s. The poses and lithe figures seen here evolved from his studies of intertwined lovers of those years and they established a composition that Rodin subtly altered to great effect in variants he exhibited beginning in the 1880s. Naming certain examples after storied lovers (*Francesca da Rimini* from Dante's *Inferno* or *Amor and Psyche* of classical myth) or simply titling them *The Kiss*,[26] the sculptor most often called the group *Spring*—presenting youthful love as an allegory of a season—or, with the alternative title *Eternal Spring*, as ideal life, alluding to Virgil's embodiment in the Georgics 2 of an idyllic Italy as the perpetual pairing of nubile earth and the divine.[27] An English critic applauded another variant of this group for exuding "an astonishing amount of passion and sweetness" and a "sensuousness" that no one familiar with Rodin's monumental "titans" would believe him capable of producing.[28] The female nude, noted his secretary, one of Germany's greatest early modern poets, Rainer Maria Rilke (1875–1926), was full of longing, embodying an urgency that contrasted with the sculptor's usual images of docile or overpowered women.[29] Rodin's *Eternal Spring* fused the bittersweet poetic resonances of love, spring and eternity, remarked the critic Léon Maillard in 1899: "Their youth so beautiful and themselves so sure of its permanence that only love seems eternal. . . . Illusion!! Illusion!! Yet hope never abandons us."[30] Rodin's group indeed suggests this double-edged vision. The sense of the beautiful dream comes through the white marble, the "purest" sculptural matter traditionally used to represent the ideal realm. The possible dangers of youthful love emerge, perhaps, in the man's unstable pose, perilously perched on what appears to be a tree trunk, his extended arm supported by a branch, and feet only lightly resting on the uneven ground.

However untraditional its concept, Rodin's embracing lovers develop the three-dimensional potential of a time-honored artistic theme, known in life-size figures, small Renaissance bronzes, and couples represented in seventeenth-century paintings of harvest feasts (such as Rubens's *Kermesse*, Louvre). The composition of the kneeling woman, passionately arched toward her seated lover, fans out from their points of contact, extending around the base to provide lively contours, masses, and voids from several viewpoints.

This sculptural group proved much in demand among art collectors. Beyond producing a successful bronze edition, Rodin executed at least ten marbles that visibly differed from one another in carving, setting, and the figures' placement within it.[31] This marble, possibly the one commissioned and executed in 1905, perhaps by Rodin's favorite carver Louis Mathet, for Georg Hirzel of Leipzig,[32] is exceptionally fine, with sharply undercut figures whose contours swell softly yet clearly, and surfaces that are sensitively worked for a range of delicate tones in natural light. The sculpture's corner placement close to the house at Sunnylands, surrounded by flowers, provided an intimate, bucolic setting for a lyrical image.

TWENTIETH-CENTURY SCULPTORS IN PARIS

Sunnylands features, in ten pieces of exceptional quality, some of the most accessible forms of avant-garde sculpture produced in Paris through the 1960s. Most fall within what certain postwar critics have called the "middle ground" between extreme realism and abstraction. This formal language carried a sense of hope for a generation, overwhelmed by war and political radicalism, that often interpreted artistic extremes politically: many rejected modern figurative art, for instance, as totalitarian because Communists and Fascists used it for their political programs.[33] Invoking nature and traditional art in gently abstract forms, this moderate approach proved especially fertile for sculptors.

JEAN ARP (1887–1966) ARTWORK AT SUNNYLANDS

Seven of the Parisian works at Sunnylands are by the Alsatian-born Jean (or Hans) Arp (1887–1966), all from his mature career. They are: *Torso*, *Leaf on Crystal*, *Souvenir d'Athènes*,

Chapeau Forêt, Demeter, Sculpture Classique, and *Simplicité Sinueuse.* They belong to a period when, after twenty years of activity, around 1930 (shortly after his move to the environs of Paris), this poet-artist began making what he called "concretions" or "biomorphs," organic masses shaped with no preconceived form or subject. Once completed, they received his titles as poetic complements rather than as descriptions.[34] The concretions epitomized Arp's credo that art grew largely on its own (without the artist) in a process akin to nature's: "Art is a fruit that grows in man, like a fruit on a plant," resulting in a piece with its own life rather than a willed copy of nature.[35] His simple forms achieve an appealing sensualism; an evocative energy animates the work and stimulates the viewer's imagination. The Sunnylands *Torso* (fig. 74) is considered one of Arp's first in this vein:[36] the shapely "body" carved with an integral base suggests a mounted antique fragment. Later examples, *Simplicité Sinueuse* (standardly translated as Entangled, rather than Sinuous Simplicity) and *Demeter* (fig. 75), similarly recall classical—and decidedly female—figures. *Leaf on Crystal* (see figs. 67, 71) instead conjoins elements that suggest flora and minerals; the least representational of the seven sculptures, *Chapeau Forêt* (literally Hat Forest) (fig. 76), links clothing with nature. Arp's fusions of human, manmade, and natural elements drew special applause from other European avant-garde sculptors who explored biotic form, such as Barbara Hepworth (1903–1975).

This "new" organic sculpture has a rich artistic heritage, from antiquity to a contemporary of Arp's also in Paris, the Romanian-born Brancusi, who rejected Rodin's loose modeling and theatrical poses for expressive subtlety and varied handling, from "primitive" carving to sleek forms in marble and bronze.[37] Arp's admiration for Brancusi, whose work is not represented in the collection, is especially clear in the Sunnylands *Demeter*, particularly with its wood base of stacked, rough-hewn bowl shapes.[38] Yet Arp's work is distinct. Whereas Brancusi's could be monumental or occupy considerable space, with multiple elements, Arp's is human, even intimately scaled: *Demeter* is life size; *Torso* and *Chapeau Forêt*, diminutive. Arp's slender *Simplicité Sinueuse* suggests proud sexuality; the ample *Demeter* (named after the ancient Greek goddess of agriculture) is earthy, supple, and responsive. His little *Torso*—thought to represent, like Rodin's *Eve*, a pregnant woman[39]—seems to dance, especially when turned, and she emanates joy. The volumes of the larger pieces undulate and swell especially when we walk around them. In so doing we realize the counterpoint of their forms: soft against hard or

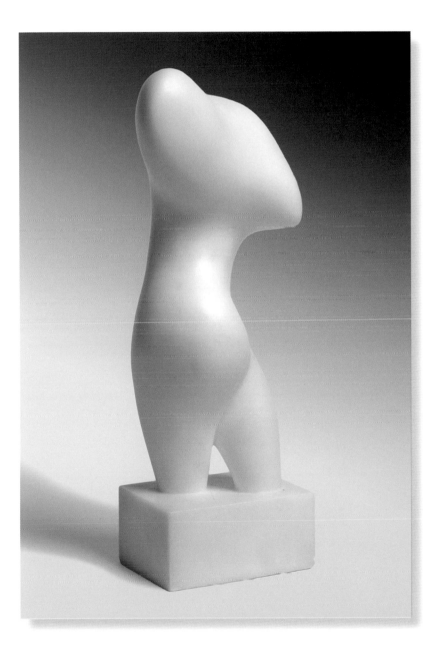

74 | *Jean Arp, Torso, 1930, marble, signed, ht. 13.5 in. (34.29 cm) (©2008 Artists Rights Society [ARS], New York/ VG Bild-Kunst, Bonn; Photograph by Graydon Wood, December 2006).*

75 | Jean Arp, Demeter, *model ca. 1960, bronze reportedly a lifetime cast, ht. 41 in. (104.14 cm), ed. 1/3 (©2008 Artists Rights Society [ARS], New York/ VG Bild-Kunst, Bonn; Photograph by Graydon Wood, December 2006).*

76 | *Jean Arp*, Chapeau Forêt, *model ca. 1960, bronze reportedly a lifetime cast, ht. 8.75 in. (22.23 cm), ed. 1/5 (©2008 Artists Rights Society [ARS], New York/ VG Bild Kunst, Bonn; Photograph by Graydon Wood, December 2006).*

ragged; edges against volumes; axial verticality against syncopated asymmetry. Their bases contrast in color, material, and form with their surmounting elements and their architectural environment.

Arp's *Sculpture Classique* (Classical Sculpture) (see fig. 67) and *Souvenir d'Athènes* (Memory or Souvenir of Athens) (see fig. 71) demonstrate this artist's innovative blurring of two- and three-dimensional sculpture. The first recalls a free-standing relief [40]—in itself an unusual form—and it is pierced repeatedly to give greater interplay between mass and space, a view through the work to the space beyond, and into the "interior" of the mass itself. Suggesting a map (but unlike any of Greece), *Souvenir d'Athènes* is one of Arp's so-called "configurations." As sculpture rather than as torn-paper collage, like others in this category, it emphasizes relief, its raised shaped forms rising sharply from its flat, blank ground. Bearing the sculptor's inscribed dedication to Walter Annenberg ("Arp à

W. Annenberg") on the back, *Souvenir d'Athènes* attests to contact between the collector and the artist in the latter's final years.

Produced as variants in several mediums, these works by Arp capitalize on their chosen material. The marble *Torso* (the only known example in the size of the surviving original plaster),[41] is finely carved, its material as evocative of ancient art as its form. The dark burnished surface of two bronzes—*Simplicité Sinueuse* and *Sculpture Classique*—emphasizes their swelling mass, and distinguishes them from Arp's polished bronzes, which emanate bright color and reflected light, dematerializing their solidity or drawing into them the changing reflected images of the world and visitors before them. The reflective surfaces especially recall those of Brancusi's bronzes. All examples at Sunnylands are reportedly lifetime works, produced in limited number (from three to five).[42]

The work of two other sculptors at Sunnylands shows affinities with Arp's. The *Coq* (Rooster) by Émile Gilioli (1911–1977) (see fig. 67) similarly invokes nature in its clean "beaked" bird shape in highly polished bronze.[43] *Belle de Nuit* (fig. 77) by Étienne Hajdu (1907–1996), a Romanian like Brancusi,[44] however, offers more than one meaning. Named after a fragrant tropical night-blooming flower (*Mirabilis jalapa*; related to the morning glory) that, in France, metaphorically signifies famous, often exotic beauties, this sculpture evokes both a sumptuous plant and an edgily voluptuous female body. The smooth pink marble could suggest either skin or floral tones—the latter especially because of its placement at Sunnylands, beside a reproduction of Fantin-Latour's still-life painting of pink roses.

These works contrast dramatically with the spectral portrait by Alberto Giacometti (1901–1966) of his brother Diego (1902–1985) (fig. 78). One of many images of Alberto's handsome, restless sibling made over the decades, the bronze bust is a telling example of this artist's complex use of portraiture in the late 1950s, especially in sculpture.[45] Diego's half-length image is placed on an elongated bronze stele to recall a classical type; the portrait of this modern man thus gains an ancient

77 | *Étienne Hajdu*, Belle de Nuit, *1958, marble, ht. 26.5 in. (67.31 cm) (©2008 Artists Rights Society [ARS], New York/ ADAGP, Paris; Photograph by Graydon Wood, December 2006).*

78 | *Alberto Giacometti*, Bust of Diego, Stele III, *model ca. 1958, bronze reportedly a lifetime cast, ht. 20.75 in. (52.71 cm), ed. 3/6 (©2008 Artists Rights Society [ARS], New York/ ADAGP/ FAAG, Paris; Photograph by Graydon Wood, December 2006).*

quality. The torso is schematized to draw attention to the head, which is flattened and simplified to emphasize Diego's strong features and gaze—for Giacometti, the source of a portrait's power and its vital link to the viewer. The turbulent surface suggests at once molten bronze and a corroded archaeological artifact as it intensifies the energy of the evocative portrayal. From his earliest years, Giacometti had admired this kind

of modeling in Rodin's portraiture. The delicate proportions of the ensemble are intended to recall what Giacometti most prized among archaeological artifacts (small ones) and to suggest we see the portrait from afar. The result is psychologically volatile, with its tense interplay between the implied distance and intimacy between subject and viewer in a portrait of a living contemporary rendered as a hallucinatory idol. The columnar bust also produces an unsettling experience for the beholder: viewed, as Giacometti intended, on a three-quarters diagonal, Diego's profile and sloping shoulders taper into the decorated stele and suggest immobile, remote strength. Seen from the front, however, Diego's flattened head, huge glaring eyes, and speaking mouth take on a living presence that shocks yet holds us.

Giacometti executed several variants of this work, cropping the bust at different points (the Sunnylands *Stele III* terminates at a lower point than most), and giving them various finishes. Unlike the gilding on some, which lends them an opulent and iconic formality, the modulated, warm-toned patina of this cast, marked third of six, adds to its archaeological aura.[46]

BERTOIA AND AGAM: SCULPTURE THAT MOVES

Bertoia and Agam gained renown in the 1950s for their kinetic sculpture, the term (from the Greek for motion) given to a type of mobile sculpture invented in the early twentieth century. This ostensibly new form, however, builds on a time-honored artistic interest.

To represent movement has always been part of the visual arts' ambition to rival nature (or the divine) by creating life. Such a quest in freestanding sculpture, which can assume the form and mass of a live being in real space, made the ponderous immobility of its standard materials (notably stone or metal) a challenge to artists and viewers. Certain observers, from the eighteenth-century English painter Joshua Reynolds (1728–1792) to the twentieth-century American critic Clement Greenberg (1909–1994), felt sculpture failed at imitating life the harder it tried.[47] Heavy stone, argued Reynolds, can neither flutter nor fly and looks ridiculous trying. It could be true to itself and its materials, all such critics asserted,

only if not forced to pretend. Nonetheless, over the centuries sculptors pursued various ways to incorporate motion in their art, to produce the illusion of life or to animate static form. Like painters, sculptors typically rendered poses that seemed to freeze action, prompting the viewer's imagination to fill in the unseen fuller story. The intertwined lovers in Rodin's *Eternal Spring* (see fig. 68), for instance, suggest a developing embrace. Certain surfaces capture motion around them: Arp's and Gilioli's polished bronzes, as said earlier, reflect the spectators' movements. Alternatively, sculptors bypassed sculpture's inescapable inertness by making the observer move instead. Walking around Rodin's *Eve* (see fig. 72) more fully reveals her intense, withdrawn gesture.

Certain works were made to be turned, on a special base like *Eve*'s if large, or in one's hand if small. As mentioned before, turning Arp's tiny *Torso* (see fig. 74) makes its asymmetrical volumes seem to undulate. Sculptors also put nature to work. Monumental figures like Augustus Saint-Gaudens's *Diana*, 1892–1894, of hammered and gilded copper (Philadelphia Museum of Art), was conceived as a gleaming artful weathervane for Madison Square Garden, to be turned by the wind high over Manhattan.[48] Officially born in the avant-garde of the 'teens and twenties, with mock industrial works that moved mechanically (Marcel Duchamp's *Bicycle Wheel* and *Roto-Reliefs*, for instance), kinetic sculpture went mainstream when the American sculptor Alexander Calder (1898–1976) made his famous "mobiles" beginning in the 1930s, abstract constructions that, suspended from a ceiling or a freestanding base, reacted to other physical forces—a breeze, our touch.[49] These works also capitalized on an emotional dimension that Calder, like Arp, advocated for art. Both artists insisted that the experience of sculpture should include childlike play; injecting such qualities especially into public, monumental forms opened new avenues for this ancient medium. Many twentieth-century artists, including Claes Oldenburg with Coosje van Bruggen, took these principles as points of departure for their own pursuits of "real" movement in sculpture.[50]

Bertoia and Agam developed the formal and psychologi-

79 | *Harry Bertoia*, Peacock, *1961, patinated bronze, ht. 70 in.*
(177.80 cm) (©2008 Estate of Harry Bertoia/ Artists Rights Society
[ARS], New York; Photograph by Graydon Wood, December 2006).

cal potential of many of these features in nonfigurative form. Bertoia, an American designer and sculptor, explored new possibilities for metal by going beyond traditional categories of craft and their assigned properties.[51] His *Peacock* at Sunnylands (fig. 79) is an excellent example, from the peak of his career in the 1950s and 1960s, of his most familiar free-standing work with metal rods, shaped and arranged to evoke dynamic nature (clouds, plants, or even volcanoes). Bertoia allegedly never titled a piece, however, aiming to free the viewer's imagination to find its own associations. It is not clear who dubbed this one *Peacock* or provided similar titles for other Bertoias in museums. The work indeed suggests the male peacock's displayed tail; close variants of it evoke starbursts or flowers (one at the Walker Art Center, Minneapolis is entitled *Dogwood VII*). Spraying gracefully from its vertical support, *Peacock*'s "feathers" wave when swept by a hand or the breeze. The sculpture asserts its manmade character through the treatment of its materials: Typically, Bertoia added molten bronze to fabricated rods to impart a crafted, light-catching surface to the industrial form, and this gives *Peacock* an especially theatrical presence at night.

Peacock's modulated delicacy contrasts with the clean industrial forms of the sculpture by Bertoia's contemporary also represented at Sunnylands, Yaacov Agam (born Jacob Gipstein, 1928), an Israeli living in Paris, but the handling of movement is similar. He is represented by eight artworks here: *Three by Six Double Frame Interplay* (1976), *Sunnylands* (1976), *Square Wave* (1976), *Situations* (1978), *Abstract Composition (1)* (1979), *Abstract Composition (2)* (1979), *Reflecting Space* (1980), and *Untitled* (1976/1980). Several geometric pieces include elements that can be turned, changing the composition at will or setting it into motion, for Agam not only believed in involving time and touch in art, he affirmed, like Arp and Bertoia, the mentally liberating power of play.[52]

Suggesting the Annenbergs' regard for this artist, the pool at the far end of the terrace prominently features his *Square*

Wave (see fig. 69), a nest of aluminum rods, forming squares bent into Vs that rock with the visitor's lightest touch—or, given its setting, with nature's. The polished rods reflect the strong desert sun when still. When activated by the famed valley breezes that stir the surrounding tree branches and the water's surface, this high-tech, geometric piece seems to dance with nature.

The façade of the house around the terrace bears examples of Agam's wall reliefs, which employ another traditional form of kinetic art: they are works with crisp vertical strips projecting from the background that are painted with different motifs on each side. The painted elements metamorphose as the spectator shifts position, recalling early optical art that Agam considers "parallel" to his work: the puzzle portraits of Giuseppe Arcimboldo (1527–1593) and Renaissance anamorphoses.[53] One Agam relief called *Situations* (fig. 80) hangs just outside the dining room and offers a painted composition when seen from one viewpoint, and seen from the opposite direction, a large "A"—linking artist and patron.

Agam's use of kinetics to include the viewer in the making of art, whether in the many compositional possibilities of moving parts or the experience of the finished piece—operates on two levels. Artistically, he participates in the broader modernist project to explore the relationship between art and spectator; philosophically, his work also embodies his metaphysical beliefs (most particularly a form of Jewish mysticism, the Cabala) in the mutability of existence and in perpetual becoming as a principle of life.

Agam's work for Sunnylands is also a testament to place, the dramatic desert world of which it is a part, and to the relationship between artist and patron. The Annenbergs met Agam in 1976, at an exhibition of his work inaugurating the new building by architect E. Stewart Williams for the Palm Springs Desert Museum, and they purchased the introductory piece in the installation, *Square Wave*, as a focal element for the Sunnylands landscape. Commissions for new work throughout their properties quickly followed, but especially for this

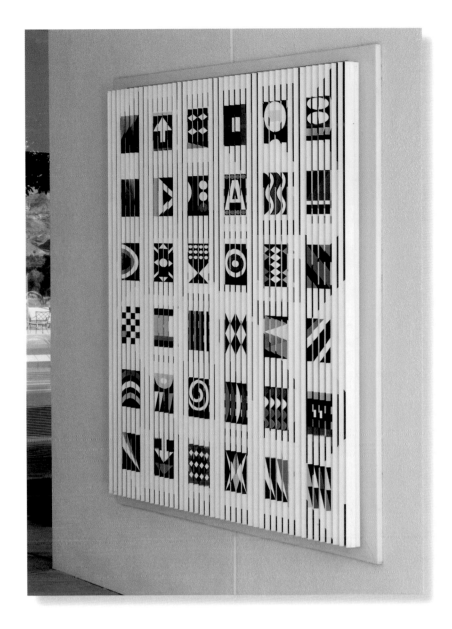

80 | *Yaacov Agam*, Situations, *1978, oil on wood, 76 × 76 in. (193.04 × 193.04 cm.) (©2008 Artists Rights Society [ARS], New York/ ADAGP, Paris; Photograph by Graydon Wood, December 2006).*

desert home. Agam and the Annenbergs worked together on-site selecting locations for new art; his outdoor painted wall pieces were consciously linked to the house and desert site: one was given the façade color in a material that would not fade in the strong sun. That technical pursuit of permanence in this outdoor relief is the rare feature of Agam's work that did not develop the concept of mutability.[54]

81 | *View across atrium from living area to entrance (Photograph by Graydon Wood, December 2006)*

SELECTED PAINTINGS AND WORKS ON PAPER

Gwendolyn DuBois Shaw

In 1991, when Walter and Leonore Annenberg gave their collection of more than fifty Impressionist and Post-Impressionist paintings to The Metropolitan Museum of Art in New York, the character of their art collection at Sunnylands shifted. High-quality reproductions of the departed paintings were hung as mementos in place of the originals (fig. 81), and the remaining canvases and works on paper by nineteenth- and twentieth-century European and American artists became objects of greater notice. Even if Claude Monet and Pierre-Auguste Renoir had left the estate, Rembrandt Peale, Andrew Wyeth, Pablo Picasso, Romare Bearden, and Jacques Villon remained and soon came to dominate the character of the more private spaces of the residence.

Five important works remained in the collection of Leonore and Walter Annenberg following an unusually heady spate of gift giving in the 1980s and 1990s. Rembrandt Peale's *George Washington* (1859), Andrew Wyeth's portrait of Walter Annenberg (1978), Pablo Picasso's drawing *Picador on Horseback* (1959), Romare Bearden's collage *Africa* (1977), and *L'Enfant au Biberon* (1952) by Jacques Villon are key to understanding specific social and historical aspects of the visual program of Sunnylands, aspects beyond points of aesthetics and the Annenbergs' inherent good taste. To consider each work fully, one must place it not only within the oeuvre of its artist, but also within the context of the house and the motivation behind its acquisition.

Two of the most important paintings at Sunnylands are installed in places of reverence in the Room of Memories, as the family calls it, an intimate space that includes an extensive library of beautifully illustrated art books and recent works of political biography. Among the floor-to-ceiling bookshelves are innumerable signed photographs of the Annenbergs with captains of industry and heads of state, memorabilia from years of diplomacy, and guest books chronicling the visits of countless notables. Presiding over this fascinating visual documentation of the Annenbergs' decades of public service to the nation, and their dedication to a tight network of close friends, are a portrait of George Washington painted by Rembrandt Peale in 1859

82 | *Rembrandt Peale*, Portrait of George Washington, *1859, oil on canvas, 35.5 × 28.5 in. (90.17 × 72.39 cm) (Photograph by Graydon Wood, December 2006).*

(fig. 82) and a 1978 portrait of Walter Annenberg by Andrew Wyeth (see fig. 84).

Like Walter Annenberg, Rembrandt Peale (1778–1860) was the industrious son of an ambitious and successful father. The second child born to the painter and naturalist Charles Willson Peale and his first wife, Rachel Brewer, Rembrandt was pushed from childhood to become an artist, completing numerous portraits of notable Philadelphians while still a teenager. The most prolific member of a family of artists, Rembrandt Peale had painted nearly one thousand portraits by the end of his life.[1]

The portrait of George Washington owned by the Annenbergs is from a series known as the "porthole" type or the *Patriæ Pater*, "father of the fatherland" in Latin. Rembrandt Peale developed the concept for the *Patriæ Pater* over a period of two decades following the president's death in 1799, before finally completing a version that satisfied him in 1823.[2] Peale's idea for the composition originated in 1795 when he first painted a portrait from life of President Washington, who was then in residence in Philadelphia, the capital of the young republic between 1790 and 1800. Ever ambitious, Peale hoped that his artistic conception of the nation's first president would become the iconic image by which the great man would be known to posterity. To that end, he reproduced the *Patriæ Pater* numerous times in an effort to aid its dissemination throughout the important government buildings and prominent households of the country. Gilbert Stuart's "Athenæum" portrait of Washington, however, which is engraved on the face of the one-dollar bill, soon eclipsed Peale's image as the ubiquitous artistic rendering of Washington—in large part due to its familiarity as currency.

Other versions of the *Patriæ Pater*, which was painted nearly eighty different times by Peale, may be found in the collection of the United States Senate and the National Portrait Gallery in Washington, D.C. Peale's inscription on parchment, affixed to the gilded frame of the portrait of Washington at Sunnylands (fig. 83), reads:

Washington sat expressly to me in September 1795—My Father, at my request, making a study of him at the same time. The Portrait from which this Picture was copied, I painted in the year 1824—being the result of a series of efforts to combine the merits of my own & my Father's studies, under the influence of extraordinary excitement & vivid recollection. . . . Though painted solely for my own gratification, it was spontaneously approved by the intimate Friends & Relatives of Washington, as the most *characteristic* likeness of him. . . . I was born the 22d of February 1778—consequently I had entered the 82d year of my age when I made this my 75th copy for John McAllister Jr. of Phila.—being now the only artist living to whom Washington ever sat for his portrait. . . . Written and signed by Rembrandt Peale. Philadelphia, June 1859.[3]

In keeping with its presence in the Room of Memories, the portrait hangs above an arrangement of invaluable presidential memorabilia and Americana. Among these unique objects is a bell from Colonial Williamsburg that is inscribed, "May the Future Learn from the Past." Beside the bell are door hinges from the Old State War and Naval Building, which were given to the Annenbergs at Christmas 1987 by President and Mrs. Ronald Reagan. To the left of the door hinges is the shell casing from the twenty-one-gun salute fired at the inauguration on January 21, 1985, for President Reagan's second term, and a crystal dish, inscribed "1st Vice President under the 25th Amendment, inaugurated, Dec. 6, 1973," a gift from President Gerald Ford, who visited Sunnylands on April 14–21, 1974. These objects, in concert with a replica of Old Glory, create a sort of shrine to the presidency and the elevation of democratic principles that George Washington has come to represent.

In addition to being a close confidant and ally of presidents and prime ministers, Walter Annenberg was also a keen supporter of the arts and as such was closely connected to one of the most important American artists of the twentieth century, Andrew Wyeth (1917–2009). Over the years the Annenbergs collected a number of paintings by the artist, including the masterpiece *The Mill* (1962), and they consistently supported exhibitions of his work under the auspices of the various charitable endowments that bear their names.

The portrait of Walter Annenberg by Andrew Wyeth re-

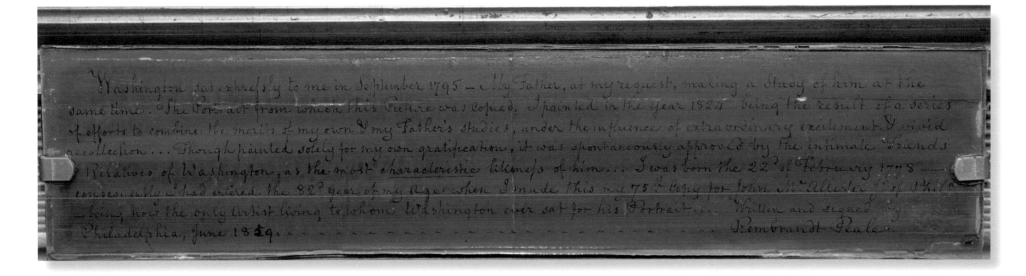

83 | *Inscription by Peale, detail of* Portrait of George Washington *(Photograph by Ned Redway, March 2008).*

84 | *Andrew Wyeth*, Portrait of Walter Annenberg, *1978, tempera on masonite, 32.5 × 28.5 in. (82.55 × 72.39 cm) (Photograph by Graydon Wood, December 2006).*

veals a very different man from the one who appears in the many photographs around the room (fig. 84). In the photographic moments that tell that story of Annenberg's life, he is always shown forging the relationships that made his political career. But rather than posing him amid the social markers of his position as a publisher or an ambassador, Wyeth chose to depict Annenberg as a man apart. Dressed in a timeless garment, an English choir robe with a high neck and long sleeves, he is shown only from the chest up, his person filling

the better part of the lower half of the canvas. An unseen light source from the left side of Wyeth's composition illuminates Annenberg's forehead and eyes, casting his cheeks and mouth in shadow. In this way, the large, empty space of the canvas that spreads out behind him becomes a space of reflection. It is in this space that we may envision the ambassador as a man whose true thoughts are remote and unknown to all but him.

The painting has a dry and austere texture to it and displays Wyeth's subtle mastery of color and the medium of tempera. On close observation, there is a surprisingly diverse range of tones and tints shading from brown and gray to beige and cream. There is also a nod to Renaissance portraiture in the way that Annenberg is posed with a slight turn toward us, presenting his shoulders as strong and firm. Beneath the

painting, a photograph of Annenberg in the robe that he wore for no less than thirty-five sittings[+] joins with the painting, as if to say, "That is indeed I" (fig. 85).

With these two remarkable paintings, of George Washington and Walter Annenberg, the Room of Memories becomes a celebration of the history of the Annenberg clan, emphasizing their connection to American history and their part in helping to make it. Photographs of the family's immediate ancestors and descendants dominate the west wall providing a view onto their personal legacy. A central roundel of Annenberg's father, Moses, rhymes nicely with the portrayal of Washington in his "porthole," while at the same time it engages the portrait of Moses' son hanging on the opposite wall. The photographs form a spatial and linear cataloging of important alliances,

85 | *Photograph of Walter Annenberg in front of his portrait by Andrew Wyeth (Photograph by Graydon Wood, December 2006, of earlier photograph).*

both revealing and inscribing a chronology of key events, from the founding of the Annenberg dynasty in America by industrious immigrants through Walter and Leonore Annenberg's service to several presidential administrations, thereby creating a perfect context for the extraordinary paintings of two singular Americans.

Moving out of the Room of Memories and into the main corridor of the private wing, we encounter *Picador on Horseback* by Pablo Picasso (1881–1973). Boldly rendered in black

86 | *Pablo Picasso*, Picador on Horseback, *1959, brush and black ink on paper, 19 × 25 in. (48.26 × 63.5 cm) (©2008 Estate of Pablo Picasso/ Artists Rights Society [ARS], New York; Photograph by Graydon Wood, December 2006).*

excitement of the line, the picador seems to be quiet and very attentive, as if he were observing an interaction between matador and bull taking place just beyond the edge of the composition. There is something about his posture—his head, rising straight in line with his back, echoing that of the horse who also stares ahead—that makes him appear deeply absorbed and relentlessly observant. This is emphasized by Picasso's prominent signature, which is found along with the date in the upper right-hand corner, "14.7.59—III—<u>Picasso</u>," just behind the head of the picador—equating the artist's importance with the bullfighter's own gravitas.

In the decade preceding the execution of *Picador on Horseback*, Picasso had been spending much of his time at Villa la Californie, his estate in Cannes, in the south of France, where he had become deeply enmeshed in the art of his native Spain, which lay less than a hundred miles to the southwest. He was looking intently at the work of the master of the Golden Age of Spanish painting, Diego Velázquez (1599–1660), completing more than forty paintings inspired by Velasquez's masterpiece *Las Meninas* between August 17 and December 30, 1957.[6] At the same time Picasso was producing numerous drawings of bullfights and bullfighters, a subject that had also been a favorite of the most famous Spanish painter of the preceding century, Francisco de Goya y Lucientes (1746–1828).

Many of Picasso's bullfighting images were inspired by days spent cheering in the hot sun at rings in nearby Vallauris and Arles, and some of them undoubtedly drew on action witnessed at bullfights performed by the celebrated matador Luis-Miguel Dominguín (1926–1996), his friend from the mid-1950s. The artist repeatedly drew and painted Dominguín over a decade culminating in 1961, when the two men collaborated on the book, *Picasso: Toros y Toreros*.

In the bullfighting season of 1959—the season during which Picasso drew *Picador on Horseback*—the intense rivalry between Dominguín and his brother-in-law Antonio Ordóñez was played out in the rings of Spain and southern France. The year before "the dangerous summer," as Ernest Hemingway would title his chronicle of the rivalry between

ink, the drawing is dated July 1959—a momentous year in the history of bullfighting in Spain and the South of France (fig. 86). The drawing depicts a picador, the mounted *torero* (bullfighter) responsible for placing sharply barbed spears in the wild bull's shoulders, enraging him yet wearing him down before his death at the hands of a matador during the preliminary stages of a traditional bullfight.[5] He holds the reins of his horse tightly and his feet are set securely in the stirrups. While the horse looks forward, he looks a little bit off to his right. The horse's tail has been braided and tied up, and the costume and plumed hat of the picador are faintly sketched: one can just make out his epaulets and the braid across his chest.

The line that Picasso uses in this bold and evocative composition is rough and jagged, broken and dry. Despite the

Ordóñez and Dominguín.[7] Picasso had chosen to leave La Californie, which had become a magnet for the artist's admirers, in favor of the fourteenth-century Château de Vauvenargues, which is situated in the shadow of Mont Sainte-Victoire, near Aix-en-Provence. For a man who had become the world's most famous artist, the Château de Vauvenargues was an exclusive retreat, providing for him the same sort of much needed respite from an increasingly demanding public that Sunnylands has provided for the Annenbergs and their guests. It was a place within which the great artist could escape the masses who clamored for his attention and where he could lavish hospitality on friends like Dominguín. It was at Vauvenargues on July 14, 1959, in relative seclusion, that Picasso drew *Picador on Horseback*, and it was also there, in continuation of an age-old tradition of commemorating place through burial, that Picasso was buried in 1973.[8]

Picasso's *Picador on Horseback* represents a moment in the artist's career when he was reexamining Spanish history and culture. The collage *Africa* (1977), which hangs opposite the drawing in the private wing's main corridor at Sunnylands (fig. 87), recalls a similar impulse by the artist Romare Bearden (1911–1988). Nearly two decades after Picasso's homage to the bullfight, Bearden too was in the process of retracing certain aspects of his own cultural and historical inheritance. *Africa* appeared on the cover of *TV Guide*, an Annenberg publication, the week that the mini-series *Roots* premiered and was kept by the Annenbergs as a memento of one of the most important television events of the era. *Roots*, a controversial and much-discussed dramatization of Alex Haley's novel, imagines his enslaved ancestors from Africa to their freedom in the post-bellum American South. The widely watched ABC mini-series inspired visceral reactions from liberal, conservative, white, and African-American viewers, and was the topic of media and scholarly debate for years thereafter. One critic noted of the controversy, "Haley's aim was . . . to fuse two seemingly disparate cultures into one continuum, and thereby bridge the gulf that has existed between Africa and America."[9]

87 | *Romare Bearden*, Africa, 1977, *paper collage, 23 × 14.75 in. (58.42 × 37.46 cm) (© Romare Bearden Foundation/ Licensed by VAGA, New York, NY; Photograph by Graydon Wood, December 2006).*

In *Africa*, the upper two thirds of the vertical composition are dominated by a teal blue paper background, while the lower third has gray paper which makes up the water on which a small slave ship sets sail. We recognize the boat as a slaver because Bearden has utilized the iconography of bodies stacked together in the hold. Linking the blue and gray grounds is the proud profile of an African American. Beneath the arc of a round, clean-shaven head, the man's features are inscribed into the surface of the paper from which he is cut, his body making up the land that the ship will encounter. His form stands for the New World and at the same time, with his face overlapping the cutout continent of Africa, he looks to his motherland. His shirt has been assembled out of red, white, and blue paper to create the American flag, and yet the blackness of his face overlapping the green continental form and the red sun rising behind it, reminds us of the colors of the African National flag, a flag that the radical activist Marcus Garvey designed in the 1910s.

Although born in Charlotte, North Carolina, Bearden spent most of his life in New York City, where he studied mathematics at New York University before taking up drawing and painting at the Art Students League in 1935 under the instruction of the German émigré artist George Grosz (1893–1959).[10] Following service in World War II, Bearden continued to pursue his wide-ranging interests and enrolled in philosophy courses at the Sorbonne in Paris under the auspices of the GI Bill. Throughout his career he grappled with American history, creating paintings, illustrations, and collages (the medium for which he is best known today) that examine the issues of class and culture experienced by African Americans yet filter them through the lens of universal human experience. For example, the same year that Bearden created *Africa* he also completed a series of collages based on the *Odyssey*, Homer's epic poem. So it is unsurprising that when the design for *Africa* was transferred to the lithographer's stone and the image was produced in a series of twenty numbered prints, the title of the image changed to *Roots Odyssey*.

At the end of the private wing's main corridor at Sunnylands, past the Bearden collage and the Picasso drawing, lies the master bedroom: an exquisitely feminine enclave characterized by Chinoiserie and Limoges porcelains, silk brocade-upholstered furnishings, and tasseled pillows. It is in this most private of spaces that is hung an abstract painting by the French artist Jacques Villon (1875–1963) (fig. 88). *L'Enfant*

au Biberon (1952), or "infant with baby bottle," is a cubistic arrangement of abstract shapes in spring colors. A patch of orange, a bit of teal blue, and a swath of lemon yellow float in the middle of the canvas, rubbing up against lime green, mossy brown, and pomegranate red. The grouping of contrasting colors that make up the painting are surrounded by a golden yellow border, colors rhyming with the yellow of the carpet and the lamps, as well as the floral-printed canopy of the four-poster bed next to it.

Born Gaston Duchamp, Jacques Villon was the oldest brother in a family of artists that included Marcel Duchamp (1887–1968), Suzanne Duchamp (1889–1963), and Raymond Duchamp-Villon (1876–1918). Although Villon is best known for his part in the development of Cubism in Paris during the 1910s and his activities with the theoretically oriented Puteaux group, he was also a painter who was highly acclaimed well into his later years, receiving the first prize at the Carnegie International in Pittsburgh in 1950, the Grand Prize for painting at the Venice Biennale in 1956, and the Grand Prize for painting at the Exposition Internationale in Brussels in 1958.[11] It was in 1952, during this mature period of remarkably fertile experimentation with color theory and the limits of abstraction, that he completed *L'Enfant au Biberon*.

Other artists at mid-century had begun to eschew explanatory titles in favor of numbering systems in an effort to discourage the viewer's literal interpretation of a work, but Villon continued to provide his paintings with specific, descriptive titles. It has been argued that this unfashionable decision was a demonstration of the artist's commitment to the basic tenets of Cubism, which advocated the deconstruction of bodies, objects, and space into planar surfaces as though seen from multiple viewpoints, but which stopped short of total nonobjectivity.[12] With this in mind, the viewer is prompted to approach *L'Enfant au Biberon* in search of a human form, and yet the reward of the painting does not lie in the ultimate reconstitution of the body of a child from within the pink, yellow, and green paint. Rather, the satisfaction imparted by the image rests largely in

88 | *Jacques Villon, L'Enfant au Biberon, 1952, oil on canvas, 25 ×
35.75 in. (63.5 × 90.80 cm) (©2008 Artists Rights Society [ARS], New
York/ ADAGP, Paris; Photograph by Ned Redway, March 2007).*

the harmonious nature of the colors themselves and the relationships produced by their evocative juxtaposition. However, the question remains: can the viewer actually find a child within the paint, or is the artist—like his brother Marcel Duchamp in his hermetic *Large Glass, or, The Bride Stripped Bare by Her Bachelors, Even*—toying with the viewer's natural inclination to seek evidence of representation?

Like Peale's portrait of Washington and Wyeth's of Annenberg, which occupy places of reverence in the Room of Memories; like Picasso's dramatic image of a picador and Bearden's collage of the Middle Passage, which speak to key moments of cultural change in the mid-twentieth century; *L'Enfant au Biberon*, with its sensuous, evanescent color harmonies, finds its natural home in the private space of Sunnylands. *L'Enfant au Biberon* is a subtle painting that elicits contemplation and quiet reflection from the viewer. As such, it is the perfect painting for the master suite at Sunnylands: an object for meditation within a private sanctuary, at the heart of the most serene and hospitable of houses.

89 | *Asian Artists in Crystal installation and a table with works from other Steuben series (By permission of Steuben Glass; Photograph by Graydon Wood, December 2006).*

THE STEUBEN GLASS COLLECTION

M. J. Madigan

The Steuben glass at Sunnylands—nearly fifty examples of engraved crystal objects made during the three decades after World War II—has been described as "the finest collection of Steuben in the world, one that could not be replicated or assembled today."[1] Its highlight is the only complete set of Steuben's *Asian Artists in Crystal* series, a project of international good will undertaken in 1954 at the request of the United States government.[2] This series is displayed in illuminated niches on shelves custom-designed by the studio of William Haines and Ted Graber, in collaboration with Harry Saunders (fig. 89), for the glass-walled corridor or "Steuben gallery" leading from the main living area to the formal dining room at Sunnylands (see fig. 47). A long console table before the central niche supports four additional examples of important engraved pieces: they represent the series of themed Steuben crystal titled *Poetry in Crystal*, 1963; *Islands in Crystal*, 1966; and *Great Explorers*, 1970 (fig. 90).

Arranged on a hexagonal table in the main living area (fig. 91) are *The Unicorn and the Maiden*, *Romance of the Rose*, and *Chinese Pavilion*—three of the nine lavishly embellished, one-of-a-kind *objets d'art* that compose the extraordinary Steuben *Masterworks* series, created between 1966 and 1980 in the spirit of Benvenuto Cellini and Carl Fabergé.[3] A fourth piece from the *Masterworks* series, *Carrousel of the Sea*, is also part of the Sunnylands collection. Casually arranged with other small objects on tables flanking a sofa in the intimate Room of Memories are a number of signature Steuben decorative designs including *Excalibur*, 1963, and *Eagle*, 1964—popular pieces that are still in production.

90 | *Works from Asian Artists in Crystal series in niches. Left to right on table: Hernando Cortes (Paul Schulz, 1970, Great Explorers series); Hawaii (Don Weir, 1966, Islands in Crystal series); Birds and Fishes (Don Pollard and Robert Vickrey, 1963, Poetry in Crystal series), and Crete (Don Pollard and Alexander Seidel, 1966, Islands in Crystal series). (By permission of Steuben Glass; Photograph by Graydon Wood, December 2006).*

91 | *On hexagonal table, Office of William Haines and Ted Graber, designers; Chinese Pavilion, Romance of the Rose, The Unicorn and the Maiden, and other glass works (By permission of Peter Schifando and Steuben Glass; Photograph by Ned Redway, March 2007). Romance of the Rose, ht. 8 × diam. top 9 × diam. bottom 8 in. (20.32 × 22.86 × 20.32 cm).*

STEUBEN GLASS: A BRIEF HISTORY

An American company, Steuben was founded in 1903 by the expatriate English glass artist Frederick Carder and the American businessman Thomas Hawkes, who owned a glass engraving factory at Corning in New York's Steuben County, from which the company takes its name.[4] Today, Steuben's local artisans still use traditional methods and tools to make crystal for the table and home, as well as for limited-edition engraved designs and one-of-a-kind sculptural pieces.

Crystal glass is created by adding as much as thirty percent lead to the standard glass formula of sand, potash, and "cullet" (broken shards of glass) before melting the mixture at high temperatures. The added lead endows the glass with weight, clarity, brilliance, and a very high index of refraction, making it ideal for engraving and forming into sculptural objects. Since lead was difficult to obtain for nonmilitary purposes during World War I, Steuben's output suffered, and in 1918 it was sold to the larger and more industrially oriented Corning Glass Works. The "Steuben Division" remained under Carder's direction until 1930, however, producing an eclectic range of colored art glass influenced by Art Nouveau, Art Deco, and various historical styles.

With the advent of modernism in the 1920s, tastes changed, and Steuben nearly went out of business. In 1933, the twenty-nine-year-old Arthur Amory Houghton, Jr. (1904–1994)—a fourth-generation member of the wealthy family that owned Corning Glass Works—took charge of the ailing Steuben Division.[5] Scholarly, urbane, and Harvard-educated, he revolutionized the company, enlisting the American sculptor Sidney Waugh as director of design. Houghton's "new" Steuben, like the crystal of Orrefors, Lobmeyer, and other fine European glasshouses, emphasized the flowing, refractive qualities of glass itself in simple heavy-walled vases and bowls compatible with the modernist aesthetic. Some of these utilitarian pieces were engraved by copper wheel, a seventeenth-century technique at which Steuben's artisans excelled. Houghton quickly phased out colored glass in favor of a new optical crystal of exceptional brilliance and purity that had recently been discovered by the scientists of Corning Glass Works. This is the brilliant, colorless glass for which Steuben is still renowned.

Arthur Houghton tirelessly promoted Steuben glass to people of taste and means, shuttling between Corning and his townhouse on Manhattan's East Ninety-first Street (a neighborhood where several Annenberg sisters also lived). He opened the first of several Steuben shops on Fifth Avenue in 1934, and commissioned Henri Matisse, Salvador Dalí, André Derain, Georgia O'Keeffe, Isamu Noguchi, and other renowned artists to create designs for engraving on the glass. Soon, Steuben's vases, bowls, and barware were *de rigueur* in discerning households, and important engraved pieces were represented in the collections of museums and private individuals. Made in America, Steuben was also favored as a gift of state by every White House incumbent from Harry Truman onward.[6] In the late 1950s, Steuben expanded its offerings to include purely sculptural forms, which by the 1960s were frequently embellished with precious metals. At that time, Steuben also introduced several themed series of sculptural glass engraved with story-telling images, often in collaboration with scholarly institutions. As noted above, examples of glass from the *Poetry in Crystal*, *Islands in Crystal*, and *Great Explorers* series are part of the Sunnylands collection.

THE ANNENBERGS AND STEUBEN

Although the Annenbergs possessed various small ornamental designs introduced by Steuben in the early 1960s (these are informally displayed on end tables in the Room of Memories at Sunnylands), it was not until 1971 that Walter Annenberg—

then serving as Ambassador to the Court of St. James and occupying Winfield House, the U.S. ambassador's residence in London—instantly established himself as an important Steuben collector with a single decisive purchase: from Steuben he bought forty-seven engraved "exhibition" pieces costing $299,075. [7] His initial intention had been only to acquire a small group of Steuben objects to leave behind upon his departure from Winfield House. "At the conclusion of my tour of service," Annenberg wrote Steuben's president Arthur Houghton in October 1970, "I will naturally want to take out the porcelain that I have [on display in Winfield House] and yet I have a desire to have something significant there for the next Ambassador and cannot think of anything any more fitting than selected pieces of Steuben. Quite frankly, I got the idea from Ambassador John Humes' residence in Vienna . . . he has a great collection of Steuben glass in his living room."[8]

Steuben immediately proposed two groups of ornamental designs "representative of our finest achievements" to fill the shelves of the Winfield House drawing room, which had been renovated by the studio of the Sunnylands interior designers William Haines and Ted Graber.[9] But Steuben's offerings consisted of large-edition pieces that anyone could buy. Annenberg (who wanted the rarest and best of everything) tactfully withdrew his request, citing a "reluctance to endow Winfield House with a built-in collection of Steuben glass which a future incumbent might not especially favor."[10] From this exchange, however, grew an Annenberg-Steuben dialogue that spanned nearly three decades. The relationship was cultivated by the Steuben sales executive Ann Pittendrigh, who continued to send the Ambassador photographs of newly introduced designs. The following summer, he responded with an unexpected, rather breathtaking idea: "It would be interesting to contemplate what would be involved in the way of investment for a total collection of all [Steuben's sculptural] work to date . . . the idea of a complete list is imaginative and appealing."[11] Pittendrigh hastily gathered photographs of fifty examples of important engraved designs, including pieces remaining from the *Asian Artists in Crystal* series of 1956. "It is very stimulat-ing to work with someone with such discerning and imaginative ideas," she replied, enclosing the list and photos.[12] With his penchant for Asian arts, Annenberg expressed interest in buying the *Asian Artists* collection, provided the missing pieces could be replicated. "Happily, this unusual collection consisting of thirty-six designs can still be made to special order," Pittendrigh assured him. "Thirteen . . . of the pieces are available, and it would take us approximately fourteen to sixteen months to make the remaining twenty-three. The overall cost amounts to $114, 875."[13]

Pittendrigh was invited to Sunnylands late in the summer of 1971 to "firm up a program regarding Steuben Crystal" for the house.[14] During her visit, the Annenbergs agreed to buy not only the entire *Asian Artists in Crystal* series but also *Carrousel of the Sea* ($47,500) and *The Unicorn and the Maiden* ($73,500)—one-of-a-kind designs from Steuben's *Masterworks* series, as well as nine other important ornamental pieces. "It was a great pleasure for me to visit your beautiful home and . . . assist with the selection of your Steuben collection," Pittendrigh wrote. "I had a very interesting meeting in Los Angeles with Mr. William Haines and Mr. Theodore Graber. It is going to be great fun working with them. . . . We plan to complete your order in time to ship it to California no later than the first week in July 1972."[15]

While Pittendrigh and the interior designers conferred on details of the installation, Annenberg weighed in from London. "Please remind the Messrs. Haines and Graber," he wrote her in October 1971, "that we need a firm base for the pieces going into the corridor at Sunnylands, because [it] is directly over the San Andreas fault and we have got to provide protection for the occasional jiggles that we have in the house. My home is built to withstand virtually 10 on the Richter Scale, but we must provide some protection for the pieces in the light of this condition. I continue to be excited about the contemplation of assembling all this work."[16] (As David Whitehouse, director of The Corning Museum of Glass, later observed after visiting Sunnylands in 1992, firm bases were indeed designed. Each object was "attached with an adhesive substance to custom-made plastic or Plexiglas bases, which fit tightly into holes in the shelves on which the objects are exhibited.")[17]

Through the winter, Pittendrigh continued to send photographs of other new designs, but Annenberg declined them all, even while passing these materials on to Prime Minister Edward Heath and others in London. "It might be prudent to examine and live with what I have on order for at least a period of a year, before I seek additional pieces," he suggested.[18] When the glass was at last in place at Sunnylands, Pittendrigh expressed delight with "your *Asian Artists in Crystal* so exquisitely displayed. The blue background and subtle lighting are superb."[19]

In the years that followed, Pittendrigh continued to send photographs of new Steuben designs, while Walter Annenberg provided her with access to influential contacts in England and the United States. She expressed thanks for his assistance in having a Steuben bowl and candlesticks selected as the White House wedding gift to England's Princess Anne.[20] But he continued to decline additional offers of Steuben for Sunnylands, sometimes tartly. "Your enclosure depicting [Steuben's] *Thousand and One Nights* is appreciated, but I am not interested—it is a little flamboyant for my taste. But then, not everybody likes spaghetti Bolognese," he wrote in early 1974.[21]

Two years later, after seeing a photograph of *Chinese Pavilion* (most likely in the luxurious limited-edition book Steuben published to document its completion), Walter Annenberg himself wrote to Arthur Houghton asking to buy this extraordinary new work in the *Masterworks* series—a Chinoiserie fantasy of engraved crystal, gold, and precious stones that was not for sale. "Surely no piece of Steuben measures up to the brilliance of this work," Annenberg wrote Houghton. "At Sunnylands, as you know, I have the Asiatic Steuben [as well as] *Carrousel of the Sea* and *The Unicorn and the Maiden*, of which we are very proud. At the risk of being presumptuous, if . . . you might consider parting with the Pavilion, I would deeply appreciate hearing from you. Ultimately, Sunnylands

will be turned over to the public and I naturally take care in the selection of acquisitions for this long-range responsibility."[22] Although newly retired, Pittendrigh nonetheless helped arrange for a duplicate of the coveted design to be made. "When my wife and I saw this superb piece . . . we simply could not resist it," Walter Annenberg wrote her in November 1976. "It will not be easy to wait approximately eighteen months for the copy to be executed but we will have to be patient in the knowledge that we will eventually have it here at Sunnylands."[23]

In July 1978—again at Pittendrigh's prompting—Walter Annenberg also agreed (albeit reluctantly) to purchase *Romance of the Rose*, another one-of-a-kind creation from the *Masterworks* series: "As you know, I am not in ecstasy over the *Romance of the Rose*, but it does belong with the other great Steuben pieces and hence I must bow in the face of the 'collector's obligation.'"[24] Although this piece was the Annenbergs' last Steuben purchase for Sunnylands, they remained friendly with Pittendrigh for years. In 1981, during Leonore Annenberg's tenure as U.S. Chief of Protocol, Pittendrigh wrote to express "how happy I am that Mrs. Annenberg chose [Steuben's] *The Crusaders* for the Royal Wedding Gift [to Prince Charles and Lady Diana Spencer], and above all, had the great wisdom to change its name for the occasion [from *The Hunt*]. It was a brilliant idea!" She added, "In spite of your enormously busy schedules I still hope that one day there will be an opportunity to catch up with you again. Your friendship and our business association has meant a great deal to me."[25]

The relationship between the Annenbergs and Steuben Glass grew more distant after Pittendrigh retired. Though he loved birds, Walter Annenberg refused Steuben's 1982 offer of their newly introduced *Belted Kingfisher*, allowing that it did "not bear a relationship to the bird I know. Perhaps this is a belted kingfisher in some other part of the world."[26] A decade later, Steuben president Susan B. King visited Sunnylands to explore the idea of borrowing the *Asian Artists in Crystal* series for an exhibition marking the ninetieth anniversary of Steuben's founding. "It would be an honor for us . . . to support an exhibition at a major New York museum or other appropriate site such as the Morgan Library," she proposed.[27] The idea was well received, and King dispatched the director of The Corning Museum of Glass to Sunnylands to ensure that the pieces could be safely transported. Although Steuben opened discussions with The Metropolitan Museum of Art, where Arthur Houghton had served as trustee, the "Asian Artists" exhibition did not come to pass.[28] In the summer of 2000, Steuben again asked to borrow objects from Sunnylands, this time for an exhibition reprising Steuben's historic *27 Artists in Crystal* series of 1940, which featured engraved drawings commissioned from Fernand Léger, Henri Matisse, Georgia O'Keeffe, Salvador Dalí, and other great artists.[29] Steuben's misunderstanding of the Sunnylands holdings was both puzzling and unfortunate. "Evidently there is some confusion about the Annenbergs' Steuben glass collection," a secretary replied on the Annenbergs' behalf. "While it is extensive, they have no pieces that were done from original artists' drawings. Theirs is an Asiatic collection, with a few assorted pieces of a sentimental nature."[30] With that modest assessment, the Annenberg-Steuben dialogue of three decades drew to a close.

THE *ASIAN ARTISTS IN CRYSTAL* SERIES, 1956

Although each piece in the *Asian Artists in Crystal* series is intriguing in its own right, it is the making of the series itself—a footnote to postwar diplomatic history—that fascinates. Created in collaboration with the U.S. government during the Eisenhower years, the collection consists of thirty-six polished crystal forms engraved with drawings commissioned from artists in sixteen "Asian" countries.[31] The idea for the show was proposed to Steuben in 1954 by Harold Stassen, then head of the United States Foreign Aid Office (FAO).[32] It was Stassen's charge to prevent the spread of communism across Asia by fostering ties of friendship with countries deemed vulnerable. Mindful of Steuben's "British Artists in Crystal" exhibition earlier that year, Stassen wrote to Arthur Houghton:

It would be possible for Steuben Glass to be of very significant service to our country. . . . There is a tendency for people to think wrongly of our country as being interested only in the materialistic and militaristic aspects. . . . We are thinking of methods by which the people of the United States might demonstrate an interest in the cultural attainments and artistic interests of the people of Asia. Noting the exceptional success of "British Artists in Crystal," it seemed if something similar could be done in relationship to Asian artists it might have a very marked result in contributing to our objective. [33]

Houghton seized the opportunity. He dispatched Karl Kup, Curator of Prints at the New York Public Library and a scholar who had traveled widely in Asia, to visit artists in sixteen countries representing "the great cultural areas of Buddhist, Hindu, and Moslem thought and tradition."[34] Included were Japan, Korea, China (represented by Nationalist Chinese artists in exile in Formosa), the Philippines, Vietnam, Indonesia, Thailand, Burma, India, Ceylon, Pakistan, Iraq, Iran, Turkey, Syria, and Egypt, the last country presumably because of its importance to Near Eastern affairs.

Although Steuben was official sponsor of the project, Kup traveled as consultant to the FAO, which paid his expenses, planned his itinerary, and organized exhibitions of local artists for him to view—an arrangement kept confidential at Stassen's request.[35] Before setting out, he was briefed on glassmaking procedures at Steuben, the better to assess which kinds of art could be translated into glass. The FAO suggested the subject matter should "please the man in the East as well as the man in the West," while Steuben asked only that the selections

92 | *George Thompson, Steuben designer, and Jamini Roy, India,* Gopis in the Grove of Vrindavana, *engraved crystal, ca. 1956, diam. 10.75 in. (27.31 cm) (By permission of Steuben Glass; Photograph by Graydon Wood, December 2006).*

93 | *Lloyd Atkins and Made Djate, Indonesia,* Balinese Funeral, *engraved crystal, ca. 1956, ht. 19 in. (48.26 cm) (By permission of Steuben Glass; Photograph by Graydon Wood, December 2006).*

be "Asian in feeling."[36] Thus instructed, Kup acquired 130 drawings, which Steuben purchased and eventually donated to the New York Public Library. Represented in the group were little-known artists along with those of established reputation. Thirty-six of the drawings were engraved on crystal forms conceived by Steuben's senior staff designers George Thompson (fig. 92), Lloyd Atkins (fig. 93), and Don Pollard (figs. 94, 95).[37] The final selections were made with input from the Steuben's copper-wheel engravers, who would bear responsibility for transferring the images to glass.

The first of two sets of the series was exhibited with great fanfare from January through March 1956, initially at the National Gallery of Art in Washington, D.C., and then at The Metropolitan Museum of Art in New York City. In their joint preface to the exhibition catalogue of the same name, museum directors David E. Finley of the National Gallery and James J. Rorimer of the Metropolitan characterized the exhibition "Asian Artists in Crystal" as "a felicitous combination of the art of the East and the craftsmanship of the West . . . another proof that art knows no boundaries and that culture is one of the strongest links between civilized men. Artists in the Far and Near East have prepared the drawings. American designers created the shapes of the glass, and American artisans skillfully interpreted the drawings on the crystal."[38]

Secretary of State John Foster Dulles officiated at the National Gallery vernissage on January 17, and President Eisen-

94 | *Donald Pollard and Kiyoshi Saito, Japan,* Bodhisattva, *engraved crystal, ca. 1956, ht. 9.5 in. (24.13 cm) (By permission of Steuben Glass; Photograph by Graydon Wood, December 2006).*

95 | *Donald Pollard and Cho Chung-Yung, China,* Sayings of Confucius, *engraved crystal, ca. 1956, ht. 7.25 in. (18.42 cm) (By permission of Steuben Glass; Photograph by Graydon Wood, December 2006).*

hower himself viewed the series during its four-week venue in Washington. The collection then traveled to The Metropolitan Museum, where the Secretary General of the United Nations Dag Hammarskjöld—along with U.N. ambassadors from each participating nation—presided over the March 9 opening ceremonies.[39] After a month, "Asian Artists in Crystal" embarked

on a two-year tour of participating nations, arranged by the United States Information Service. The first stop was the National Museum in Seoul, Korea; last was the Cairo Museum of Modern Art in Egypt. As a gesture of goodwill, the U.S. government presented each nation's museum or head of state with its representative pieces at the close of the tour. "Asian

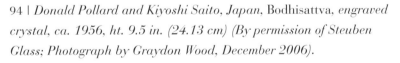

Artists in Crystal" was positively received in the arts press, although the journal *Oriental Art* groused that "the selection of artists from the different countries seems to have been made with little discernment, and simply by virtue of their official eminence. They are the 'senior civil servants' of each country's art."[40]

The duplicate set of "Asian Artists" pieces, meanwhile, was exhibited at The Corning Museum of Glass in the summer of 1956 to mark the fifth anniversary of the Museum's founding by Steuben president Arthur Houghton. Afterward, Steuben sent selections from this set to be offered for sale in its regional shops. Thirteen of the thirty-six objects in that set remained unsold and eventually became part of Walter Annenberg's initial Steuben purchase in September 1971, forming the nucleus of the Sunnylands collection.

single sculpture." Marianne Moore, Conrad Aiken, Denise Levertov, W. H. Auden, and other acclaimed poets were among the contributors who received a $250 honorarium. Completed in two years, the *Poetry in Crystal* collection was unveiled at Steuben's Fifth Avenue gallery on April 18, 1963, with a benefit for the Poetry Society. To document the series, Steuben published all the poems with full-page photogravure images of the crystal interpretations in a bound book of the same name. Two pieces from this series—interpretations of poet Melville Crane's "To Build a Fire" (an abstract flamelike sculpture designed by Steuben's Lloyd Atkins) and poet Robinson Jeffers's "Birds and Fishes" (fig. 96)—a wavelike form designed by Steuben's Donald Pollard and engraved with a drawing by artist Robert Vickrey—are at Sunnylands.

THE *POETRY IN CRYSTAL* SERIES, 1963

Throughout the 1940s and 1950s, Steuben used copper-wheel engraving primarily to ornament utilitarian items like vases and bowls, but by the 1960s the engravings grew more complex, often dictating the shape of the object. This melding of engraving and form is clearly seen in the *Poetry in Crystal* series, an "experimental" joint venture undertaken in 1961 by Steuben Glass and the Poetry Society of America. Steuben commissioned thirty-one representative American artists selected by the Poetry Society to write poems that would "not concern crystal or glass and . . . be no fewer than eight nor more than forty lines in length."[41] The manuscripts were anonymously circulated among Steuben's designers and contributing artists; the poets' names were revealed only after selections had been made. Each glass artist was challenged "not to illustrate the poem but to express its imagery in a

96 | *Donald Pollard and Robert Vickrey,* Birds and Fishes, *engraved crystal, 1963, ht. 8.25 in. (20.96 cm) (By permission of Steuben Glass; Photograph by Graydon Wood, December 2006).*

101

THE *ISLANDS IN CRYSTAL* SERIES, 1966

An ardent bibliophile with close ties to the academic world, Steuben's president Arthur Houghton dominated the company's artistic direction throughout the 1960s and early 1970s. His interest in antique maps fueled the *Islands in Crystal* series, which was organized in collaboration with Alexander D. Vietor, curator of maps at the Yale University Library.[42] In this imaginative series, maps and symbols of twelve islands—actual, mythical, and fictional—were engraved on sculpted pieces of crystal designed by Steuben's in-house staff. Sketches for some of the engravings were taken from early maps, including those in the Yale collection. Chosen for their appeal to the romantic imagination or for their contribution to civilization's progress were Atlantis, Baffin Island, Bermuda, Capri, Crete, Easter Island, the Galapagos, Hawaii, Nantucket, Robinson Crusoe's island, Tahiti, and Treasure Island. When the series was completed in about a year's time, it was exhibited at Steuben's Fifth Avenue gallery, where it was well received by the press.

The *Islands in Crystal* series is represented at Sunnylands by both *Hawaii* and *Crete*, a tribute to the mythology of the ancient Minoan island said to be the birthplace of Zeus (see fig. 90). *Crete* is engraved with figures depicting the story of Theseus, Ariadne, and the Labyrinth of the Minotaur. In the mythological tale, the young Athenian Theseus sails to Crete to kill the Minotaur—a fearsome beast with the head of a bull and the body of a man. The Minotaur dwells in a labyrinth built by King Minos of Crete, enemy of Athens. Each year a dozen Athenian youths and maidens are sacrificed to the beast. Theseus slays the Minotaur, then escapes from the labyrinth using the twine given him by Minos's daughter Ariadne, who has fallen in love with him. The two then sail back to Athens in a craft with two white sails—the inspiration for the boat-shaped form of this crystal sculpture.

THE *GREAT EXPLORERS* SERIES, 1970–72

Yet another series of themed ornamental designs reflecting Arthur Houghton's personal and scholarly interests is *Great Explorers*, begun in 1970. By 1972, it had grown to include nine freeform glass sculptures engraved with images and symbols relating to the famous explorers Hernando Cortes, Lewis and Clark, Leif Erikson, Ferdinand Magellan, David Livingstone, Henry Hudson, James Cook, Christopher Columbus, and Robert Falcon Scott. This series is represented at Sunnylands by the crystal sculpture *Hernando Cortes* (see figs. 89, 90), honoring the Spanish explorer who conquered the Aztec empire ruled by Montezuma in 1519 and later voyaged up the Pacific Coast of Mexico, claiming Baja California for the Spanish king. This design takes the form of a rough-hewn block of crystal suggesting Aztec architecture. It is engraved with symbols of Aztec civilization, and with stylized figures of the conqueror Cortes and the emperor Montezuma II.

THE STEUBEN *MASTERWORKS* SERIES, 1966–1980

By the early 1960s, Steuben began to accent its engraved glass sculptures with precious metals, a trend championed by Arthur Houghton, who admired the work of Cellini and Fabergé. Houghton fervently believed that "many, perhaps most, of the greatest objects that have ever been made combined more than one material."[43] His conviction was ultimately expressed in Steuben's *Masterworks* series, created between 1966 and 1980—nine unique objects of crystal engraved in narrative detail and ornamented with gold, silver, platinum, pearls, and precious stones. Each piece was to be "the imaginative con-

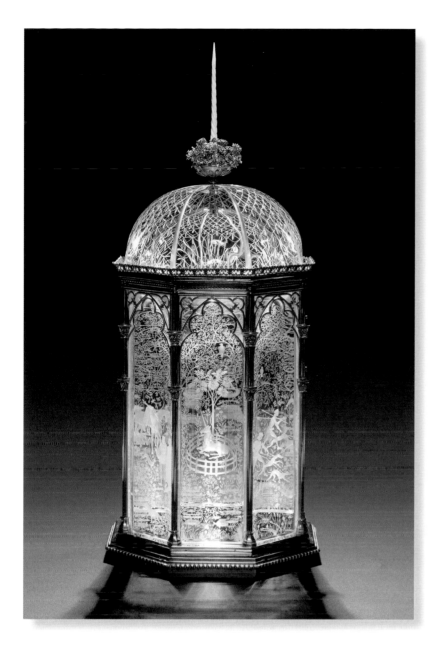

98 | *Donald Pollard, Alexander Seidel, Roland Erlacher, and Louis Feron,* Chinese Pavilion, *gold, jade, and jewel-mounted engraved crystal, 1975, ht. 12.25 in. (31.12 cm) (By permission of Steuben Glass; Photograph by Graydon Wood, December 2006).*

97 | *Donald Pollard, Alexander Seidel, Ladislav Havlik, and Peter Schelling,* The Unicorn and the Maiden, *1971, gold-mounted and jeweled engraved crystal, ht. 15 in. (38.1 cm) (By permission of Steuben Glass; Photograph by Graydon Wood, December 2006).*

cept of a senior staff artist, free to call upon associate artists, designers, artisans, engravers, and goldsmiths to bring into being under his direction a unique object of the finest design and craftsmanship."[44] Individual *Masterworks* drew inspiration from renowned works of literature, art, or scholarship and required two to four years to complete. When each piece was finished, it was documented with a luxurious limited-edition book of photographs highlighting each detail of the design and referring to its inspiration. Four of the nine Steuben *Masterworks* are represented in the Sunnylands collection—George Thompson's *Carrousel of the Sea*, 1970, and three designs by Donald Pollard: *The Unicorn and the Maiden*, 1971 (fig. 97), *Chinese Pavilion*, 1974 (fig. 98), and *Romance of the Rose*, 1978. *Chinese Pavilion*—an exact copy of the original, commissioned from Steuben by Walter Annenberg expressly for Sunnylands—is the only object in the one-of-a-kind series that Steuben ever duplicated.

99 | *View from terrace looking into living area (Photograph by Graydon Wood, December 2006).*

DECORATIVE ARTS

Donna Corbin

The European decorative arts at Sunnylands are notable for the variety of their medium, date, and country of origin. Reflecting a lifetime of acquisitions through purchase and gifts, they range from elegant English crystal candelabra of the early nineteenth century to a ceramic plate decorated by Pablo Picasso in 1957, and from eighteenth-century jars made at the Meissen porcelain factory in Germany to a jade, quartz, and enamel "Mystery" clock made by the firm established by Louis-François Cartier in Paris in 1847 (fig. 99).

Within this broad category, by far the most important group of objects is the English silver. The Annenbergs, who were known for elegant and gracious entertaining, acquired silver for use at Sunnylands as well as at Inwood, their estate outside Philadelphia. A number of pieces of silver, including the silver-gilt tray and basket discussed below, were purchased from the sale of the important collection of Mrs. Jay Plohn of New York, which took place at Sotheby's in London on October 15, 1970, while Walter Annenberg was serving as Ambassador to the Court of St. James's, and the Annenbergs were entertaining at Winfield House, the American ambassador's residence in London.[1]

Of particular interest is a set of seven silver-gilt baskets that were acquired by the Annenbergs in 1976. Six of the baskets bear the stamp of William Pitts and Joseph Preedy (partnership 1791–1799) and date from 1793–1794; the seventh basket bears the stamp of Joseph Preedy (active from 1773) and dates from 1802–1803. The baskets, which are engraved on the interior with the cipher and coronet of Queen Charlotte, wife of George III, must have been the gift of five of her children: their ciphers appear on the bottoms. They descended in the family of Ernest Augustus, Duke of Cumberland, fifth son of George III, who was King of Hanover (1837–1851)—all in all, a remarkable provenance.

AN EPERGNE OF 1761–62

Changes in dining customs in the seventeenth century, including the introduction of a style of dining that came to be known as *service à la française*—reflecting its origins at the tables of the French nobility—necessitated the invention of a range of specialized forms for serving and eating. Dining *à la française* required that an array of dishes from which diners helped themselves and each other were symmetrically placed on the table at the beginning of the meal and then, at the end of each of several courses, were cleared leaving only containers for spices and condiments on the table. Among the newly introduced forms was the *surtout de table* or epergne,[2] which was intended as a visual focus for the diners at the same time that it united cruets, containers for salt, pepper, and spices, and, in many cases, candlesticks, in the center of the table. Early French references to surtouts include four delivered by the silversmith Nicolas Delaunay to the Crown in September 1685, works described in the *Journal du Garde-meuble*.[3]

By the beginning of the eighteenth century, the fashion for dining *à la française* had spread throughout Europe, taking with it many of the associated forms. Documentation indicates that surtouts or epergnes of English manufacture were probably produced as early as the 1720s, though none of these are known today. The early English examples tended to follow the French form of a central bowl or dish flanked by attached smaller dishes and candle branches with clusters of casters at each end.

Although the centerpiece never lost its ornamental purpose, by the mid-eighteenth century, particularly in England, its primary function had become that of a rather grand fruit stand that was placed on the table at the beginning of the meal and enriched with additional dishes of fruits and sweetmeats at the dessert course. The Sunnylands epergne is an example of this type (fig. 100). Along with changes in the function came changes in the design, and by the mid-1740s, under the influence of the emerging Rococo style, epergnes become lighter in form, in part the result of the introduction of pierced decoration and a general attenuation of the parts. The Sunnylands epergne is a marvelous example of the delicacy and elegant whimsicality of the most successful epergnes of the Rococo period. There the naturalistic elements of the Rococo style merge with elements, both observed and imaginary, borrowed from the arts of Asia. Compendiums of Rococo ornament, such as the works of carvers like Matthias Lock and Lock and Copeland published in the 1740s and 1750s, may have inspired some of the elements.[4]

The Sunnylands epergne is the most elaborate and among the earliest of a group of epergnes stamped by the London silversmith Thomas Pitts I (active from 1744). Judging from the number of epergnes he is recorded as providing to the London retailer-goldsmiths John Parker and Edward Wakelin, it appears that the Pitts workshop specialized in these centerpieces.[5] The basic canopied form of this epergne has a precedent in published designs such as those by the English architect William Kent,[6] which themselves ultimately derive from French-made examples. The Chinese bell-hung, pagoda-style canopy, here in a rare double version,[7] however, was monopolized by Pitts.

A BASKET OF 1797–98

In 1800, when William Beckford (1760–1844), one of the greatest and perhaps most idiosyncratic collectors, connoisseurs, and patrons of his time, entertained Lord Nelson and Sir William and Lady Emma Hamilton at his partially completed home, Fonthill Abbey, it was recorded that, "after various entertainments, a collation was provided in the library consisting of various sorts of confectionary, served in gold baskets . . . after which Emma Hamilton performed some of her celebrated attitudes."[8] The baskets displayed in the library on the occasion of the Nelson-Hamilton visit may have been

0//⊠ *Epergne, stamped by Thomas Pitts I, London, 1761–62, silver with later gilding, 26.5 × 28 × ht. 30 in. (67.31 × 71.12 × 76.2 cm) (Photograph by Graydon Wood, December 2006).*

a pair of monumental gilded-silver baskets, dated 1797–98, that bear the Beckford crest, a heron with a fish in its beak. Today, one of the baskets is at Sunnylands (fig. 101).[9]

Beckford, who is perhaps best known as the builder of the sprawling and fantastic neo-Gothic Fonthill Abbey, was born into a family that made its tremendous fortune in the West Indies sugar trade. In 1822, with the failure of his sugar plantation, Beckford was forced to sell most of the enormous collection of objects he had amassed at Fonthill Abbey, including the pair of gilded-silver baskets. These appear as lots 75 and 76 in the 1822 Christie's sale catalogue: "A magnificent basket, formed of ears of wheat, of the finest workmanship" and "A ditto, ditto."[10]

Throughout his long life Beckford commissioned a prodigious amount of silver —some two hundred pieces have been identified—that was evidently displayed with great effect at the Abbey.[11] Beckford's admiration for French silver, particularly that of Parisian silversmith Henri Auguste (1759–1816), had been established during his long stays in France, beginning in 1788; and during the 1790s he patronized the French decorative painter and silver designer Jean-Jacques Boileau (active ca. 1787–1827).[12] The silver that Boileau designed for Beckford is largely in a late French Neoclassical style, and it probably includes these baskets, whose sides are formed by outward-turning ears of wheat. Of the Beckford/Boileau-designed silver that has been identified, most bears the mark of the London silversmith Paul Storr (1771–1844).[13] Storr, the son of a silver chaser who first registered his mark in 1792, became one of the most celebrated goldsmiths of the Regency period in England.

101 | *Basket, stamped by Paul Storr, London, 1797–98, gilded silver, width 20 in. (50.8 cm) (Photograph by Graydon Wood, December 2006).*

A TRAY OF 1807–8

Throughout the eighteenth century, the *service à la française* style of dining dominated in Europe; but by the nineteenth century a new style was introduced. It may have originated at the Russian court and was named *service à la russe*. Unlike *service à la française*, in which all the dishes for a particular course were laid out together on the table, *service à la russe*

required servants to pass the food to the diners, and all but a few items, such as cruet stands, sauceboats, and decoration, were banished from the table. At the beginning of the nineteenth century, this change in dining etiquette brought about a demand for extensive dinner services and massive pieces of silver. The sideboard now became the focal point of display in the dining room, fueling the need for large and impressive pieces of silver such as this tray to be massed there (fig. 102). In addition, silver of scale, whether functional or purely ornamental, was increasingly in demand by the substantial num-

102 | *Tray, stamped by Benjamin Smith II, London, made for Rundell, Bridge & Rundell, London, 1807–8, gilded silver, length 29.75 in. (75.57 cm) (Photograph by Graydon Wood, December 2006).*

ber of British landowners who had grown wealthy through the Napoleonic Wars, which drove up the prices of commodities such as grain and beef.[14]

In the period, Rundell, Bridge & Rundell, the most fashionable and successful of the London retailer-goldsmiths, who counted among their clients the prince regent and the dukes of Norfolk and Wellington, were major providers of large-scale objects in silver and silver-gilt. Indicating the firm's prodigious output, the Rundell shop was said to have "massive silver vases, &c.&c. strewed on the floor as if they were articles possessing neither external beauty, [n]or intrinsic value."[15]

The firm of Rundell & Bridge was established in 1787 by Philip Rundell, a jeweler, and John Bridge, a silversmith; from about 1804, the same year in which the firm was appointed Principal Royal Goldsmiths and Jewellers, Edmond Walker Rundell, the nephew of Philip, joined the firm, and it was renamed Rundell, Bridge & Rundell; Rundell's closed in 1843. In 1802, the firm, which had previously relied on a network of silversmiths to supply the hollow wares they sold, established its own workshop. In addition, Rundell's retained a number of skilled artists who provided designs and models from which the silversmiths worked, thus creating a distinctive look for the silver they marketed.

Among the silversmiths who managed the Rundell workshop over the years was Benjamin Smith II (1764–1823), whose stamp appears on the tray in the Sunnylands collection.[16] Smith, a native of Birmingham who had been in the employ of Matthew Boulton in that city, worked almost exclusively for Rundell's between 1802 and 1814. Under Rundell's strict aesthetic control, the silver Smith produced is often indistinguishable from that of other silversmiths working in the period, including the well-known maker Paul Storr, who was associated with Rundell's beginning around 1800.

The Annenberg tray is one of a group of silver-gilt objects including trays, baskets, and salvers with an identical pierced grapevine border.[17] The pattern, which proved to be among the firm's most successful, was in production for over a decade.[18]

A PAIR OF MEISSEN COVERED JARS

When Augustus II (the Strong), Elector of Saxony and King of Poland (1670–1733), announced the formation of his porcelain factory in Meissen in 1710, he became the first European successfully to produce true or hard-paste porcelain of the type that Europeans had been coveting and importing from Asia for centuries. As would be expected with so complicated a venture, the factory's establishment was trumpeted but then followed by years of experimentation, and it was decades before Meissen, as it came to be known, assumed its position as the foremost porcelain factory in Europe.

Augustus himself was one of Europe's most legendary collectors of Asian ceramics, amassing huge numbers of both Chinese and Japanese porcelains. The collection was largely formed beginning in 1715, suggesting that Augustus's passion for Asian porcelain was driven in part by the success of his own porcelain manufactory.

In 1717 Augustus acquired a palace on the banks of the Elbe River in Dresden from his cabinet minister, Count Jakob von Flemming, from whom he also purchased a collection of Asian porcelain. The palace, soon named Japanische Palais (Japanese Palace), was the site of some of the celebrations surrounding the marriage of the crown prince to the archduchess Maria Josepha in 1719. By 1727 Augustus's plans for a palace devoted to his collection of more than twenty thousand pieces of porcelain had been formalized and a massive remodeling of the Japanese Palace began. The project was unfinished upon Augustus's death in 1733, but from the architects' plan for the sumptuous interiors we know that the Asian and Meissen porcelains were to be exhibited on separate floors in some thirty-two rooms or galleries—the porcelain displayed in formal patterns over the walls—with each room dominated by porcelain of one color or type. Galleries devoted to porcelain with a yellow ground, such as that on the

jars in the collection at Sunnylands (fig. 103), were included in both the Asian and Meissen galleries.[19] Meissen's use of ground colors with areas of white held in reserve for painted decoration was borrowed from Chinese porcelain. The yellow, which ranged from a pale to a brightly saturated hue, was among the earliest ground colors developed at Meissen,[20] and it appeared on Meissen pieces with both Asian-inspired and European style decoration.

From the factory's inception, Asian ceramics provided models for the production,[21] but it was not until after the arrival in 1720 of the painter Johann Gregorius Höroldt (1696–1775) that the factory succeeded in producing enamel decoration imitating that on Asian ceramics. The decoration on the jars at Sunnylands is derived from a style of Chinese painting that originated in the Kangxi reign. Because of the predominance

103 | *Pair of covered jars, made at the Meissen Porcelain Factory, ca. 1730–35, hard-paste porcelain, ht. 14.57 in. (37 cm) (Photograph by Graydon Wood, December 2006).*

of green decoration in this style, in the nineteenth century it was given the name *famille verte*. The scheme, which consisted mainly of green, yellow, aubergine, iron red, black, and blue, exerted a tremendous influence on the decoration of European porcelain from Saint Cloud in France to Chelsea in England to Meissen. The Sunnylands jars—the oviform shape of which is taken from a Chinese model—are decorated on four sides with landscapes, exotic birds on flowering prunus, and flowers issuing from rockwork, a decoration that is typical of *famille verte*.

PIECES FROM THE FLORA DANICA SERVICE

After several earlier attempts at producing true or hard-paste porcelain in and around Copenhagen in the mid-eighteenth century, a factory was established there in 1775 by a Danish scientist, Frantz Heinrich Müller (1732–1820). Although Müller himself shouldered the cost of the initial experiments, in 1774, members of the royal family, who surely saw the benefits of a Danish porcelain factory, responded to a call for investors by purchasing shares in the firm.[22] The early years of the factory were fraught with difficulties, and the first piece of porcelain was not sold until the end of 1779. In that year King Christian VII bought the remaining shares, and the factory took the name the Royal Copenhagen Porcelain Manufactory, which it retains today. From the outset the goal was to pro-

duce an attractive porcelain that could be used every day and be sold at a reasonable price; the emphasis was on porcelain with an underglaze blue decoration that required only two firings and was thus inexpensive to manufacture. At the same time, however, the factory produced a more expensive line of luxury objects, including richly decorated vases, coffee and tea services, and ornamental figures.

The porcelain produced at the Copenhagen factory in the eighteenth century was for the most part stylistically dependent on the production of other European porcelain factories, with one notable exception, the Flora Danica service (fig. 104).[23] Commissioned by King Christian VII in 1790, the Flora Danica service may have been intended as a gift from the king to Empress Catherine of Russia.[24] In 1802, some seven years after Catherine's death, when production was called to a halt, the service comprised 1,802 pieces.[25] The decoration on the pieces was taken from engravings from the botanical work *Flora Danica*, the first volume of which appeared in 1761. This important publication, which embodies the eighteenth-century fascination with the recording and classification of natural history, is celebrated on the porcelain service. The engravings were faithfully copied onto the porcelain almost single-handedly by the flower painter, Johan Christoph Bayer (1738–1812). The service was much used by the royal family, beginning in 1803, when a number of dessert pieces were delivered to the court confectioner for a dinner in honor of the king's birthday. A second service was ordered in 1863 at the time of the marriage of Princess Alexandra, daughter of Christian IX, to Albert Edward, Prince of Wales, and since that time the service has been in continuous production.

104 | *Pieces from the Flora Danica service, made at the Royal Copenhagen Porcelain Manufactory, after 1922, hard-paste porcelain, plate diam. 11 in. (27.94 cm), ice dome and stand ht. 11 in. (27.94 cm), basket diam. 10 in. (25.4 cm) (By permission of Royal Copenhagen; Photograph by Graydon Wood, December 2006).*

A PAIR OF CANDELABRA AND A TUREEN BY GEORG JENSEN

The acclaimed Danish silversmith Georg Jensen (1866–1935) was thirty-eight years old in 1904 when he opened his first shop on a fashionable street in Copenhagen; from this rather modest beginning grew the internationally renowned silverwares firm that today still bears his name. Jensen was born into a working-class family in Raadvad, Denmark, a small industrial town north of Copenhagen, and at the age of fourteen, after the family's move to Copenhagen, he was apprenticed to a silversmith there. It was Jensen's ambition, however, to be a sculptor, and in 1887 he entered the Royal Danish Academy of Fine Arts, from which he graduated in 1892. His sculptures received some favorable critical notice but unfortunately did not sell, and thus, in order to support his young family, Jensen found employment for a time as a modeler in the ceramics industry. Perhaps more important, in 1901 he went to work for the painter-metalsmith Mogens Ballin (1871–1941), whose innovative approach to pewter design reinvigorated that industry in Denmark.

When Jensen established his own silversmithing workshop in 1904, he did so with two guiding principles: the first of these, to improve the standard of silver production, he borrowed from Ballin and from the Arts and Crafts movement of the late nineteenth century; the second, that nature was his source of inspiration, came from his early experiences in the idyllic countryside that surrounded his home, and from the then-current Art Nouveau movement, which he studied both in Copenhagen and Paris. Known in Denmark as *skønvirke* (literally "beautiful work"), the "new" style aimed to liberate itself from historical conventions and to be a language that spoke to the age in which it was created.

Jensen's first metalwork designs were for a line of inexpensive jewelry; its early success gave him the capital he needed to design and produce tablewares in silver. The table-

105 | *Tureen, designed 1920, silver, diam. 14 × ht. 12 in. (35.56 × 30.48 cm), Pair of candelabra, designed 1930, silver, ht. 26.5 × diam. 19 in. (67.31 × 48.26 cm), Georg Jensen, designer; Sideboard, Office of William Haines and Ted Graber, designers, ca. 1965, painted wood, 34 × 84 × 21 in. (86.4 × 213.4 × 53.3 cm) (By permission of Peter Schifando; Photograph by Graydon Wood, December 2006).*

wares, like his jewelry, found an immediate audience, and Jensen's silver quickly won an international reputation. He opened shops in Berlin (1909), Stockholm and Paris (1918), London (1921), and New York (1924), and he won prizes at international exhibitions in San Francisco (1915), Barcelona (1923), and Paris (1925).

The four magnificent pieces of silver at Sunnylands—a pair of five-armed candelabra, a covered tureen (fig. 105), and a footed dish—are among the most opulent objects designed by Jensen and made by his firm. Throughout his lifetime, Jensen continued to describe himself as a sculptor—the sign over his workshop read "Sculptor, Georg Jensen, Silversmith"—and his work in silver, as evidenced by the soft, organic contours of these pieces, was always informed by this. Jensen created his own unique interpretation of the Art Nouveau style, fusing new decorative silver forms with stylized motifs, such as the leaves and fruit derived from nature on the Sunnylands pieces.

As their inscriptions indicate, the Jensen pieces were gifts of Walter Annenberg's father, Moses Annenberg, to his wife, Sadie Cecelia Friedman, in 1935 and the following year (when Moses purchased the *Philadelphia Inquirer*). One of Jensen's earliest American patrons was William Randolph Hearst, who first encountered the silversmith's work at the 1915 Pan-Pacific Exposition in San Francisco, and with whom Moses Annenberg had worked.

A PLATE DECORATED BY PICASSO

In 1946 while Pablo Picasso (1881–1973) and Françoise Gilot (b. 1921) were living at Golfe-Juan on the French Riviera, they were invited to visit the Madoura pottery of Georges and Suzanne Ramié, in Vallauris.[26] The Ramiés were among the young potters who before and after World War II established factories in Vallauris in an effort to revive the ceramics industry that had existed there since Roman times. During the visit Picasso was persuaded to try his hand at the craft and he modeled a couple of small figures. The somewhat unpredictable medium, which can combine the properties of painting and sculpture, must have appealed to the artist, and the following year he returned to the pottery with sketches of what he wanted to make. From that time until his death, Picasso made and decorated thousands of pieces of ceramics in and around Vallauris.[27] He left more than 3,200 such works in his estate.[28] Picasso never learned to work the potter's wheel, instead relying on others to throw pots for him that he then decorated; or he decorated shapes produced at Madoura, on occasion manipulating the malleable unfired pots into unique forms. He exploited the full range of techniques; the decoration on his ceramics is painted, incised, gouged, applied, and raised. The themes he employed

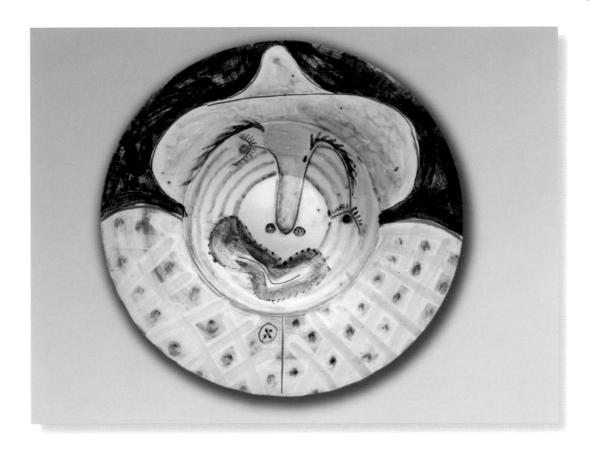

106 | *Plate, decorated by Pablo Picasso, 1957, earthenware, diam. 17 in. (43.18 cm) (©2008 Estate of Pablo Picasso/ Artists Rights Society [ARS], New York; Photograph by Graydon Wood, December 2006).*

are often either slyly or openly comic, such as the colorful clown's face on the Sunnylands plate (fig. 106),[29] and they include the same themes—animals, portraits, bullfights and still lifes—that he employed elsewhere in his work.

FURNITURE DESIGNED BY WILLIAM HAINES AND TED GRABER

In 1963, when the firm that William Haines had founded began working for the Annenbergs on the Sunnylands project, he had been designing interiors and furniture for some thirty

107 | *Console table, Office of William Haines and Ted Graber,*
designers, marble and wrought iron, ca. 1965, 32.75 × 66 in. (83.19 ×
167.64 cm) (By permission of Peter Schifando; Photograph by Graydon
Wood, December 2006).

108 | *Chair, Office of William Haines and Ted Graber, designers, ca.
1965, walnut and leather upholstery, 23 × 22 × 32.5 in. (58.42 ×
55.88 × 82.55 cm) (By permission of Peter Schifando; Photograph by
Graydon Wood, December 2006).*

years.[30] His career as a movie actor in the 1920s and early 1930s coincided with the period when America was discovering and embracing what came to be called the Art Deco style. In fact, it was in Hollywood movies such as *Grand Hotel* (1932) that it is said the Art Deco style "reached its full potential for fantasy, glamour and mass popularity."[31]

In his approach to interior design, Haines appears to have largely rejected the Hollywood brand of Art Deco. The style he helped popularize, one more rooted in tradition, has come to be known as "Hollywood Regency," a reference to the style that was current in England at the beginning of the nineteenth century, during the Regency of George IV. Nevertheless, the furniture designed by Haines's firm, throughout its history and including pieces for Sunnylands, owes a debt to furniture design of the 1920s and 1930s.

The Exposition Internationale des Arts Décoratifs et Industriels Modernes, held in Paris in 1925, was the landmark event in the history of the Art Deco style. In retrospect the term Art Deco embraced not one, but many styles that shared a common language of visual elements, all filtered through a modern lens. These included a reliance on historical styles, both non-Western and Western, particularly ancient ones; a tendency toward abstracted, simplified forms; and an emphasis on surface effects. For example, shagreen or sharkskin, an exotic and luxurious material, was used as a surface covering for everything from furniture to makeup cases. Many designers in the period also explored the possibilities inherent in new technologies and materials like stainless steel and plastics.

Although American designers and manufacturers did not participate in the 1925 Paris Exposition, a great number of Americans visited the show, and the new style was disseminated in the United States by newspapers, magazines, and museums. In 1926 an exhibition of more than four hundred objects that had been shown in Paris traveled to nine major American art museums. Over the next few years department stores from Lord & Taylor in New York to Barker Brothers in Los Angeles promoted the modern style, mounting their own exhibitions and creating new furniture lines that copied the originals, often in less expensive materials. Haines, whose first design project in 1926–27 was his own home (at 1712 North Stanley Avenue in Los Angeles), was surely aware of the excitement engendered by the new style.

The characteristics of the Art Deco style cited above turn up in subtle ways in the furniture at Sunnylands designed by the office of William Haines and Ted Graber. There is no better example of this than the sideboard in the dining room, which today displays three pieces of the magnificent Georg Jensen silver that Walter Annenberg inherited from his mother (see fig. 105). A pure geometric shape, the sideboard is devoid of decoration save that provided by two rectangular cutouts serving as door pulls, a series of parallel lines incised into the front of the piece, and the texture of the painted surface, which in its subtle pale green suggests the shagreen surfaces of the most extravagant Art Deco furniture. The rosewood dining table with its ivory inlaid top and pedestal base recalls the furniture of such French Art Deco designers as Jacques-Émile Ruhlmann (1879–1933), at the same time that it evokes the work of Regency cabinetmakers like George Bullock (ca. 1738–1818; see fig. 49).

Of the furniture that the office of Haines and Graber designed for Sunnylands, perhaps none is more directly related to furniture design of the 1920s and 1930s than two wrought iron and marble console tables in the main living area (fig. 107). In style and material these tables mimic examples designed in the 1920s by Edgar Brandt (1880–1960), the French metalworker and designer. Brandt, whose architectural metalwork was particularly admired in America, opened a branch of his metalworking business in New York in 1925 under the name Ferrobrandt. The wrought iron and marble tables Brandt designed proved to be immensely popular, and they were copied by many anonymous French designers in the 1930s and 1940s.

For the main living area at Sunnylands, the office of Haines and Graber designed a version of the firm's so-called Conference Chair (fig. 108). A chair of this design with a solid back had previously been used by Haines in 1949 in his new studio at 446 South Canon Drive in Beverly Hills. The Conference Chair, along with Haines's Hostess Chair, are variations on the ancient Greek klismos chair, which had experienced a revival during the Regency period.[32] It was a theme also explored by furniture designers in the 1920s and 1930s. Among them was Aage Rafn (1890–1953), who included klismos chairs, along with other classically inspired furniture, in his furnishings for the Danish pavilion at the widely publicized 1925 Exposition.

Perhaps the most famous designer of the period to experiment with the klismos chair was the British interior and furniture designer T. H. Robsjohn-Gibbings (1905–1976). When Robsjohn-Gibbings set up his office in New York City in 1936, he furnished it with furniture based on his extensive studies of ancient art. In the following years he included klismos chairs—some of them accurate recreations of the classical models, some reinterpretations of the originals—in his interiors from New York to California,[33] and he counted among his clients the young Walter Annenberg, for whom he designed an apartment in Philadelphia in the late 1930s.[34]

109 | *Detail, Figure of priest, Jaina, Maya Late Classic period (Photograph by Graydon Wood, December 2006).*

A MAYA FIGURINE IN JAINA STYLE

Jeremy A. Sabloff

On view at Sunnylands, this beautiful ancient Maya pottery figurine (figs. 109, 110) is an example of a Late Classic Period (600–800 C.E.) style that was centered on the small island of Jaina off the west coast of the Yucatan peninsula and the adjacent mainland region in the modern Mexican state of Campeche.[1] Similar figurines are also found to the southwest in the Tabasco lowlands. Many figurines of this kind were discovered in excavations by Mexican archaeologists during the 1940s, 1950s, and 1960s on Jaina,[2] but, unfortunately, much of the island and adjacent areas have been looted over the years and many of the pieces that are found in museums and collections around the world do not have documented provenances.[3]

Recent archaeological research has revealed that the ancient Maya civilization, with its remarkable achievements in art and science, flourished for more than two millennia, beginning as early as 700 B.C.E. and ending with the Spanish Conquest in the sixteenth century C.E., in an area that is centered on the Yucatan peninsula and that now includes southern Mexico, Guatemala, Belize, and parts of El Salvador and Honduras. Scholars generally view the artistic and political height of Maya civilization as having occurred in the southern lowland base of the peninsula during the Classic Period, from 300 to 800 C.E. This was a time when major cities filled the landscape; the powerful rulers of the largest urban centers, such as Tikal and Calakmul, vied for influence; and the architecture and art of the Maya reached the apogee of sophistication. It is in this thriving cultural context that the distinctive Jaina-style figurines were created.

The island of Jaina, situated in the northern Maya lowlands, is separated from the Campeche coast by a relatively narrow channel and may have originally been connected to the mainland. Several groups of small Classic structures are present on Jaina, but the island is renowned for the thousands of burials found there. These discoveries have led some archaeologists to call Jaina a necropolis where Maya communities in western Campeche buried their dead. The burials apparently are of ancient Maya commoners because the grave goods are limited, but include at least one figurine in an individual burial. These figurines are either mold-made or hand-modeled or sometimes a combination of both. The hollow examples often functioned as whistles or rattles. The details on some are quite striking in their lifelikeness, with features such as facial tattooing still visible. The figurines frequently retain their multicolored post-fire painting, and the distinctive Maya blue paint is most prominent. This mineralogically based paint is a unique feature of Maya art.

The figurines depict a wide variety of personages and activities, from mortals to deities and from ball players to weavers.[4] The art historian Mary Miller, in a study of Jaina materials, has stressed that the "Jaina figurines are not simple folk art. On the contrary, they are sophisticated works of art."[5] This judgment is based on a variety of factors, most particularly the rich iconographic and ritual symbolism of the figurines. In fact, she hypothesizes that the figurines are associated with rituals relating to the underworld, in keeping with Jaina's location on the western edge of the Maya world, where the sun could be seen setting in the ocean (thus making Jaina similar to the important ancient pilgrimage site of the island of Cozumel on the opposite coast of the Yucatan peninsula, where the sun could be seen rising from the ocean each morning). In this way, Miller argues, the Jaina figurines "brought art to the common man."[6]

The freestanding Maya figurine at Sunnylands is eleven inches tall and still retains some of its original paint. When it was purchased, its provenance was listed as coastal Campeche.

A photograph and a brief caption about this piece were published nearly forty years ago by Hasso Von Winning in his volume *Pre-Columbian Art of Mexico and Central America*, which identifies it as a "standing male holding a serpent scepter" and notes that both the scepter and the shield on the figure's back are removable.[7] Simon Martin and Mary Miller, both leading Maya scholars, have suggested that the man depicted in the figurine represents a Maya ruler, as the figure radiates strength and power and is dressed in all the regalia of a king, from the elaborate earplugs, belt, necklace, and chest ornament, to the shield, headdress, and loincloth. They further speculate that he may have originally held a snake in his two hands that was broken off sometime in the past,[8] although this suggestion clearly cannot be confirmed. But his right hand certainly held something that has been broken off, the removable scepter in his left hand, which is definitely a snake's head, does not support this speculation. This pose is an unusual one, however, with each hand apparently holding an object, perhaps indicating that the piece had been modified in the past.

In sum, this small pottery figure is an aesthetically beautiful example of the important Jaina-style figurines that were used as burial furniture in Late Classic Maya civilization. It has all the typical features, including physiognomy, clothing, and regalia, of a Maya ruler and is a striking exemplar of the achievements of ancient Maya craftspeople during the height of their civilization.

110 || *Figure of priest, Jaina, Maya Late Classic period (600–800 C.E.), terracotta with remains of pigments, ht. 11 in. (27.94 cm) (Photograph by Graydon Wood, December 2006).*

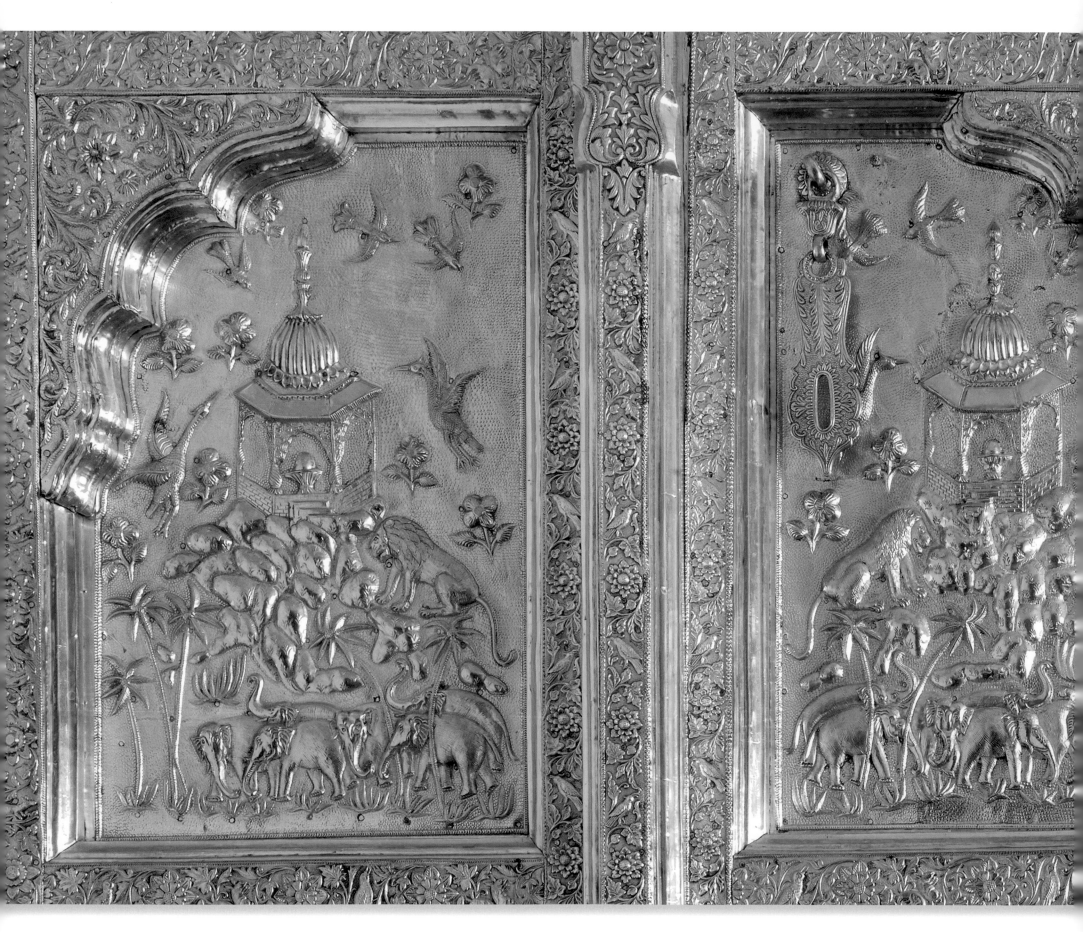

111 | *Upper panels of Hindu doors (Photograph by Graydon Wood, December 2006).*

TWO HINDU TEMPLE DOOR PANELS WITH SILVER REPOUSSÉ

Michael W. Meister

Displayed in the hall leading to the private wing of Sunnylands, this pair of door panels, covered with silver repoussé, represents fine South Asian Indian craftsmanship of perhaps the late eighteenth or early nineteenth century (figs. 111, 112). Comparable door panels may still be found in temples in Vrindavan,[1] Jaipur, Nathadwara, and elsewhere in western India and the Gangetic plains. Their eclectic themes and ornamental sources reflect the composite societies of northern India in the late Mughal period.

An important temple built late in the sixteenth century at the sacred site of Vrindavan, near the Mughal capital of Delhi, to serve an important community worshipping the Hindu deity Vishnu, can act as a touchstone for the Sunnylands doorway. Although this temple has sometimes been called a "Mughal temple" because of its royal patronage and imperial craft guilds, art in this period had many patrons, users, and artisans from a variety of communities, Hindu and Muslim.

Whether or not Sunnyland's silver doors had royal patrons, they might best be labeled northern Indian style from the later Mughal period.[2] Segmented into three levels, with ornate frames, these doors simulate a type of cusped niche often found in miniature paintings and architecture of the period. The foliated vine motif, inhabited by birds and animals, that frames each segment can be compared to late Mughal ornamentation or to the carved patterning on the Krishna temple at Vrindavan mentioned above, built with the patronage of the greatest of the Mughal emperors, Akbar, but for Hindu use.

The tall central frame of the left-hand door (fig. 113) contains a standing figure of Vishnu's flute-playing incarnation, Krishna, the cowherd god, a peacock feather in his hair. He gazes over his left shoulder toward his beloved, Radha, on the other door. She holds a garland as if offering it to her lover. Both have haloes and stand on lotus pedestals, symbolic of their divinity.[3] Peacocks stand at their feet. Other birds and flowers are scattered over the field. These scenes are framed by ornate half pillars, resembling pillars of the

112 | *Pair of Hindu doors, South Asian Indian, silver repoussé, 71 × 34.5 in. (180.34 × 87.63 cm) (Photograph by Graydon Wood, December 2006).*

Diwan-i-Am or hall of public audience at Amber, near Jaipur, and seem to support an elegant cusped filigree-arch above.[4] Two doorknockers take the form of elephant busts with heavy rings in their trunks. An elaborate cartouche on the doorframe between Krishna and Radha contains an image of Ganesh, the rotund elephant-headed deity who grants favors and brings good fortune. At the top left of the upper right-hand panel an elaborate slotted clasp hangs down, meant to secure the doors to a frame above (see fig. 111).

Northern India in the sixteenth and seventeenth centuries saw a great outpouring of devotion to Krishna and Radha, centered on a sect called Gaudiya Vaishnavism and led by a saint named Chaitanya (1486–1534).[5] A center of this devotional sect was the town of Vrindavan, but the worship spread widely from Bengal to Rajasthan, where these two doors may have been made for a temple or domestic shrine.[6] The two lower panels refer to the famed forests of Vrindavan, with crenellated ponds at the bottom, filled with lotus flowers and cranes, a field of grasses and flowers, and, at the top, an array of tall palms and grasses as a setting for a graceful long-tailed tiger, which first stalks an antlered stag on the left panel and then attacks on the right (fig. 114).

The two cusped panels at the top of the doors raise intriguing questions about the nature of the sectarian dedication of these two domestic-shrine doors. If they include references to Shiva's worship, then the ecumenical ambience of Vaishnavism might be the issue. If not, the enthusiastic devotionalism of Gaudiya-Vaishnava adoration can be seen as perfuming the door panels and unifying their themes. These upper panels show hexagonal garden pavilions set on rocky outcrops, with birds and flowers above and lions seated to the side, in nearly symmetrically mirrored images. Below are groves of tall palms and grasses enjoyed by families of elephants. Sheltered in these pavilions are hourglass pedestals supporting egg-shaped aniconic stones. At first glance the symbolic objects appear to be *linga*s, the phallic emblem of Shiva, but they are more probably Vaishnava equivalents—*shalagram-as*—anemonite (or fossil) stones used by Vishnu worshippers.

The many varieties of sacred *shalagrama*s marketed today include a Shiva-*linga shalagrama*, the worshipping of which, according to a popular source, "increases family harmony, and the environment of the house and the workplace of the beholder becomes like a temple."[7] Another source, a priest and scholar writing on the Web, reports that "the area within a radius of twenty-four miles from where a *shalagrama-shila* is worshipped is counted as a holy place."[8] Consonant with the scenes in these doors' lower panels of the tiger chasing and capturing a stag is the saying "as deer flee upon seeing a lion in the jungle, so all types of sins run away from one who sees a *shalagrama*."[9]

As doorways to a Krishna shrine within a Vaishnava household, these silver-covered frames proclaim the importance of a transcendent devotion, a communal system of belief, and integration with the natural world. Intense in their imagery, and profound in their emotional effect, these doors are extensions of the mental visions invoked by Krishna's devotees. Ornament is not their function; faith is.

> *If remembering Krishna enriches your heart,*
> *If his arts of seduction arouse you,*
> *Listen to His speech*
> *In these sweet lyrical songs [and scenes].*[10]

113 | *Middle panels of Hindu doors (Photograph by Graydon Wood, December 2006).*

114 | *Lower panels of Hindu doors (Photograph by Graydon Wood, December 2006).*

115 | *Figure of recumbent water buffalo, Qing dynasty (1644–1911) or Republican period (1911–1949), nineteenth or early twentieth century. Pale green jadeite, 8.75 × 20 × 16.5 in. (22.23 × 50.8 × 41.91 cm) (Photograph by Graydon Wood, December 2006).*

CHINESE ART

Virginia Bower

Leonore and Walter Annenberg had far more than a casual interest in Chinese art. Indeed, their affection and appreciation for this part of their art collections is manifest in its omnipresence at Sunnylands. Chinese ceramics are especially plentiful, ranging from Tang dynasty tomb sculptures of rough earthenware to Qing dynasty export wares of fine porcelain—a span of almost thirteen centuries. Less ubiquitous than the ceramics, but impossible to overlook, are brilliantly colored Ming and Qing dynasty enamels, including rare examples of *cloisonné*-embellished furniture. Also to be found are bronzes and jades dated as early as the Shang dynasty (ca. 1600–ca. 1050 B.C.E.) and as late as the Republican period (1911–1949).[1] Of note among the jade carvings is an exceptionally large recumbent water buffalo.[2] This twenty-inch-long creature was a particular favorite of Walter Annenberg's and came to be referred to as "Walter" (fig. 115).[3]

Judging from published accounts, the Annenbergs were inspired to collect Chinese art primarily by an appreciation of its aesthetic qualities, especially the colors and forms similar to those found in the Impressionist and Post-Impressionist paintings they avidly acquired. A sixteenth- to seventeenth-century *cloisonné* enamel plaque (fig. 116), for example, particularly captivated Walter Annenberg because "the vigorous movement of colors, the bold forms reminded me so much of van Gogh."[4] Leonore Annenberg, too, seemed primarily stirred by the beauty of Chinese art, and favorite works included the colorful *cloisonné* furniture that their interior designer William Haines persuaded them to purchase and the many Chinese export porcelains, especially those bearing the "peacock pattern" (see fig. 120).[5] At the same time, the Annenbergs were also occasionally intrigued by the original function and history of certain Chinese works, such as an archaistic jade carving in the shape of a ceremonial scepter held by courtiers at imperial audiences.[6]

The story of the Annenbergs' art collections in general and of their Chinese art collection in particular

116 | *Plaque of landscape, Ming dynasty (1368–1644), sixteenth to seventeenth century. Cloisonné enamel, 24 × 15.5 in. (60.96 × 39.37 cm) (Photograph by Graydon Wood, December 2006).*

predated the construction of Sunnylands and their association with William Haines, even though his predilections influenced certain of their acquisitions for the estate. It was in the early 1950s that the couple began to collect art seriously, often visiting galleries in New York City with some of Walter's sisters and their husbands. Enid and Ira Haupt, Lita and Joseph Hazen, and Evelyn and William Jaffe were especially knowledgeable and serious about art, including Asian art.[7] (It

is no surprise that Evelyn's collection of fine Ming and Qing porcelains was auctioned off with great success in the spring of 2006,[8] and Lita and Joseph Hazen's daughter, Cynthia Hazen Polsky, went on to become a renowned collector of Indian art.)[9] As the Annenbergs frequented the New York galleries of Knoedler and Wildenstein with and without their relatives, they also became acquainted with various leading venues for Asian art, such as the Ralph M. Chait Galleries, located in the same general neighborhood of Manhattan.[10] Their focus was first on embellishing Inwood, Walter Annenberg's home in Wynnewood, outside Philadelphia. Inwood, which Leonore Annenberg undertook to redecorate and remodel in 1951 after

117 | *Pair of figures of tomb guardian warriors, Tang dynasty, late seventh to first half of the eighth century. Earthenware with traces of paint and gilt, ht. 34 in. (86.36 cm) (Photograph by Graydon Wood, December 2006).*

nenbergs' collecting. Although Sunnylands had some Chinese art in it from the beginning as shown by letters to Walter Annenberg from William Haines about the proposed conversion of Chinese ceramic figures to lamps—its Chinese art holdings increased over time. In some instances, this was because of a recommendation from Haines, and at other times because the Annenbergs themselves transferred a work of Chinese art from Inwood, or they made a purchase in this area.[12] Acquisitions continued well after Sunnylands was completed: among the later additions, for instance, was a large pair of painted and gilt Tang dynasty tomb guardians (fig. 117).[13] Yet the goal is not a comprehensive collection of the whole of Chinese art, anymore than the Annenberg collection of paintings and sculpture was intended to be a comprehensive collection of nineteenth- and twentieth-century Western art. Rather, the Chinese art at Sunnylands reflects the Annenbergs' personal interests and tastes; it is unique in its twin emphases on ceramics and enamels.

THE COLLECTION
IN CONTEXT

the Annenbergs' marriage, was naturally the prime repository of much of their art collecting before the building of Sunnylands.[11]

As recounted by David De Long elsewhere in this volume, the vision that would become Sunnylands evolved as the estate was constructed, and the design continued to change as it responded to the evolving demands of its owners. With the decision in 1974 to move the Impressionist and Post-Impressionist paintings from Inwood to Sunnylands, as well as the addition of more paintings, sculpture, and other artifacts, the Rancho Mirage home became less an "unembellished desert retreat," as De Long notes, and more a magnet for the An-

To appreciate the importance of Chinese art at Sunnylands, one need only imagine the estate without it—no porcelains in pastel hues, no dramatic tomb sculptures, no vivid enamels, no jade "Walter." When Thomas Hoving likened Sunnylands to the "finest 'stately homes'" of England, he was referring to the rich aesthetic ambiance of those homes, an ambiance also encountered at Sunnylands.[14] An important aspect of those great houses is the almost universal presence of Chinese and Japanese artifacts.[15] This is still the case for various nineteenth- and twentieth-century mansions in North America, some now turned into museums.[16] What distinguishes Sunnylands from many of these homes, whether European or

American, is its modern interior. It is not filled with antique American, English, or French furniture of dark or gilt wood, but custom-designed furnishings of contemporary appearance, mostly in light shades designed by the William Haines studio (see fig. 45). Thanks to the interiors' generally pale colors and the many large windows, a sense of airiness and light prevails through much of Sunnylands. The sometimes soft, sometimes brilliant colors of the Impressionist and Post-Impressionist paintings housed here were made fully visible by this décor. So, too, was the palette of the Chinese artworks. Despite the quantity of art—which increased at Sunnylands over the years—there is no sense of overwhelming splendor (at best) or clutter (at worst), which is a characteristic of many "stately homes" in England or the United States. Sunnylands is certainly in the tradition of the great houses of the past, but it is a simpler, more open type, one not seen before the twentieth century. Chinese art can be found in most of its interiors, carrying on a long-standing Western tradition. Credit for the success of this integration must go to William Haines, his associates, and his discerning clients.

The display of Chinese artifacts in European and American residences, whether grand or modest, can be traced to the seventeenth and eighteenth centuries when, through the expansion of trade, Chinese goods were no longer as rare as in the fourteenth century, the dawn of export to Europe, when a single treasured piece of porcelain was set in gilt-silver mounts.[17] By the 1600s, aristocrats and the merely wealthy aspired to show off and occasionally even use "Oriental" porcelain of Chinese or Japanese manufacture. In the mid-to-late seventeenth century, however, Japanese porcelain became popular abroad as Chinese porcelain manufacture contracted during the disorder that followed the fall of the Ming dynasty and the delayed consolidation of the Qing. But by the eighteenth century Chinese porcelain regained its dominance in the export market after the kilns at Jingdezhen, still the main center of China's porcelain production, were rebuilt during the reign of the Kangxi emperor (r. 1662–1722), and at about the same time, Japan, because of a change in government policy, severely restricted

its foreign trade.[18] Great European collections were formed: among the most noted were those of Queen Mary II of England (1662–1694), and the porcelain-mad Augustus II (the Strong), King of Poland and Elector of Saxony (1670–1733).[19] The "secret" of true porcelain was discovered in Europe by Johann Frederick Böttger, working for Augustus II (the Strong) in the eighteenth century; and manufacture began in 1710 at the Meissen factory sponsored by that monarch, eventually followed by other European factories. But Chinese porcelain did not immediately lose its position as an object of value.[20] Many eighteenth-century palaces and wealthy residences continued to showcase their Chinese porcelains along with their European examples. As time passed and European and eventually American production of various kinds of ceramics increased, however, the demand for Chinese products declined. This coincided with disorder in China and a related decline in the quality of Chinese ceramics. Thus they were predominantly collected by those who could not afford better.

In the late nineteenth century, collecting trends changed again, as a widespread interest in many aspects of "Oriental" art appeared in both Europe and North America. There are many reasons. China and Japan were opened to wider travel and trade, which exposed Americans and Europeans, including artists and collectors, to a broader scope of art and culture to appreciate, collect, or imitate. Some felt dissatisfied with their own art and culture, and sought out new inspirations and fields of collecting. Among those especially interested in East Asian art were artists such as James McNeill Whistler (1834–1903), whose work was also acquired by such wealthy collectors of Chinese porcelain as Henry Clay Frick (1849–1919). A large assemblage of Chinese porcelain is part of the exquisite furnishings of the Frick Collection, once Frick's New York home, perhaps best known for its Old Master and nineteenth-century paintings, including some by Whistler.

As for Chinese ceramics in the late nineteenth and early twentieth centuries, there was not simply a revival of interest in collecting them by the wealthy, but also the beginnings of their systematic study. The dispersal of much of J. Pierpont

Morgan's (1837–1913) porcelain collection in 1915–1916 enriched the homes of Frick, John D. Rockefeller, Jr. (1874–1960), and Joseph Widener (1872–1943) with these primarily eighteenth-century works. As to their Morgan ceramics, the Rockefellers gave some to The Metropolitan Museum of Art, New York, but others remained with the family in lavish residences, including the Rockefeller estate called Kykuit, Pocantico Hills, New York, where some can still be seen.[21] The Rockefeller interiors show that as late as the mid-twentieth century the grand style of interior design with period furnishings and Chinese porcelains remained popular, even as other trends in interior design appeared. Sunnylands epitomizes one of these recent trends—not the complete rejection of tradition, but the combination of the antique with the contemporary.

In reviewing the design career of William Haines, which began in the 1930s, it appears that he seldom (if ever) produced interiors in exclusively grand or conventionally modernist style. Homes might feature antiques, but they usually also included comfortable contemporary furniture. While modern, these interiors were not minimalist, and they were noted for a skillful use of accessories. Consistently Haines employed East Asian artifacts in his décor as stand-alone objects or as lamps, and he combined them with antique Chinese wallpapers and Chinese-inspired decorative objects.[22] Such works are usually referred to as his "Chinoiserie."[23] A term derived from the French *chinois* (Chinese), this became widely known after the publication in 1961 of Hugh Honour's *Chinoiserie: The Vision of Cathay*, but its application can be traced at least to the nineteenth century. Honour and other scholars generally use Chinoiserie to signify non-Chinese interpretations of Chinese art and culture, made with varying degrees of fidelity from the Middle Ages through the nineteenth century.[24] However, in his use of East Asian, and usually Chinese, artworks at Sunnylands and elsewhere, Haines did not seem intent on creating anyone's "vision of Cathay," but on enhancing the ambiance of a variety of California interiors, whether more modernist or more traditional. In many instances the Chinese artworks, as at Sunnylands, are so successfully integrated within the interior design that the casual visitor may not immediately notice them. At the same time, the knowledgeable will appreciate the subtlety of their placement.

CHINESE CERAMICS

Chinese ceramics encompass unparalleled variety.[25] They range from low-fired glazed and unglazed earthenwares to glazed and unglazed stonewares, the latter group including porcelains, a type of highly refined white-bodied stoneware. Examples of all major varieties of Chinese ceramics may be seen at Sunnylands.

The estate is especially rich in multicolored porcelains specifically created for foreign markets during the last of China's dynasties, the Qing (1644–1911; figs. 118–122). Though richer in export ware, the collection also includes a few early Qing dishes, more likely made for domestic consumption, whose vivid greens and yellows contribute to the bright ambiance.

118 | *Teapot or water dropper, Qing dynasty, Kangxi reign (1662–1722). Porcelain with enamels used as glazes on the biscuit, diam. 4.88 in (12.4 cm) (Photograph by Ned Redway, February 2008).*

119 | *Chocolate or coffee pot with European subject for export trade, Qing dynasty, mid-eighteenth century. Porcelain with overglaze famille rose enamels and gold, ht. 10 in. (25.4 cm) (Photograph by Graydon Wood, December 2006).*

120 | *Charger, one of a pair for export trade, Qing dynasty, eighteenth century. Porcelain with "peacock pattern" in overglaze famille rose enamels, diam. 16.25 in. (41.28 cm) (Photograph by Graydon Wood, December 2006).*

Other domestic wares, including impressive Tang (618–907 C.E.) dynasty mortuary figures (figs. 123, 125) and charming Ming (1368–1644) dynasty rabbit-form roof tiles (fig. 124), play an important role in the décor of Sunnylands. Indeed, the Chinese ceramic sculptures, whether created for export or the domestic market, are displayed at Sunnylands with as much care as the examples of modern sculpture exhibited there.

The Chinese ceramics at Sunnylands generally fall into two categories: containers or vessels (bowls, dishes, flagons or jugs, pots, vases, and so on), and sculptures (architectural, decorative, mortuary, and the like), the latter group including some of the more significant works. What follows here, after an introduction to the development of Chinese ceramics, is an examination of these ceramic vessels and ceramic sculpture.

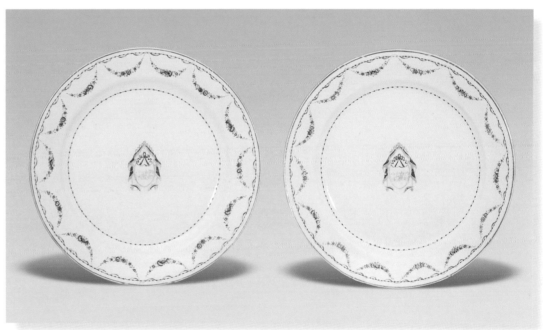

121 | *Monteith for export trade, Qing dynasty, ca. 1740. Porcelain with overglaze famille rose enamels and gold, length 21 in. (53.34 cm) (Photograph by Graydon Wood, November 2005).*

122 | *Chargers, pair for export trade, Qing dynasty, late eighteenth century. Porcelain with ribbon-tied swag-draped shield with monogram with overglaze famille rose enamels and gold, diam. 18 in. (45.6 cm.) (Photograph by Ned Redway, February 2008).*

123 | *View of five Tang dynasty works, late seventh to first half of the eighth century, in alcove adjacent to atrium. Earthenware with three-color (sancai) glaze and pigments (Photograph by Graydon Wood, December 2006).*

124 | *Pair of rabbit-form roof tiles, late Ming dynasty, sixteenth to seventeenth century. Glazed earthenware or stoneware, ht. 11.5 in. (29.21 cm) (Photograph by Ned Redway, February 2008).*

125 | *Five Tang dynasty works, late seventh to first half of the eighth century. Earthenware with three-color (sancai) glaze and pigments. Left to right: Tomb guardian warrior, ht. 42 in. (106.68 cm); camel, ht. 26.5 in. (67.31 cm); official, ht. 31.5 in. (80.01 cm); official, ht. 42 in. (106.68 cm) (Photograph by Graydon Wood, December 2006).*

A THUMBNAIL HISTORY OF CHINESE CERAMICS

Surprisingly, considering its ultimate dominance in the world of ceramics, China is apparently *not* where the world's earliest ceramics were made, nor where the earliest advances in ceramic technology occurred. Low-fired unglazed earthenwares have been found in Japan dating to about 11,000/10,500 B.C.E., compared to examples from China dating to about 9000 B.C.E.[26] Glazed earthenware was produced in the Middle East as early as 2000–1000 B.C.E., but it only became common in China during the Warring States period (481–221 B.C.E.).[27] And unglazed high-fired stonewares found in Iraq and Turkey date to about 2800/2300 B.C.E., compared to Chinese examples dating to about 1600/1500 B.C.E.[28] At almost the same time that they mastered the high-temperature kiln, Chinese potters produced the world's earliest glazed stonewares, around 1400/1300 B.C.E. These became the foundation of several of China's most famous products, such as those described as having a *qing* glaze (blue-green to gray-green to olive-green), usually translated as "celadon," sometimes simply as "green" glaze.[29] While most associated with the Song (960–1279) and Yüan (1279–1368) dynasties, celadon wares were made both before and after those dynasties, and were always part of the domestic and export markets.[30] A handsome example of celadon at Sunnylands is a carved Ming dynasty jar in ovoid form (fig. 126).

Perhaps China's most celebrated ceramic achievement is the creation of the world's earliest porcelains (ca. 600 C.E.).[31] These came to be especially treasured outside of China, prized for their whiteness and translucency. But in traditional Chinese ceramic literature, these white-bodied stonewares are not classified apart from dark-bodied high-fired stonewares, or given a special name; they were regarded as part of a grand continuum of extremely sturdy ceramics that could be adorned with an array of glazes; the emphasis was on the strength of the ware rather than on its whiteness. In fact, some Chinese connoisseurs most value certain Song dynasty stonewares whose buff, gray, and brown bodies influence the glazes applied to them, evoking the appearance of jade, for example. On the other hand, the white ground of porcelain made it an ideal surface for a wide range of décor and glazes so it is not surprising that it came to predominate among Chinese ceramics made for the imperial court during the Ming and Qing

126 | *Carved celadon ovoid jar, Ming dynasty, fourteenth to sixteenth century. Stoneware with celadon glaze, ht. 13.5 in. (34.29 cm) (Photograph by Ned Redway, March 2008).*

dynasties. Other East Asian ceramic-producing regions such as Korea and Japan made porcelain some centuries later, and in the early eighteenth century porcelain was finally made in Europe.[32]

In China, porcelains do not appear to have been manufactured or exported in any quantity until the Song and Yüan dynasties. By about 1300 C.E., examples of white porcelain reached Europe.[33] During the Yüan, if not sooner, white porcelain was embellished by blue or red underglaze painted décor; this, too, was exported, first reaching the Middle East and then Europe a bit later.[34] By the sixteenth century at the latest, Chinese ceramics, especially "blue and white" porcelains, as the underglaze blue-decorated wares are generally known, were collected in some numbers abroad, and by the late seventeenth century they became an important part of the décor of the homes of the European elite where they frequently play that role today.[35] At Sunnylands, however, another type predominates—polychrome porcelain—a type that enjoyed growing popularity in Europe and North America from the late nineteenth century on.

Continuing advances in ceramic technology during the Ming and Qing dynasties enabled the creation of an astonishing variety of Chinese porcelains, sometimes fired multiple times to allow for the most elaborate overglaze decoration.[36] Production of porcelain for both the domestic and export markets expanded, with only some interruption following the collapse of the Ming during the seventeenth century and the consolidation of Qing rule.[37] Ceramics created for foreign markets were familiar to Chinese potters before European (and eventually American) merchants began to make special orders and requests, but the extent to which Chinese ceramics were made to order for these markets, especially in the eighteenth and nineteenth centuries when whole services in "Western" forms were created with various coats of arms or other "Western" designs, is apparently unprecedented.[38]

EARTHENWARE AND STONEWARE VESSELS AT SUNNYLANDS

Sunnylands holds relatively few Chinese earthenware and stoneware vessels. The most noteworthy is a *Tang sancai* ("Tang dynasty three-color ware") tripod (fig. 127) displayed on a table in the living area at Sunnylands along with a *Tang sancai* camel and three *Tang sancai* figures.[39] All were originally intended for placement in the tomb of someone of rank. Because of their funerary associations, such works, whether vessels or figures, were not collected or regarded as artworks

127 | *Tang sancai tripod, Tang dynasty (618–907), late seventh to first half of the eighth century. Earthenware with three-color (sancai) glaze and pigments, ht. 5.5 in. (13.97 cm) (Photograph by Ned Redway, February 2008).*

by the Chinese until the twentieth century. Japanese, European, and American collectors and scholars became fascinated with Chinese mortuary ceramics as they began to be unearthed from ancient burials during railway construction in China in the early part of the twentieth century and eventually Chinese collectors turned their attention to them, too.[40] Only then does one find Chinese mortuary ceramics displayed in galleries, homes, and museums.

PORCELAIN VESSELS

The majority of Chinese ceramics at Sunnylands are Qing dynasty porcelains, many with overglaze enamels, and sometimes also with gilding. Only a small number were created for the domestic Chinese market, the rest for export.

Among the Chinese vessels at Sunnylands probably intended for domestic use are works found in the living room including a splashed glaze "egg and spinach" water coupe and a teapot (or water dropper) glazed in green and ocher (see fig. 118).[41] These, along with a multipart "sweetmeat set" with typical *famille verte* enamels on the biscuit, are all attributed to the Kangxi period (1662–1722) of the Qing dynasty, that is to the reign of this emperor.[42] *Famille verte* or "green family" was a term apparently coined, along with *famille rose* or "rose family," by the French ceramics collector and historian Albert Jacquemart (1808–1875), to discriminate between these two enamel color schemes. *Famille verte* appeared earlier than *famille rose*, and the latter was only fully mastered during the reign of Kangxi's successor, Yongzheng, who ruled from 1732 to 1735.[43] Distinguished by its carefully applied translucent colors, with strong greens and yellows, *famille verte* enamels might be applied to an already glazed and fired surface or to a fired but unglazed porcelain surface. The brilliant hues of the *famille verte* and other Kangxi wares at Sunnylands not only complement the colors occasionally seen in certain

of the estate's Impressionist and Post-Impressionist paintings, but also the greens and ambers of the *Tang sancai* mortuary wares.

Famille rose features pinks and roses, of a type previously unknown in overglaze porcelain decoration, and also an opaque white.[44] The *famille rose* palette seen at Sunnylands harmonizes well with those Impressionist works with softer colors; the *famille rose* wares are the most numerous among the Chinese porcelains throughout the house.

An example of export *famille rose* at Sunnylands that would have required multiple firings because of its extensive gilding is the handsome mid-eighteenth-century export chocolate or coffee pot with a European-inspired design of huntsman, hounds, and stag (see fig. 119).[45] The scholars David Howard and John Ayers have identified the likely inspiration of this in a print dated to about 1730 by a German artist, Johan Elias Ridinger (1698–1767); versions of this design appear on export porcelains including plates and chocolate or coffee pots.[46] Displayed in the living area, the vessel is a good example of a Chinese work whose décor and shape were no doubt created for export.[47]

Another noteworthy *famille rose* work at Sunnylands, also to be seen in the living area, is a large monteith, or wine glass cooler, with bird and flower décor dated to ca. 1740 (see fig. 121). Monteiths, purportedly named after a "fantastical Scot," are noted in late seventeenth-century English texts. Though sometimes mistaken later for punch bowls and used as such, monteiths became popular in America and Europe, surviving in a number of forms and media, with the older versions more circular in shape. Not surprisingly, Chinese porcelain examples eventually appeared beginning in the eighteenth century. Apparently the notched rim was utilized for chilling the wine glasses, and this rim is one key to their identity.[48] Mounted on ball and claw feet, in size and oblong form somewhat resembling an earlier *famille verte* example now in the collection of the Metropolitan Museum of Art, the large monteith at Sunnylands brings to mind the American and European furniture of the late seventeenth and eighteenth centuries that also feature ball and claw feet.[49]

Other *famille rose* works of interest at Sunnylands include a pair of jars and covers dated to ca. 1750; these are placed under tables framing the fireplace in the living area (see fig. 45 for a distant view of both jars). These were probably once part of a set or garniture of jars and beakers (usually three, five, or seven) intended to be displayed on a chimney mantel or high cupboard. Most familiarly known by the French term *garniture de cheminée*, they are also sometimes referred to by the Dutch word *kaststel*, after the Dutch tall cupboard, the *kast*. Such sets were made in large quantities in China for export in the eighteenth century, and they remain popular among American and European collectors of Chinese export porcelain.[50] The Sunnylands jars, decorated with four flower-filled baskets between ruby-colored borders, resemble two in a five-vessel set that were part of the Benjamin Altman bequest to The Metropolitan Museum of Art.[51]

A particular favorite of Leonore Annenberg is the *famille rose* "peacock pattern," which features a pair of peacocks perched on rocks, framed by flowers.[52] The Sunnylands holdings include four platters in the living room as well as two large chargers in the master bedroom (see fig. 120). Described by a scholar as a "stock" export pattern during the eighteenth century, this was popular from "Canada to Florida."[53] Services in it were owned not only by wealthy Americans, but also by members of the Portuguese royal family who took them to Brazil when they fled from Napoleon in the early nineteenth century. Eventually the pattern was copied by the Spode factory in the early nineteenth century.[54]

Much Chinese porcelain was decorated with patterns that were made to order during the eighteenth and nineteenth centuries. Among the most often encountered are those with a coat of arms, often placed on a large service. There are quite a few such armorial porcelains at Sunnylands, including dishes, platters, and drinking vessels variously known as "Toddy jugs," a type of flagons. Among the most artfully painted of armorial wares at Sunnylands are four platters with a design of birds on rockwork and landscape vignettes as well as the arms of William Davis, an assistant governor of Bengal, all datable to about 1746.[55] Also appealing is a pair of late eighteenth century chargers. These are decorated with swags of flowers on the border surrounding a ribbon-tied swag-draped shield with a faint monogram; whether these shields are arms or another type of made-to-order design is as yet undetermined (see fig. 122). Classifying and identifying armorial porcelains, which were apparently first made to order in quantity during the eighteenth century, is complex and specialized, especially as armorial services were made for individuals of several countries.[56]

CERAMIC SCULPTURE

Chinese ceramic sculpture at Sunnylands ranges from striking Tang dynasty mortuary figures through charming Ming dynasty architectural accoutrements to elegant Qing dynasty export models. Items whose original purpose was funerary or religious are displayed individually or in groups; they are treated as worthy of concentrated attention like other sculpture at the residence. Works created with a decorative aim generally continue to play that role at Sunnylands. To a surprising extent, this relatively small collection at Sunnylands embodies the rich panoply of Chinese ceramic sculpture.

Significant amounts of ceramic sculpture first appear in China during the middle to late Neolithic era (ca. 5000–2000 B.C.E.).[57] Images of females associated with the Hongshan culture of Northeast China likely had a ritual purpose, and the small figures of humans and animals associated with the Shijiahe culture of south-central China may have been a trade good.[58] In later periods, religious and export images made of ceramics were not uncommon, and in some instances, such as an exceptionally large eighteenth-to-nineteenth-century *Blanc de Chine* or Dehua ware Buddhist figure now displayed in the dining room at Sunnylands, an image might be religious or for export, or possibly both at once (fig. 128; see fig. 48).

128 | *Figure of Guanyin ("Goddess of Mercy"), Qing dynasty, late eighteenth to nineteenth century. Porcelain with clear glaze (Dehua ware, Fujian Province), ht. 33.5 in. (85.09 cm) (Photograph by Graydon Wood, December 2006).*

MORTUARY SCULPTURE

Ceramic sculpture deliberately made for placement in Chinese tombs can be documented during the successive Bronze Age dynasties, especially the Eastern Zhou (771–256 B.C.E.), when ceramic and wooden figures began to be more widely used to supplement animal and human sacrifices in the graves of the elite.[59] Examples of this, thus far unique in scale and number, are the thousands of life-size earthenware statues, the world-famous "Terra-cotta warriors," unearthed at the necropolis of Ying Zheng (259–210 B.C.E.), Qin Shihuangdi. This title can be translated as Qin [dynasty] First August Emperor, the honorific that Ying Zheng gave himself upon unifying China into an empire in 221 B.C.E. In English, he is generally referred to as the First Emperor.[60] Although the custom of using ceramic mortuary models persisted into the Qing dynasty, they are most prevalent from the Qin (221–206 B.C.E.) through the Tang dynasties. Tang dynasty works, such as those found at Sunnylands, whether glazed or painted, placid or dynamic, are noted for their robust three-dimensionality.

As explained above, Chinese tomb sculptures were not collected in China until the twentieth century, and only then thanks in part to outside interest, which only began in the early part of that century. Thus tomb sculpture does not figure in the ceramics displayed in the "great houses" of England in the seventeenth through the late nineteenth centuries, nor in the collections or homes in North America of such magnates as Frick or Morgan. After World War I a shift in taste among Western collectors and scholars toward earlier Chinese wares (and away from once-favored Qing porcelains) caused Chinese tomb sculpture to be added not only to museum holdings, but also to homes. After Nelson Rockefeller moved into Kykuit in 1963, for example, he added Han and Tang mortuary wares to the Ming and Qing ceramics already displayed there, enhancing, but not changing, the richly appointed interiors.[61] The ambiance of Sunnylands is simpler, if no less impressive.

The latter approach reflects the wishes of the Annenbergs, who avoided traditional settings at Rancho Mirage in contrast to those at their home in Wynnewood, outside Philadelphia. The successful mixture of Chinese antiquities (in this instance tomb sculpture) with modern design should also be credited to William Haines, who had previous interest in this conception.[62]

Prominently positioned on a long table in the alcove adjacent to the atrium at Sunnylands are five fine examples of *Tang sancai* ("Tang dynasty three-color ware"), all datable to the late seventh century through the first half of the eighth century, the heyday of this glazed earthenware.[63] Whether seen in the ambiance of Sunnylands (see figs. 42, 123), or in the seclusion of a photographer's studio (see fig. 125), these are striking works. Of these *Tang sancai* examples, the one vessel, a tripod, is discussed above. In the tombs in which such funerary ceramics were placed, there was always a mixture of vessels and figures, as seen here.

Tang government regulations sought to insure that deceased individuals were supplied only with grave goods deemed appropriate to that person's status.[64] Based on their large size and the careful quality of their modeling and glazing, the four Sunnylands figures are typical members of the "retinue" of tomb sculptures supplied to high-ranking individuals. Controlled excavations reveal that Tang tombs generally had within this retinue what has been termed "a core group" of two oversize figures in military attire (a type of tomb guardian warrior); two oversize chimerical animals (additional tomb guardians); two oversize figures dressed as officials; an oversize pair of camels with their grooms; an oversize pair of horses with their grooms. This retinue also included many smaller figures.[65] Usually the figures dressed as officials have dignified and placid expressions such as those on the right in figure 125, whereas those who function as tomb guardian warriors have fiercer miens and sometimes gesticulate in a threatening manner, like the armored figure on the left.

Judging by their impressive size, which is coordinated appropriately among them, and the similar application of their predominantly green and yellow glazes, it is likely that

129 | *Figure of official, Tang dynasty, late seventh to first half of the eighth century. Earthenware with three-color (sancai) glaze, including blue, and pigments, ht. 31.5 in. (80.01 cm) (Photograph by Graydon Wood, December 2006).*

three—the larger official, the camel, and the military figure—originated from the tomb of someone of high status, though not necessarily the same tomb.[66] The smaller official, adorned with rare blue glaze, probably came from a tomb with similar smaller figures, figures that were probably embellished with a similar blue glaze (fig. 129). Some collectors believe that only the most important individuals merited *Tang sancai* with blue glaze, but recent research has revealed that some less important tomb occupants were accorded it, and sometimes important ones were not.[67] Consequently, the smaller official's blue glaze offers no clue to the rank of the person from whose tomb this came. As to where the tombs were located, the most likely candidates are in the Xi'an area of Shaanxi province and the Luoyang area of Henan province, the sites of the Tang dynasty's primary and secondary capitals, and the locale of the majority of tombs yielding *Tang sancai*.

Because of their alluring and often well-preserved glazes, *Tang sancai* mortuary ceramics have tended to overshadow those that are merely painted, or painted and gilded. However, as better-made and better-preserved unglazed works have become available, more collectors and scholars have come to appreciate the immense amount of labor that they represent. In fact, earthenware further adorned with gold is sometimes the material of the most important figures in imperial tombs.[68] Among the latest additions of Chinese art at Sunnylands is a pair of lively military figures, tomb guardian warriors shown standing on bulls (see fig. 117).[69] Of a type popularly referred to as "Lokapalas" (a Sanskrit term) or "Heavenly Kings," after these Buddhist deities whose iconography came to influence tomb sculpture, the two figures are notable for their well-preserved original paint and gilding.[70]

Ceramic tiles play an important role in Chinese architecture. Among the more attractive architectural ceramics are various glazed earthenware and stoneware ornaments, often in the form of animals, placed on roof ridges, among other spots.[71] A pair of late Ming dynasty rabbit-form roof tiles now occupy a place on a table at Sunnylands in front of a reproduction of Pablo Picasso's *Au Lapin Agile* (1905) in the living area (see fig. 124). Grace Glueck, writing shortly after this painting's purchase, described Walter Annenberg: "Stepping in front of the new Picasso, whose subject is a harlequin at the café called Le Lapin Agile, he gleefully pointed to a pair of frisky Chinese porcelain rabbits he had placed as accents beneath it."[72] This work, now at The Metropolitan Museum of Art, might also be more literally called "At the Nimble Rabbit," that being a direct translation of the name of the bar frequented by Picasso.[73]

Decorative ceramic sculpture was made in China for both the domestic and export market as early as the Song dynasty, with the bulk that reached the Americas and Europe dating to the Qing. Among the Qing export porcelain sculptures to be found in the living area at Sunnylands, a pair of mid-eighteenth-century figural candlesticks deserves comment for their charm (figs. 130, 131). Decorated with overglaze *famille rose* enamels, each takes the form of a presumably Chinese figure seated among rocks with a bird perched on the figure's hand. The pair epitomizes a type of "Chinoiserie" popular outside of China, and may reflect Walter Annenberg's interest in images of birds.[74]

By the Ming and Qing dynasties the vast majority of Chinese porcelain was made, if not always completely decorated, at Jingdezhen, in Jiangxi province, still today the center of China's ceramic industry. Only a few other regions of Chi-

130 | *Pair of figural candlesticks for export trade, Qing dynasty, mid-eighteenth century. Porcelain with overglaze famille rose enamels, ht. 8 in. (20.32 cm) (Photograph by Ned Redway, February 2008).*

131 | *Detail of one of a pair of figural candlesticks for export trade, Qing dynasty, mid-eighteenth century. Porcelain with overglaze famille rose enamels, ht. 8 in. (20.32 cm) (Photograph by Ned Redway, February 2008).*

na produced ceramics that could successfully compete with those from Jingdezhen, and only through a unique product that Jingdezhen could not duplicate. Such was and is the case with the kilns of Dehua, located in Fujian province.[75] Their most famous product, now often called Dehua ware but long known as *Blanc de Chine* in the West, consists of creamy white porcelain particularly suited for the modeling of figures.[76] Of those figures, the most famous is Guanyin, also known by the older Romanization "Kuan-yin," the Chinese version of the Bodhisattva Avalokitesvara, the most beloved of these compassionate Buddhist figures. This originally male figure underwent a transformation in China, ultimately coming to be regarded as a "Goddess of Mercy" by many during the Ming and Qing dynasties.[77] It is that form which was a specialty of the potters of Dehua. An unusually large figure of a Guanyin in Dehua ware or *Blanc de Chine* may be seen at Sunnylands in the dining room (see figs. 48, 128). Because of its style this religious figure has been judged to date to the Qing period.[78] Whether it was made for domestic use or the export market is difficult to determine.[79] What is undeniable is the monumentality of this particular statue. With enrobed body and kindly expression, it cannot help presenting a stark contrast to Rodin's *Eve* (see fig. 72).

THE ENAMELED METALWARE

Relatively few American and European collectors have concentrated their attention on Chinese enameled metalware, much less integrated it so thoroughly into the décor of their home as have the Annenbergs at Sunnylands.[80] Here, over forty Ming and Qing dynasty works are judiciously arranged so that their typically brilliant colors match or complement the palette of the Annenbergs' other art. Especially noteworthy is a pair of seventeenth-century enamel-embellished wooden stools, now used as tables in the living area, which William Haines correctly described as "so fantastic and like nothing we have ever

seen, that we felt it would be remiss not to bring them to your attention" (fig. 133).[81]

The living area boasts the great bulk of the fine, and in some instances quite rare, Chinese enameled metalware (see fig. 45).[82] A large part of the collection is Ming and Qing dynasty *cloisonné*, some of imperial quality (e.g., fig. 132). But it also includes examples of Qing dynasty painted enamel, among them an outstanding pair of large dishes decorated with images of "Westerners" (fig. 134). Some technical and historical information may help to indicate their achievement.

Enamel is a glass paste that when fired at a low temperature achieves a smooth and vitreous appearance. Enamels applied to ceramics and to metals are similar in that they both fuse at a relatively low temperature, about 700–800 degrees Celsius. Generally, when describing an object or objects as "enamel ware" or "enamels," it is understood that the objects are made of metal—brass, bronze, copper, gold, silver—perhaps because of the long and relatively continuous history of enameled metal in Europe and Western Asia.[83] On the other hand, if the subject under discussion is Chinese ceramics, they might also be termed "enamel ware," but seldom as "an enamel" or "enamels." Here, unless otherwise specified, references to "enamel ware" or "an enamel" or "enamels," will mean enameled *metal*.[84]

Chinese enamel-decorated ceramics (stoneware) date to as early as twelfth century, only slightly later than the Iranian enamel-decorated glazed ceramics that were apparently among the world's earliest examples of enamels used in this manner.[85] During the Ming dynasty, enameled porcelain became widely available.[86] By the late seventeenth century, during the Qing, the importation of European enameled metalware, especially that with a strong pink, influenced the enamels applied to Chinese ceramics by potters, evidently inspiring the creation of the ware known as *famille rose*, as exemplified by the Sunnylands "peacock pattern" chargers (see fig. 120).[87]

Painted enamels were produced in European locales as early as the fifteenth century, including Belgium and the Netherlands, with the sixteenth- and seventeenth-century products

132 | *Three cloisonné enamel vessels. Left. Plum-blossom vase (Meiping) with applied gilt-bronze beaded chains, Qing dynasty, Kangxi reign, ht. 14.25 in (36.2 cm). Center: Archaistic bird-form vessel, Qing dynasty, mark and period of Qianlong (1736–1795) reign, ht. 14 in. (35.56 cm). Right: Archaistic jar (Hu), Qing dynasty, eighteenth century; ht. 16 in. (40.64 cm) (Photograph by Graydon Wood, December 2006).*

133 | *One of pair of stools, Ming dynasty (1368–1644), seventeenth century. Cloisonné enamel, wood, 19.5 × 24 in. (49.53 × 60.96 cm) (Photograph by Graydon Wood, December 2006).*

of Limoges, France, becoming particularly celebrated.[88] From the Jesuit missionaries who brought various painted enamels to China, some of whom could practice the craft, Chinese artisans apparently learned how to make the pink enamel seen on these foreign works, and also how to create painted enamels.[89]

Before the late seventeenth and eighteenth centuries, the primary techniques of enameling in China had been *cloisonné* and *champlevé*. In *cloisonné*, metal wires are applied to the surface of an item, creating barriers that form cells into which enamel is placed before firing or fusing: the name derives from the French for "cell." In *champlevé*, the metal surface is carved out to form grooves or fields into which glass paste is placed before firing or fusing: the name derives from the French for "raised field."[90] These methods, also practiced elsewhere in Europe and in Western Asia, mitigate the tendency of enamels to run during firing and to detach from the metal they are fused to. Close-up views of fine *cloisonné* such as that at Sunnylands reveal the crisp distinctions of color

134 | *Two dishes for export trade, Qing dynasty, first half eighteenth century, Kangxi (1662–1722) or Yongzheng (1722–1735) reigns. Enamel on copper; interior view on left, diam. 13.25 in. (33.66 cm); exterior view on right, diam. 13.25 in. (33.66 cm) (Photograph by Graydon Wood, December 2006).*

that this process makes possible (see fig. 116). The success of European and eventually Chinese painted enamels depended on the application of grounding layers of less fusible enamel over a metal surface. Colored enamels were then applied, and the item was fired again. If all went well, the painted designs, executed in more fusible enamel, would not run, and the now-decorated ground layer would bond securely with the metal (see fig. 134).[91]

Some contend that production of Chinese *cloisonné* began as early as the eighth century, but the evidence for this is not universally accepted. However, few dispute a continuous tradition of Chinese *cloisonné* (and to a less extent *champlevé*) beginning as early as the thirteenth century or the fourteenth century, that is, during the late Yuan or early Ming dynasties, most likely stimulated by Byzantine and Western Asian examples. Mongol domination of the continent at this time would have facilitated such cultural interaction.[92] The Chinese enamels at Sunnylands date to the Ming and Qing dynasties.

The painted Chinese enamels in the Annenberg collection include an outstanding pair of large dishes, works featuring Westerners in their central décor, which were most probably created for export (see fig. 134).[93] These colorful dishes may date as early as the last years of the reign of Kangxi (1662–1722) or to the reign of Yongzheng (1722–1735), judging from the red enamel in the palette and the yellow diaper pattern.[94] Women and children predominate in the slightly varying compositions, although there are also a few men: the

135 | *Pair of covered boxes with Shou characters, late Ming dynasty, sixteenth to seventeenth century. Cloisonné enamel, ht. 3.25 in. (8.26 cm) (Photograph by Ned Redway, March 2008).*

subject combines European motifs and Chinese elements, and most likely does not derive from any specific Western model.[95] Especially unusual is the elaborate décor lavished on the exterior walls, consisting of landscapes in cartouches, and the lion-like beast on the base of each of these dishes.[96]

The Annenberg collection of Ming and Qing *cloisonné* comprises both typical and atypical works, all made of copper or copper alloy (brass or bronze), in some instances further embellished with gilt bronze ornament. Three items bear authentic four-character engraved reign marks of the Qianlong emperor (r. 1736–1795), indicating their use in an imperial palace. Differences in refinement between Ming and Qing *cloisonné* may be explained by a variety of technological advances, such as the practice of drawing the wires that make up the cells through a die rather than hammering them so that they split less frequently, and their being glued to the metal body rather than soldered, thus lessening their weight. New enamel colors, most importantly rose pink, were developed or introduced from abroad. However, the ubiquity of turquoise

as a ground color during both periods makes this difference less immediately noticeable. Ming *cloisonné*, which may be heavier and simpler in color scheme than that of the Qing, can present a refreshing contrast to the sometimes overly fussy work of the later dynasty. On the other hand, the exuberant archaism of Qianlong *cloisonné* vessels directly or vaguely inspired by ancient bronzes of the Shang (or Zhou) or the Han dynasties can be endearing.

With its vigorous colors and bold forms, a Ming dynasty sixteenth- to seventeenth-century plaque typifies the direct appeal of much Ming *cloisonné* (see fig. 116).[97] It was in this period that such pictorial scenes evidently began to appear.[98] Some of these panels, especially those finished on both sides, may have been inset into small wooden table screens or metal stands, but others may always have been intended to function as ornamental pictures; indeed, examples in that form survive in the National Palace Museum in Taiwan.[99] Other Ming *cloisonné* in the Annenberg collection includes a large covered tripod censer of Han dynasty form, with gilt bronze fittings and a pair of foliate-shaped covered boxes of a type usually termed "mallow-form" after the hibiscus-like Chinese flower, featuring red *Shou* or "Longevity" characters in a repetitive pattern (fig. 135).

Most important in the Sunnylands enamel collection, as mentioned above, are the two seventeenth-century wooden stools embellished with *cloisonné* now used as tables (see fig. 133). Few examples of wooden furniture with *cloisonné* survive, and what does is generally associated with imperial use. Works that can be cited include a throne attributed to the eighteenth century now in the New Summer Palace, or Yiheyuan, in the outskirts of Beijing, and a pair of barrel stools, most likely of eighteenth- or nineteenth-century date, now held in the Forbidden City (Imperial Palace) in the center of Beijing.[100] The Annenberg stools have been dated to the seventeenth century not only on the basis of the period design and technique of the enamel, but also because the stools resemble unembellished wooden furniture of that time.[101] This dating and the refinement of their *cloisonné* make them rare, indeed.

After the disruptions in the late Ming and early Qing dynasties, order was restored to the empire under the Kangxi emperor. This order extended into the arts and crafts, with the rebuilding of the imperial porcelain kilns and resumption of work there. It was at this time, in the seventeenth century, that the Jesuits brought painted enamels to China, as noted above.[102] Few works of enamel anywhere can be directly linked to the Kangxi period through their markings. But a work in the Annenberg collection is attributed to this era, perhaps because of certain bold Ming elements within its design: an unmarked *cloisonné* vessel of *meiping* (plum-blossom vase) shape with applied pendant gilt-bronze beaded chains suspended from *Ruyi* (As You Wish) trefoil heads and *Shou* (Longevity) medallions (see fig. 132, left).[103] Another unmarked *cloisonné* vase in *meiping* form with somewhat similar beaded chain ornament exists in the former imperial collection housed at the National Palace Museum in Taiwan; that work, however, has been credited to the reign of the Qianlong emperor (1736–1795), perhaps because of its extreme refinement.[104] This demonstrates the complexity of dating unmarked works, especially in the case of unusual artifacts.

During the Ming dynasty, reign marks, usually of four or six Chinese characters, indicating that an item was made during the reign of a particular emperor, began to be regularly applied to works used in imperial palaces, though not necessarily used by the emperor himself. However, not all works destined for a palace received these marks, and they were not consistently applied during the reigns of certain emperors. Furthermore, such marks were copied, sometimes in tribute to an admired earlier model, but sometimes also to deceive.[105]

The Annenberg collection includes three *cloisonné* works with Qianlong reign marks, a pair of joss-stick or incensestick holders, and an archaistic bird form vessel. These reflect this emperor's interest in antiquities. The joss-stick holders evoke Ming dynasty *cloisonné* in their restricted palette and archaic dragon and lotus décor.[106] The bird-form vessel (see fig. 132, center) is remotely related to Shang and Zhou dynasty animal-formed bronze vessels, but more directly to what the Qing perceived as ancient Han dynasty bronze vessels. Illustrations in a mid-eighteenth century book show similar items described as Han "bird-chariots."[107] Another Qianlong marked vessel of this type has been published, as have other unmarked models.[108] Without a Qianlong mark, and therefore only attributable to the eighteenth century, is a brilliantly colored covered jar whose form and monster-mask design owe much to Shang and Zhou bronzes (see fig. 132, right). A fascination with ancient artifacts was not exclusive to the emperor during this period: this vessel might well have been made for another member of the elite.[109]

The Annenberg enamel collection includes other Qing dynasty works. Among them are many images of birds, especially pairs of cranes both large and small. This may reflect Walter Annenberg's fondness for these creatures.[110] Large pairs of *cloisonné* cranes were frequently put in Qing dynasty throne rooms, perhaps because of their association with longevity and immortality and perhaps also because their name, *he*, is homophone for harmony. At Sunnylands, a pair of these birds, in size comparable to those just mentioned, was placed in front of the fireplace in the living room (see fig. 45).[111]

At Sunnylands peace and harmony prevail. Contributing to that ambiance are the Chinese artifacts assembled there by the Annenbergs, who responded to them as they did to the other art they brought to Rancho Mirage, with appreciation and curiosity and love. The vast span of history offered by the Chinese artworks offers a counterpoint to the elegant modernism of the architecture. The collection, unusual in its scope but universal in its appeal, reveals much about the ancient culture that created it: the evolution of technique can be observed, and the results of interaction with other artistic traditions can be understood. The collection also reflects the confident and discerning taste of the Annenbergs, especially as it contributed to the creation of Sunnylands.

Distant view of main house; in right foreground, Art Price, Birds of Welcome, *ca. 1971, bronze, diam. 60 in. (152.4 cm), ht. 96 in (243.84 cm) (Photograph by Graydon Wood, April 2006).*

AFTERWORD

Anne d'Harnoncourt

Sunnylands means a great deal to many people—the grand and the good, the talented and the beautiful, the famous and those less famous. So many people over the years have been embraced by its magic (and I think that's the right word) and, above all, by the civility and good will of its owners.

I remember once saying after a long weekend with the Annenbergs that the effect of the house was very much like that of Venice. From the first turn at the corner of Bob Hope and Frank Sinatra drives and through those low pink gatehouses, you enter into a special "other" realm, the suavity and comfort of which you don't fully comprehend until later, after you're rudely wrenched away to the blunt realities of terra firma just outside those gates.

Which is not to say that reality, blunt and otherwise, wasn't in full focus at Sunnylands. International affairs, politics, social issues, and the arts were central—for nearly everyone met there—and were vigorously and candidly discussed often with those most in the know and best equipped to handle the complexity of the information in play. But it was an elevated reality, pursued with diplomacy, tolerance, and ease. Frequently and in open and engaged conversation, on long walks (over to the totem pole or the pink pagoda at the distant green), during golf games or swims, and especially over an endlessly inventive variety of delicious meals—we considered ideas in a context of leisure, in the absence of haste. We were all set a little out of time, in a golden place that seemed to bring out the best in everyone—in wit or charm or quality of insights. Listening and talking!

From the splendor of the art at Sunnylands—the very best of its kind—and the legions of kind people who seemed to be there solely to please, to the high rank of many of one's fellow guests, along with a kind of old-fashioned formality, one would assume an implicit social hierarchy. But I never encountered it.

At every turn, be it at a banquet-scale gala with everyone dressed to the nines or an intimate barefoot lunch, evenhandedness was the rule. Conventional formality was nowhere in sight. Lee Annenberg was masterly at drawing people out and would, even in fairly large groups, ask the very question of someone (like an ex-President of the United States) that we were all dying to ask.

Walter could get deeply involved in discussions of heavy social or political ideas, but he always made sure that everyone was following and, very often, was heard. Particularly with their friends who had not been in the house before, a "ramble" looking at the paintings after dinner with Walter was a delightful ritual. It's hard to convey to those who didn't know him well the depth of his charm and delight in pleasing, as he told what he liked best about any given object and then quizzed his audience. But even works of art of this magnitude did not dominate the house, as splendid as they were on those beautiful Mexican lava rock walls and wooden panels. No, that was the role of the Ambassador who, without any force or staging, was completely the epicenter of the household, even when in his office working (as he was many mornings) and not to be seen until lunch.

Attention to their guests was the Annenbergs' central mode. I remember a lovely story told by Colin Powell at Walter's memorial service at the Academy of Music in Philadelphia. He recalled his and Alma's first visit to Sunnylands when he developed a near strep throat which he proudly thought he'd kept well hidden from his hosts, only to be confronted in his bedroom long after dinner by both Walter and Lee, in dressing gowns and slippers, demanding to take his temperature and then driving him to the local clinic.

Informality doesn't, of course, mean absence of order. Meals were precisely timed and promptness was assumed. Optional outings and entertainment were thoroughly described, including the big-screen movies in the game room after dinner. Your companions were carefully listed, often with their newest publication and news clippings waiting in your room upon arrival. Walter sometimes took charge of the outings himself, and was particularly proud of touring the local hospital (which he supported), the best medical service in the region, which he had supplied with full-scale reproductions of famous medical paintings, including Thomas Eakins's

Gross Clinic. A special treat was to drive the few blocks over to Frank Sinatra's house where the star would demonstrate his collection of toy trains, three sets on different tracks, housed in their own station. But mostly the world came to Sunnylands, and one should never underestimate, even for the titled folks and high-ranking politicians, the kick it was to have Bob Hope cracking jokes at lunch or simply to watch Mary Martin, exuding her Peter Pan joie de vivre, enter the room.

Yet there was still an encapsulated Venetian quality to the place. Thanks to the clever landscape design (described in David De Long's essay), a flat desert lot, and a very big one at that, was adjusted in such a way that, once inside the gates, one literally saw nothing of the burgeoning housing developments and country clubs that now surround Sunnylands. From every vantage point there was a direct, unpopulated view, over rolling lawns (and sand traps) to the east into the desert or west to the wall of the San Joaquin Mountains, gold in the morning, purple at dusk. All this, within an ingenious surround of running oleander hedges, gave a sense of isolated vastness.

And, of course, everything within those hedges was lush and green. I recall once being present when a crew of photographers and conservators set up, in high summer, a kind of "art camp" at Sunnylands, recording and cataloguing the collection. I decided to hoof it across an undeveloped scrub lot outside a nearby service gate. Though farther than I had planned to go in the blistering sun, I was nonetheless amused to watch a fine gray fox patrolling, as it were, the fenced embankment, looking for a way into that Eden and to the migrating birds and plump desert quail for which the Sunnylands landscape and its lakes are a lovely sanctuary. I was delighted he succeeded.

Many of these memories date to the distant past. This animated house does, indeed, have a long history. I remember seeing a photograph of Dwight Eisenhower, in retirement, flycasting in one of the newly dug ponds. At the other end of this era, a certain courtly grandeur departed with the death of Ambassador Annenberg. Therefore, it was heartening during a recent visit with Lee Annenberg, then on her own but

in wonderful company, to see the house in full swing, a piano set up on the terrace, everyone dancing, and the famous New Year's parties continuing.

How satisfying to know that Sunnylands, which has served so long as an international and diplomatic point of retreat for candid exchange and good fellowship, will be preserved prop-erly and opened to the public. And, above all, that its spirit of hospitality and informal comradeship over the past decades will continue as, one hopes, a standard for the sharing of ideas so central to the values of its creators.

NOVEMBER 2007

NOTES

FOREWORD

1. Conversation with Kathleen Hall Jamieson, February 12, 2009.
2. Christopher Ogden, *Legacy: A Biography of Moses and Walter Annenberg* (Boston: Little, Brown, 1999), 401.

THE DESIGN OF SUNNYLANDS

1. Among Annenberg biographies are Gaeton Fonzi, *Annenberg: A Biography of Power* (New York: Weybright and Talley, 1969); John Cooney, *The Annenbergs* (New York: Simon and Schuster, 1982); and Christopher Ogden, *Legacy: A Biography of Moses and Walter Annenberg* (Boston: Little, Brown, 1999). The biographical information that follows is drawn from these accounts.
2. As recounted in Ogden, *Legacy*, 303–8, and Fonzi, *Annenberg*, 43.
3. In conversaion with her daughter in July 2008, Leonore Annenberg recalled that their actual meeting took place in nearby Boca Raton, at a party given by J. Myer Schine in the private club he owned, the Boca Raton. Junious Myer Schine owned numerous properties in the area; he purchased the Boca Raton resort and club in 1945 and held it until 1956. In 2008 it was still operating as a private resort and club. I am grateful to Mrs. Annenberg's daughter, Diane Deshong, for sharing her mother's recollections and to Cheryl Pauley for checking details of Schine's ownership.
4. As described in Adele Cygelman, *Palm Springs Modern: Houses in the California Desert* (New York: Rizzoli, 1999), esp. 17–19.
5. Cygelman, *Palm Springs Modern*, 19–23.
6. Ogden, *Legacy*, 137; Cooney, *Annenbergs*, 72.
7. Ogden, *Legacy*, 396.
8. Peter H. Binzen, "The Walter Annenbergs," *Sunday Bulletin* (Philadelphia), June 23, 1974, 6–12ff.
9. Letter, William Haines to Walter and Leonore Annenberg, January 31, 1963; Haines correspondence file, The Annenberg Foundation Trust at Sunnylands (hereafter Annenberg Foundation Trust).
10. Information on this sequence of events is drawn from my interview with Leonore Annenberg at Sunnylands on February 11, 2006, and from my interview with estate manager Linda S. Brooks on February 7, 2006. Details are also confirmed by Jean Mathison, an associate of Haines and Graber, in a letter to me of December 19, 2005. Information on Haines and Graber's clients comes from William J. Mann, *Wisecracker: The Life and Times of William Haines, Hollywood's First Openly Gay Star* (New York: Viking, 1998), esp. 338–39, and also from Peter Schifando and Jean H. Mathison, *Class Act: William Haines, Legendary Hollywood Decorator* (New York: Pointed Leaf Press, 2005); the Brody house is described on p. 135; work for the Deutsch family (and the inaugural dinner party) on p. 206. For additional information on the Deutsch family, see Todd S. Purdum, "Armand S. Deutsch, 92, Hollywood Fixture," obituary, *New York Times*, August 18, 2005, A21.
11. Letter, Walter Annenberg to A. Quincy Jones, February 21, 1963; Jones correspondence file, Annenberg Foundation Trust.
12. Problems with the title had led to a delay of a first meeting, originally planned for March 15, 1963; letter, Walter Annenberg to William Haines, February 21, 1963; Haines correspondence file, Annenberg Foundation Trust.
13. Letter (five pages), A. Quincy Jones to Mr. and Mrs. Walter H. Annenberg, April 17, 1963; A. Quincy Jones archive, collection 1692, box 1234, folder 1, Department of Special Collections, Young Research Library, University of California, Los Angeles (hereafter Jones archive, UCLA).
14. Letter, William Haines to Walter Annenberg, April 22, 1963; Haines correspondence file, Annenberg Foundation Trust.
15. Biographical information on Jones is drawn primarily from Cory Buckner, *A. Quincy Jones* (London: Phaidon, 2002), esp. 9–15.

16. Information on Saunders's involvement with Sunnylands comes from my interviews with him on April 27 and May 31, 2006, and from interviews with Linda S. Brooks at Sunnylands in May 2005 and February 2006.

17. For information on the Eichler Homes, see Paul Adamson and Marty Arbunich, *Eichler: Modernism Rebuilds the American Dream* (Salt Lake City: Gibbs Smith, 2002), esp. 19–105 and 119–21.

18. As reflected in Zahid Sardar, "Child's Play," *San Francisco Chronicle Magazine*, July 11, 2005, 12–15.

19. Among the more recent publications on the Case Study House program is Ethel Buisson and Thomas Billard, *The Presence of the Case Study Houses* (Basel: Birkhauser, 2004); for Jones's contribution, 173–74.

20. Biographical information on Haines is drawn primarily from Mann, *Wisecracker*, and Schifando and Mathison, *Class Act*.

21. Betsy Bloomingdale with Burt Boyar, "*Class Act*: A New Book on Hollywood Designer Billy Haines Inspires Betsy Bloomingdale's Memories of Her Dear Friend," *Vanity Fair* (October 2005), 148.

22. Interview with Leonore Annenberg at Sunnylands, February 11, 2006.

23. Mann, *Wisecracker*, xi.

24. Ibid., 169–72, 212, 247–85, 319–21.

25. Schifando and Mathison, *Class Act*, 10, 224; Mann, *Wisecracker*, 325.

26. John Chase as quoted in Mann, *Wisecracker*, 245.

27. Schifando and Mathison, *Class Act*, 29.

28. Ibid., 207.

29. Joseph Rosa, "Modern Times: A Quintessential West Coast Designer," in Schifando and Mathison, *Class Act*, 157.

30. Interview with Leonore Annenberg, February 11, 2006. The Maya theme is mentioned in several publications on the house, perhaps most clearly in Bob Colacello, "Palm Springs Weekends," *Vanity Fair* (June 1999), 192–211.

31. The diversity of response is suggested in a book by Marjorie Ingle, *The Mayan Revival Style: Art Deco Mayan Fantasy* (Salt Lake City: Peregrine Smith, 1984).

32. As I discuss in "Frank Lloyd Wright: Designs for an American Landscape, 1922–1932," in *Frank Lloyd Wright, Designs for an American Landscape, 1922–1932*, ed. David G. De Long (New York: Harry N. Abrams in association with the Canadian Centre for Architecture, the Library of Congress, and the Frank Lloyd Wright Foundation, 1996), 36–38.

33. Letter, William Haines to Walter Annenberg, August 8, 1963; Haines correspondence file, Annenberg Foundation Trust.

34. Esther McCoy, as quoted in Ruth Weisberg, "Travel Sketches," *Process Architecture* 41 (Tokyo: Process Architecture Publication Co., 1983), 7–9.

35. Letters, Nancy Kane, Secretary, to Walter Annenberg, August 14, 1963; Quincy Jones to Walter Annenberg, September 16, 1963; boxes 1234 and 1235, Jones archive, UCLA.

36. Letter, Quincy Jones to Walter Annenberg, September 16, 1963, box 1234, Jones archive, UCLA.

37. The film *Kings of the Sun* was produced by the Mirisch Company; letter, Walter Annenberg to William Haines, September 18, 1963. Issues of *National Geographic* sent to Haines were March 1913, June 1914, February 1922, January 1925, July 1931, November 1935, November 1936, August 1939, November 1942, January 1948, January 1959, and October 1961; letters, Walter Annenberg to Franc Shor, *National Geographic*, October 4, 1963 (in which he discusses the Maya theme); Franc Shor to Walter Annenberg, October 8, 1963; Shirley Keane Neff (secretary to Shor) to William Haines, October 11, 1963; correspondence files, Annenberg Foundation Trust.

38. Letter, William Haines to Walter Annenberg, October 7, 1963; Haines correspondence file, Annenberg Foundation Trust.

39. Letters, Walter Annenberg to William Haines, August 29, 1963; William Haines to Walter Annenberg, October 7, 1963; Haines correspondence file, Annenberg Foundation Trust.

40. Letter, William Haines to Walter Annenberg, October 7, 1963; Haines correspondence file, Annenberg Foundation Trust.

41. Letter, Walter Annenberg to William Haines, October 8, 1963; Haines correspondence file, Annenberg Foundation Trust.

42. Letter, William Haines to Leonore Annenberg, May 18, 1964; Haines correspondence file, Annenberg Foundation Trust.

43. Letter, Quincy Jones to Walter Annenberg, September 25, 1963; box 1235, Jones archive, UCLA. In this same letter, Jones acknowledges Annenberg's request for the additional rooms, service passages, and windows.

44. Letter of transmittal, Quincy Jones to Dick Wilson, September 17, 1963; box 1235, Jones archive, UCLA.

45. Letter, Quincy Jones to Walter Annenberg, October 22, 1963; box 1235, Jones papers, UCLA.

46. Interviews with Harry Saunders, May 2006.

47. Letters, Quincy Jones to Walter Annenberg, September 25, 1963; Quincy Jones to Joseph Harvey, December 3, 1963; box 1235, Jones archive, UCLA. Joseph Harvey was hired as the clerk-of-the-works.

48. Regarding well locations, see letters, Quincy Jones to Philip Abrams, December 3, 1963, and December 16, 1963; letter of transmittal to Haines, December 7, 1963; box 1235, Jones archive, UCLA.

49. Walter Annenberg as quoted in Ogden, *Legacy*, 398; the quotation is repeated in Cygelman, *Palm Springs Modern*, 180. For Leonore Annenberg, De Long interview, February 11, 2006.

50. Telephone interview with Rolla J. Wilhite, March 8, 2006. Harry Saunders further confirmed Wemple's involvement; De Long interview, January 5, 2007.

51. Letter, Quincy Jones to Walter Annenberg, January 24, 1964; Box 1236, Jones Papers, UCLA.

52. Letter with enclosed architect's notes, Quincy Jones to Walter Annenberg, February 24, 1964; box 1236, Jones archive, UCLA.

53. Interview with Harry Saunders, April 27, 2006.

54. As described in Schifando and Mathison, *Class Act*, 165.

55. Letter, Quincy Jones to David Anderson, February 27, 1964; box 1236, Jones archive, UCLA.

56. Interview, Leonore Annenberg, February 11, 2006. Debate on the siting of the house is confirmed by a letter, Harry Saunders to Walter Annenberg, February 14, 1964; confirming the staking out of the house, Quincy Jones to Philip Abrams, March 8, 1964; both letters in box 1236, Jones archive, UCLA.

57. Letter, Harry Saunders to David Anderson, March 20, 1964; box 1236, Jones archive, UCLA.

58. Interviews with Leonore Annenberg, February 11, 2006, and Harry Saunders, April 27, 2006.

59. The final statement for the model was enclosed in a letter, Quincy Jones to Walter Annenberg, March 30, 1964; box 1236, Jones archive, UCLA.

60. David Anderson, progress reports, March 20, 1964; April 10, 1964; April 23, 1964; May 16, 1964; correspondence files, Annenberg Foundation Trust.

61. Joseph Harvey, progress reports, July 31, 1964; August 31, 1964; correspondence files, Annenberg Foundation Trust.

62. Interview with Leonore Annenberg, February 11, 2006.

63. Joseph Harvey, progress reports, July 31, 1964; September 14, 1964; correspondence files, Annenberg Foundation Trust.

64. Interview with Harry Saunders, May 31, 2006.

65. Interview with Harry Saunders, April 17, 2007.

66. Joseph Harvey, progress reports, September 15, 1964; October 22–23, 1964; correspondence files, Annenberg Foundation Trust.

67. Letter, Quincy Jones to Walter Annenberg, November 4, 1964; box 1239, Jones archive, UCLA.

68. E.g., letter with drawings enclosed, Quincy Jones to Walter Annenberg, box 1239, Jones archive, UCLA.

69. Interview with Leonore Annenberg, February 11, 2006.

70. Ogden, *Legacy*, 399.

71. Interviews with Rolla J. Wilhite, ASLA, July 2005 through May 2006.

72. Interview with Leonore Annenberg, February 11, 2006.

73. Schifando and Mathison, *Class Act*, 65, 73, 80, 106–7.

74. Letter, William Haines to Walter Annenberg, July 1, 1964; Haines correspondence, Annenberg Foundation Trust.

75. Schifando and Mathison, *Class Act*, 59.

76. Jean Mathison, interview with Harry Saunders, April 17, 2007; reported to De Long, April 18, 2007.

77. Mann, *Wisecracker*, 322, 336; Schifando and Mathison, *Class Act*, 123–25.

78. As described by Rolla J. Wilhite, interviews, April and May 2006.

79. Printed announcement among unsorted papers and photographs from Elaine K. Sewell, Jones archive, UCLA.

80. As described by Harry Saunders, interview, April 27, 2006. Liets's name appears on working drawings for the house, a full set of which are housed at Sunnylands.

81. Some designed by John and Marilyn Neuhart, designers in Hermosa Beach, California; letter, Harry Saunders to John and Marilyn Neuhart, November 8, 1965; box 1239, Jones archive, UCLA.

82. For references to the Pennsylvania Sunnylands, see Ogden, *Legacy*, 145, 257. Jones and Haines made suggestions to the Annenbergs in letters, Quincy Jones to Walter Annenberg, March 30, 1964; William Haines to Walter Annenberg, June 11, 1964; filed with the Annenberg correspondence, Jones and Haines files, Annenberg Foundation Trust.

83. Interview with Leonore Annenberg, February 11, 2006.

84. Ibid.

85. Apparently these were in place by 1966; letter, Walter Annenberg to Rolla J. Wilhite, August 4, 1966; Annenberg-Wilhite correspondence, Annenberg Foundation Trust.

86. Letter, Walter Annenberg to Quincy Jones, June 20, 1968; Jones correspondence, Annenberg Foundation Trust. Walter Annenberg made arrangements for this replica with Pedro Ramirez Vasquez, an architect; letter, Walter Annenberg to Donald Aspinwall Allan, September 27, 1971, Box 1, folder 74, Annenberg Foundation Trust. Linda S. Brooks, estate manager at Sunnylands, reports that the Maya column at Sunnylands is a one-quarter size replica of the original now displayed in the patio of the National Museum of Anthropology in Mexico City; the archaeologist Luis Avereyra Arroya de Anda was involved with the installation.

87. As recorded on drawings for the enclosure now in the possession of Harry Saunders. I am grateful to Mr. Saunders for bringing this to my attention.

88. Letter, William Haines to the Hon. and Mrs. Walter H. Annenberg, February 29, 1972; correspondence files, Annenberg Foundation Trust.

89. Interview with Leonore Annenberg, February 11, 2006; regarding the design of the cases, interview with Harry Saunders, April 17, 2007.

90. Letter, Walter Annenberg to Ted Graber, February 18, 1974; Annenberg correspondence, Annenberg Foundation Trust.

91. Interview with Harry Saunders, April 17, 2007.

92. Interviews with Harry Saunders, April 17, 2006, and Leonore Annenberg, February 11, 2006. Saunders left Jones to open his own

93. Ogden, *Legacy*, 316–18, 520–28. At the time of the gift, they were valued at one billion dollars. Among reports on the purchase from Enid Haupt, see Enid Nemy, "Enid A. Haupt, Philanthropist, Dies at 99," obituary, *New York Times*, October 27, 2005, B13. Mrs. Annenberg described the hanging of the pictures to me in the interview of February 11, 2006.

94. Interview with Harry Saunders, April 2006. Saunders's drawings for the changes to the walls are dated 1984.

95. Interview with Leonore Annenberg, February 11, 2006.

96. Drawings for the conversion in Harry Saunders's possession are dated May 1977.

97. Drawings for this addition in Harry Saunders's possession are dated May 1977.

98. Drawings for the pavilion in Harry Saunders's possession are dated July 1976.

99. Interview with Harry Saunders, April 17, 2007. Linda S. Brooks reports that the bench is a replica of one on the Greek island of Galu; the marble is from the same quarry as the original and the bench was shipped to Sunnylands in October 1980.

100. In addition to drawings in the possession of Harry Saunders that document alterations to the main house and gardens, drawings for the perimeter wall, by John Vogley & Associates, dated late 1995, are kept in the drawing files at Sunnylands. I am grateful to Ken Brooks for helping locate these and other drawings and for explaining the reason for the change, a reason also given by Leonore Annenberg.

101. I am grateful to Judy Kenwood, Operations Assistant at Sunnylands, for supplying preliminary numbers and to John Berley of Frederick Fisher and Partners for more detailed numbers. Other less official estimates vary, as suggested in Ogden, *Legacy*, 394, and Cooney, *Annenbergs*, 315.

102. Ogden, *Legacy*, 92–93, 137; Mann, *Wisecracker*, 11, 128–30. Biltmore, for George W. Vanderbilt, Asheville, N.C., 1890–95, was designed by Richard Morris Hunt (1827–1895); San Simeon, the William Randolph Hearst estate in California, 1919–1951, was designed by Julia Morgan (1872–1957).

103. Walter Annenberg, as quoted in Ogden, *Legacy*, 510.

104. Walter Annenberg, as quoted by Leonore Annenberg, interview, February 11, 2006.

105. Letter, Quincy Jones to Walter Annenberg, June 28, 1965; Jones correspondence, Annenberg Foundation Trust.

106. Betsy Bloomingdale, as quoted in William J. Mann, "William Haines: Creator of a Smart New Look for the Hollywood Scene," *Architectural Digest* 57 (January 2000), 184–87.

107. Cooney, *Annenbergs*, 10; Ogden, *Legacy*, 393; and Robert Sam Anson, *Exile: The Unquiet Oblivion of Richard M. Nixon* (New York: Simon and Schuster, 1984), 59.

108. Mann, *Wisecracker*, 347.

109. Interviews with Leonore Annenberg, February 11, 2006, and Harry Saunders, May 31, 2006.

110. Letter, Walter Annenberg to Nancy Reagan, May 31, 1966, as quoted in Ogden, *Legacy*, 493.

111. Thomas Hoving, "Inside Sunnylands: A Visit with Ambassador Annenberg," *Connoisseur* 213, no. 855 (May 1983), 76–84.

112. I am grateful to estate manager Linda S. Brooks for this information.

113. As suggested in Ogden, *Legacy*, 400.

114. Unless otherwise noted, the names and dates of guests that will be mentioned are confirmed by the Sunnylands guest books, which I examined in May 2005.

115. Leonore Annenberg, as quoted in Bob Colacello, "Palm Springs Weekends," *Vanity Fair* nos. 464–66 (June 1999), 192–211.

116. As recounted in Ogden, *Legacy*, 401–20, and Fonzi, *Annenberg*, 212.

117. Richard Nixon, handwritten entry in guest book, September 8, 1974. It was while at Sunnylands on this visit that Nixon was diagnosed with acute phlebitis, as recounted in John C. Lungren, M.D., and John C. Lungren, Jr., *Healing Richard Nixon* (Lexington: University of Kentucky Press, 2003), 12.

118. Nancy Reagan, February 22, 1975; Ronald Reagan, January 2, 1981.

119. George H. W. Bush, March 8, 1980, part of an album in the Room of Memories commemorating his visit; Barbara Bush, March 21, 1995.

120. Rosalynn Carter, January 18, 2003.

121. Interview with Leonore Annenberg, February 11, 2006.

122. Interview with Michael Comerford, February 12, 2006.

123. As reported in Ogden, *Legacy*, 510.

124. Leonore Annenberg, as quoted in Ogden, *Legacy*, 503.

125. As reported in Jon Nordheimer, "Prince Charles' Palm Springs Visit," *New York Times*, March 19, 1974.

126. Truman Capote, February 25, 1968.

127. Philippe de Montebello, January 25, 1988, in an album of letters presented by Leonore Annenberg to Walter Annenberg in celebration of his eightieth birthday, March 13, 1988, album in the Room of Memories.

128. Some are described in Ogden, *Legacy*, 499.

129. William Haines, March 23, 1967; Ted Graber, December 7, 1983.

130. The work is described in Ogden, *Legacy*, 449–50; and Mann, *Wisecracker*, 365–72.

131. Letter, Walter Annenberg to William Haines, June 22, 1971; correspondence files, Annenberg Foundation Trust.

The top of the page (before note 93):

office in 1966. Dated drawings in Saunders's possession document the date of this and other alterations.

132. As noted by Mann, "William Haines: Creator of a Smart New Look," 185; and Pilar Viladas, "A Designer's Designer," in Schifando and Mathison, *Class Act*, 219.

133. The building is illustrated and described in Buckner, *Quincy Jones*, 20–21.

134. Letter, Elaine K. S. Jones to Walter Annenberg, July 18, 1990; correspondence files, Annenberg Foundation Trust.

135. Interview with Rolla Wilhite, March 8, 2006.

136. William H. Davis and the Editors of Golf Digest, *100 Greatest Golf Courses—and Then Some* (New York: Simon and Schuster, 1982), 266–67.

THE MODERN SCULPTURE

1. Digital replicas of Impressionist and Post-Impressionist paintings now on the walls at Sunnylands represent those given by the Ambassador to the Metropolitan Museum of Art.

2. Grace Glueck, "The Successful Stalker," *International Herald Tribune*, April 28,1990 (clipping, Archives, Musée Rodin, Paris); Christopher Ogden, "Trouble in Paradise," *W*, June 1999, 191–93; and idem, *Legacy: A Biography of Moses and Walter Annenberg* (Boston: Little, Brown, 1999), 521.

3. Florence Rossi, letter dated December 20, 2005, to the author; Paul Rossi, "All This You Must Imitate," undated brochure, Annenberg Foundation Trust at Sunnylands.

4. Rossi letter, dated December 20, 2005, to the author; Paul Rossi, "The Great Saddles of the West," undated computer-generated brochure. www.rossistudios.com/prossi2, as of September 30, 2008.

5. A prominent theme in Ogden, *Legacy*.

6. Ogden, *Legacy*, 522.

7. The Arp *Souvenir d'Athènes* was cited as in the "Collection W. Annenberg, Philadelphia" in Margareta Hagenbach, "Documentation," in Carola Giedion-Welcker, *Jean Arp*, trans. Norbert Guterman (Stuttgart: Thames & Hudson, 1957), 104; interview with Sunnylands estate manager, Linda S. Brooks, October 31–November 1, 2005.

8. David De Long, interview with Leonore Annenberg, February 11, 2006.

9. Ogden, *Legacy*, 520–28; Robert Montgomery Scott and Anne d'Harnoncourt, "Foreword," *Masterpieces of Impressionism and Post-Impressionism: The Annenberg Collection*, exh. cat. (Philadelphia: Philadelphia Museum of Art, 1989), xi–xii.

10. Interview with Linda S. Brooks, October 31–November 1, 2005.

11. Ibid.; Rossi letter to the author dated December 20, 2005. For Agam, see further in the text.

12. John L. Tancock, *The Sculpture of Auguste Rodin: The Collection of the Rodin Museum, Philadelphia* (Philadelphia: Philadelphia Museum of Art, 1976), 89–181; and Ruth Butler, *Rodin: The Shape of Genius* (New Haven: Yale University Press, 1993), 141–49, 214–25.

13. Ruth Butler, "Religious Sculpture in Post-Christian France," *The Romantics to Rodin: French Nineteenth-Century Sculpture from North American Collections*, ed. Peter Fusco and H. W. Janson, exh. cat. (New York: Los Angeles County Museum of Art in association with George Braziller, 1980), 83–95.

14. Butler, "Religious Sculpture," 92–94.

15. There is considerable debate about the identity of the model. See particularly Jacques de Caso and Patricia B. Sanders, *Rodin's Sculpture: A Critical Study of the Spreckels Collection* (Rutland, Vt.: The Fine Arts Museums of San Francisco in association with Charles E. Tuttle, 1977), 143–47; and Antoinette Le Normand-Romain, in Antoinette Le Normand-Romain, with the collaboration of Hélène Marraud and Diane Tytgat, *The Bronzes of Rodin: Catalogue of Works in the Musée Rodin*, 2 vols. (Paris: Éditions de la Réunion des Musées Nationaux and the Musée Rodin), vol. 1: 345.

16. Monique Laurent, "Observations on Rodin and His Founders," *Rodin Rediscovered*, ed. Albert E. Elsen, exh. cat. (Washington, D.C.: National Gallery of Art, 1981), fig. 14-4; Le Normand-Romain, *Rodin en 1900: L'Exposition de l'Alma*, exh. cat. (Paris: Musée du Luxembourg, 2001), 268; Le Normand-Romain, in Le Normand-Romain et al., *Bronzes*, vol. 1: 340 (under "Other casts"), 347–48; e-mail correspondence between Le Normand-Romain and the author dated November 16–17, 2005; Henri Duhem, letters dated April–August 1899 to Rodin; Archives, Musée Rodin, Paris; Rodin, letter dated July 19, 1900, to Duhem, courtesy of Wildenstein & Co, Inc. I offer grateful thanks to Antoinette Le Normand-Romain, then conservateur général, Musée Rodin, and now Directeur général, Institut National d'Histoire de l'Art, Paris, and Virginie Delaforge, formerly at the Musée Rodin, Paris, and to Joseph Baillio of Wildenstein & Co., New York, for their generous help.

17. [First name unlocated] Berville, *Patrie*, April 30, 1899; [anonymous] *Weekly Register*, May 6, 1899, both clippings; Archives, Musée Rodin. Unless otherwise indicated, all reviews derive from this archive.

18. For example, Henri Frantz, "Art: Les Salons de 1899," *La Critique* 101 (May 5, 1899), 69–70.

19. Ibid.

20. *Weekly Register*; Gustave Schneider, "La Sculpture," *Moniteur Général de l'Exposition de 1900* [*sic*], May 16–17, 1899; Arsène Alexandre, "Salon de 1899," *Le Figaro*, April 30, 1899.

21. Alexandre, "Salon de 1899." The caryatid had been a common motif in Rodin's work since the early 1880s.

22. Tancock, *Sculpture of Auguste Rodin*, 150.

23. For his payments for *Eve*, see Duhem, letters dated June 29, 1899, through August 26 [1899] to Rodin; for its presence in Rodin's 1900 Pont de l'Alma exhibition, see Rodin's letter to Duhem dated July 19, 1900 (see above, note 16). For its installation in Duhem's garden, see his letter of August 26 and his photographic postcard to Rodin dated July 1907 (Archives, Musée Rodin, Ms. 561; in Le Normand-Romain, in Le Normand-Romain et al., *Bronzes*, vol. 1: 348, fig. 10.).

24. Le Normand-Romain, in Le Normand-Romain et al., *Bronzes*, vol. 1: 348, n. 42.

25. Alain Beausire, *Quand Rodin exposait* (Paris: Éditions Musée Rodin, 1988), 23.

26. Ibid., 96, 104, 131.

27. Rodin typically used language centered on human relations, particularly between the sexes.

28. M. H. Spielmann, "Sculpture at the Paris Salons," *Magazine of Art*, October 1897, 321.

29. Rainier Maria Rilke, *Rodin*, trans. Robert Fermage (Salt Lake City: Peregrine Smith, 1979), 42.

30. Léon Maillard, *Auguste Rodin statuaire* (Paris: H. Floury, 1899), 122.

31. Collector Maurice Masson specified the unique features of the marble of *Eternal Spring* that he commissioned from Rodin (presently at the Museo Nacional de Bellas Artes, Buenos Aires). See Le Normand-Romain, *Rodin en Buenos Aires*, exh. cat. (Buenos Aires: Museo Nacional de Bellas Artes, 2001), 154; Le Normand-Romain, in Le Normand-Romain et al., 2007, vol. 1: 331–37; *Éternel Printemps* dossiers, archives, Musée Rodin, Paris; personal research files, Le Normand-Romain, Paris.

32. Le Normand-Romain, in Le Normand-Romain et al., 2007, vol. 1: 331, under "Related Works, no. 6."

33. Andrew Carduff Ritchie, "Foreword," *The New Decade: 22 European Painters and Sculptors*, exh. cat. (New York: Museum of Modern Art, 1960), 9–10.

34. Herbert Read, *The Art of Jean Arp* (New York: Harry N. Abrams, 1968); Margherita Andreotti, *The Early Sculpture of Jean Arp* (Ann Arbor: UMI Research Press, 1989).

35. "Notes from a Diary," *Transition* no. 21, 1932; in Giedion-Welcker, *Jean Arp*, xxvii; *Hommage à Jan Arp*, exh. cat. (Strasbourg: Ancienne Douane, 1967); Jack Burnham, *Beyond Modern Sculpture: The Effects of Science and Technology on the Sculpture of This Century* (New York: George Braziller, 1982), 87–94.

36. Andreotti, *Early Sculpture*, 181–82.

37. William Tucker, *Early Modern Sculpture* (New York: Oxford University Press, 1974); Burnham, *Beyond Modern Sculpture*; Con-

stantin Brancusi 1876–1957, exh. cat. (Philadelphia: Philadelphia Museum of Art, 1995).

38. For a brief study of Arp's formal tributes to Brancusi, see Andreotti, *Early Sculpture*, 106–8.

39. Ibid., 182.

40. A form begun early in his career; see Andreotti, *Early Sculpture*, 96–104; Bernd Rau, *Jean Arp: The Reliefs: Catalogue of Complete Works* (New York: Rizzoli, 1981); Daniel Klébaner, *Arp demi-sommeil. Les Reliefs de Jean Arp* (Paris: Maeght Éditeur, 1999).

41. Andreotti, *Early Sculpture*, 268, cat. 17.

42. Hagenbach, "Documentation," in Giedion-Welcker, *Jean Arp*, 108, cat. 5; François Arp, "Catalogue of Sculptures," in *Jean Arp, Sculpture, His Last Ten Years*, trans. Karen Philippson (New York: Harry N. Abrams, 1968), 104, cat. 5; 113, cats. 212a, 213, 227; and 114, cats. 231, 240a.

43. For studies of his work, see Jerome Mellquist, *Dictionnaire de la sculpture moderne* (Paris: F. Hazan, 1960), 115–16, s.v. "Gilioli, Émile;" and *Gilioli: Sculptures*, exh. cat. (Paris: Centre Georges Pompidou, 1979).

44. Denys Chevalier, *Dictionnaire de la sculpture moderne* (Paris: F. Hazan, 1960), 128–30, s.v. "Hajdu, Etienne." The artist's name is often misspelled as "Hadju."

45. The following comments are based on discussions in James Lord. *Giacometti: A Biography* (New York: Farrar, Straus and Giroux, 1985); Angela Schneider, ed., *Alberto Giacometti: Sculpture. Paintings. Drawings*, trans. Elizabeth Clegg (New York: Prestel-Verlag, 1994); and Laurie Wilson, *Alberto Giacometti: Myth, Magic, and the Man* (New Haven: Yale University Press, 2003).

46. For a photograph of artisans working on Giacometti's portrait-stele of Diego at the Susse foundry, see Élisabeth Lebon, "La Fonte d'art au XXe siècle," *Dictionnaire des fondeurs de bronze d'art. France 1890–1950* (Perth: Marjon, 2003), 82–83, repro.

47. Suzanne G. Lindsay, "Western Figurative Sculpture: Foundations and Functions," in *The National Sculpture Society Celebrates the Figure*, ed. Jean Henry, exh. cat. (New York: National Sculpture Society in association with the Port of History Museum and Drexel University Museum, 1987), esp. 14–15.

48. Wind damage quickly immobilized the figure; see Kathryn Greenthal, *Augustus Saint-Gaudens: Master Sculptor* (New York: Metropolitan Museum of Art, 1983), 138–39.

49. Burnham, *Beyond Modern Sculpture*, 185–262.

50. E.g., Hans Dickel, *Lipstick (Ascending) on Caterpillar Tracks* (Freiburg im Breisgau: Rombach, 1999); Germano Celant, ed., *Claes Oldenburg, Coosje van Bruggen* (Milan: Skira, 1999).

51. June Kompass Nelson, *Harry Bertoia: Sculptor* (Detroit: Wayne State University Press, 1970); Nancy N. Schiffer and Val O. Bertoia, *The World of Bertoia* (Atglen, Pa.: Schiffer Publishing, 2003).

52. Günter Metkin, *Agam* (New York: Harry N. Abrams, 1977), un-paginated; a comprehensive study of Agam's life and work is Frank Popper, *Agam* (New York: Harry N. Abrams, 1976).

53. Metkin, *Agam*, unpaginated.

54. Sayako Aragaki, *Agam: Beyond the Visible*, rev. ed. (Jerusalem: Gefen Publishing House, 2003), 103–5. I thank Kathleen Hall Jamieson, Program Director, Annenberg Foundation Trust at Sunnylands, for providing this source.

SELECTED PAINTINGS AND WORKS ON PAPER

1. For detailed information about Rembrandt Peale, Charles Willson Peale, and the other members of the Peale family, see Lillian B. Miller, ed., *The Peale Family: Creation of a Legacy, 1770–1870* (New York: Abbeville, 1996).

2. For an in-depth discussion of Rembrandt Peale's portrait of George Washington, see William T. Oedel, "The Rewards of Virtue: Rembrandt Peale and Social Reform," in Miller, ed., *The Peale Family*, 151–67.

3. This inscription is written in Rembrandt Peale's hand and secured to the front of the painting's picture frame. The transcription here, given in toto, observes Peale's punctuation.

4. Ira Berkow, "Jewels in the Desert," *ArtNews* 97, no. 5 (May 1998), 145.

5. James A. Michener, intro., in Ernest Hemingway, *The Dangerous Summer* (1960; repr., New York: Charles Scribner's Sons, 1985), 24.

6. Jane Fluegel, "Chronology," in *Pablo Picasso: A Retrospective*, ed. William Rubin (New York: Museum of Modern Art, 1980), 417.

7. Hemingway's *The Dangerous Summer*, written in 1959–60 and published in part in *Life* (September 5, 1960), was not published as a book until 1985, long after his suicide in 1961.

8. See David De Long's note of this tradition in his preceding essay, on the architecture of Sunnylands, with its special designation as a memorial park.

9. Professor George Whitfield, as quoted in Margaret Styles Ambrose, "Roots: A Southern Symposium," *Callaloo* 2 (February 1978), 125.

10. Ruth Fine, "Romare Bearden: The Spaces Between," in *The Art of Romare Bearden*, ed. Ruth Fine (Washington, D.C.: National Gallery of Art, 2003), 7.

11. "Chronology," in *Jacques Villon*, ed. Hélène Lassalle, exh. cat. (Paris: Éditions des musées nationaux, 1975), 137–39.

12. David S. Rubin, "Jacques Villon's Abstraction," *Arts Magazine* 50, no. 8 (April 1976), 78–80.

THE STEUBEN GLASS COLLECTION

1. Susan B. King to Walter Annenberg, January 14, 1992; Annenberg family papers, The Annenberg Foundation Trust at Sunnylands, Radnor, Pennsylvania. (Except where noted, all letters to or from Walter Annenberg cited below are from this source.) "The 'Asian Artists' series and the individual masterworks such as *Carrousel of the Sea* and *Chinese Pavilion* are the most ambitious projects ever undertaken by Steuben, and . . . represent a style and quality of artistry that we might well revisit," she added.

2. Mary Jean Madigan, *Steuben Glass: An American Tradition in Crystal* (1981; rev. ed., New York: Harry N. Abrams, 2003), 217–18. This book offers the first comprehensive history of Steuben glass and its wares, including an illustrated catalogue of virtually every piece produced from 1932 through 2001.

3. Madigan, *Steuben Glass*, 127–30.

4. Ibid., 49, citing Paul V. Gardner, *The Glass of Frederick Carder* (New York: Crown, 1971). Gardner's book is considered to be the definitive account of Steuben's first thirty years, from 1903 to 1932. Gardner was Carder's assistant and later served as Curator of Ceramics and Glass at the Smithsonian Institution's National Museum of History and Technology.

5. Arthur Houghton was a dedicated bibliophile, philanthropist, and Anglophile (his uncle Alanson Houghton, president of Corning Glass Works, was U.S. ambassador to the Court of St. James's in the 1920s). The Houghton Library at Harvard was endowed to house Arthur Houghton's Keats collection, for which he remained honorary curator. Like Walter Annenberg, Houghton later served as a trustee of The Metropolitan Museum of Art. He was also a trustee of the New York Public Library, the Morgan Library, and Lincoln Center, where, as chairman, he presided over its official opening in 1962. In 1951, he spearheaded the founding of The Corning Museum of Glass with a collection of rare historical glass that remained from the Fifth Avenue Steuben shop's "Antique Glass Room"—created to augment the shop's dwindling inventory of new glass during World War II, when lead (a critical component of crystal) was strictly rationed. As the longtime chairman of The Corning Museum, Houghton hired its first director, Tom Buechner, who was later named president of Steuben.

6. Madigan, *Steuben Glass*, 121. Truman gave Steuben's *Merry-Go-Round Bowl* to England's then-Princess Elizabeth as a wedding gift in 1947. In the 1960s, Steuben reserved a special group of engraved vases and bowls—the so-called "OX Collection"—for exclusive sale to the White House and Department of State. To assist government officials in choosing appropriate gifts of state, three sets of books picturing these designs were made—one for Steuben's Fifth Avenue shop, one for the U.S. Department of State, and one for the White House.

7. Walter Annenberg to Ann Pittendrigh, September 14, 1971. Confirming the purchase to Steuben's sales executive Ann Pittendrigh, he wrote, "it seems that we are off to something of an adventure in crystal, and this is indeed appealing to us."

8. Walter H. Annenberg to Arthur A. Houghton, Jr., April 22, 1970.

9. James A. Thurston to Walter Annenberg, November 27, 1970.

10. The Honorable Walter Annenberg to James H. Thurston, May 18, 1971.

11. Walter Annenberg to Ann Pittendrigh, June 30, 1971.

12. Ann Pittendrigh to Walter Annenberg, July 16, 1971.

13. Ann Pittendrigh to Walter Annenberg, July 26, 1971.

14. Walter Annenberg to Ann Pittendrigh, July 29, 1971.

15. Ann Pittendrigh to Walter and Leonore Annenberg, September 10, 1971. She enclosed a list confirming each item on the order. In addition to the *Asian Artists in Crystal* series and the two *Masterworks* series pieces *Carrousel of the Sea* and *The Unicorn and the Maiden*, the purchase included *Birds and Fishes* ($9,750), *To Build a Fire* ($3,600 to be made), *Hernando Cortes* ($9,500 to be made), *Crete* ($6,750 to be made), *Easter Island* ($7,500), *Hawaii* ($7,000), *Prismatic Column* ($2,600 and one of the few pieces not pictorially engraved), *Rotating Square* ($3,000, not engraved), and *The Wilderness Trilogy* ($13,500 for a three-piece engraved set). Except where noted, all pieces were engraved with story-telling designs that related to the Annenbergs' travels and interests.

16. Walter Annenberg to Ann Pittendrigh, October 13, 1971. In the same letter, he promised to pass along Steuben's Christmas catalogue to Britain's Prime Minister Edward Heath, and wrote, "Because of Mr. Heath's great interest in Steuben glass I would very much appreciate your sending me a set of black and white pictures representing my purchase. I would like to be able to show him the pieces that are going in my California home."

17. Memo, David B. Whitehouse to Susan B. King, June 4, 1992, on the condition of the *Asian Artists* collection at Sunnylands. Enclosure in letter from Susan B. King to The Honorable and Mrs. Walter Annenberg, June 4, 1992.

18. Walter Annenberg to Ann Pittendrigh, March 17, 1972.

19. Ann Pittendrigh to Walter Annenberg, May 23, 1973.

20. Ann Pittendrigh to Walter Annenberg, October 7, 1973.

21. Walter Annenberg to Ann Pittendrigh, February 12, 1974.

22. Walter Annenberg to Arthur Houghton, March 25, 1976.

23. Walter Annenberg to Ann Pittendrigh, November 8, 1976.

24. Walter Annenberg to Ann Pittendrigh, July 14, 1978. Newly returned from a trip to the Greek islands, Annenberg was feeling the press of mortality. "The islands off Greece are wondrously impressive and yet terribly sobering," he wrote her. "Sobering in the sense that we, too, will be plowed under and another will take our place." But he closed with a bit of wry humor: "Beware of the hippies in your part of the world."

25. Ann Pittendrigh to the Ambassadors Walter and Leonore Annenberg, August 8, 1981. Mrs. Reagan's purchase of Steuben's *Crusader's Bowl* caused a flap in the press when a reporter discovered that Steuben's price for the bowl—which took 670 hours to make and was a rare example of the difficult Hochtschnidt style of copper-wheel engraving—was $75,000, far more than the $1,000 federal spending limit for gifts of state. Mrs. Reagan was obliged to say she had acquired it from Steuben for just $800. (See Madigan, *Steuben Glass*, 175.)

26. Walter Annenberg to James A. Thurston, June 23, 1982.

27. Susan B. King to The Honorable and Mrs. Walter Annenberg, January 14, 1992.

28. Susan B. King to The Honorable and Mrs. Walter Annenberg, June 4, 1992.

29. James R. Houghton to The Honorable Walter Annenberg, July 21, 2000.

30. Renée A. Rogen to James R. Houghton, July 28, 2000.

31. *Asian Artists in Crystal: Designs by Contemporary Asian Artists Engraved on Steuben Crystal* (New York: Spiral Press, 1956).

32. Author's interview with Steuben marketing executive Isobel Lee Beers, September 15, 1980, in preparation for the first edition of *Steuben Glass: An American Tradition in Crystal*. See p. 117, rev. ed., for the history of the *Asian Artists in Crystal* series. Beers became acquainted with many high-level officials, including Stassen, during her wartime service in the Red Cross, and their friendship continued after the war. She kept him apprised of events at Steuben and encouraged him to approach Houghton with his idea.

33. Harold Stassen to Arthur Houghton, Steuben Permanent File, cited in Madigan, *Steuben Glass*, 117. A three-time Republican presidential candidate, Stassen released his votes to Dwight Eisenhower in the 1952 primary and was appointed head of the U.S. Foreign Aid Office when Eisenhower became president. He exerted considerable influence in Washington.

34. Karl Kup, "Asian Artists in Crystal," *Metropolitan Museum of Art Bulletin* 14 (March 1956), 174–80. Kup was the chief of the Art Division, Curator of Prints, and Curator of the Spencer Collection of the New York Public Library.

35. Madigan, *Steuben Glass*, 117.

36. The participation of the United States Information Service (which organized group exhibitions in various countries to facilitate Kup's efforts) was later acknowledged. Steuben Permanent File, quoted in Madigan, *Steuben Glass*, 117.

37. Kup, "Asian Artists," 175.

38. David E. Finley and James J. Rorimer, foreword, *Asian Artists in Crystal*.

39. Madigan, *Steuben Glass*, 118, citing *Asian Artists in Crystal* cor-

respondence and final report, Steuben Permanent File, Steuben Glass, New York City.

40. P. S. Rawson, "Asian Artists in Crystal," *Oriental Art* 2, no. 4 (Winter 1956), 153.

41. John Monteith Gates, intro., *Poetry in Crystal* (New York: Spiral Press, 1963).

42. Madigan, *Steuben Glass*, 130, citing Alexander D. Vietor letters, Steuben Permanent File, Steuben Glass, New York City.

43. Interview with Arthur A. Houghton, Jr., taped by author on May 12, 1981, in preparation for first edition of *Steuben Glass*.

44. Arthur A. Houghton, Jr., intro., *Five Masterworks* (New York: Spiral Press, 1972).

DECORATIVE ARTS

1. Information provided in 2006 by Michael Comerford, Sunnylands Head Butler.

2. The origin of the word "epergne," which was not used in France, is unknown.

3. Paul Micio, "Early French *Surtouts*: Unpublished Drawings and Documents," *Silver Studies: The Journal of The Silver Society* 19 (2005), 82.

4. Michael Snodin, ed., *Rococo: Art and Design in Hogarth's England* (London: Victoria and Albert Museum, 1984), cat. R10.

5. Arthur G. Grimwade, *London Goldsmiths, 1697–1837* (London: Faber and Faber, 1990), 626.

6. Inigo Jones, *Some Designs of Mr. Inigo Jones and Mr. William Kent* (London: John Vardy, 1744; repr., Farnsborough, UK.: Gregg International Publications, 1967), 27.

7. Another example of this model is in the collection of the Colonial Williamsburg Foundation: see John D. Davis, *English Silver at Williamsburg* (Williamsburg, Va.: Colonial Williamsburg Foundation, 1976), 112.

8. Quoted in Derek E. Ostergard, ed., *William Beckford, 1760–1844: An Eye for the Magnificent* (New Haven: Yale University Press, 2002), 315.

9. The other basket is in the Gilbert Collection, Somerset House, London. See Timothy B. Schroder, *The Gilbert Collection of Gold and Silver* (Los Angeles: Los Angeles County Museum of Art, 1988), 324–27.

10. *Magnificent Effects at Fonthill Abbey*, sale cat., Christie's, Fonthill, scheduled October 1, 1822. The announced public offering of the Abbey's contents never took place; the house and contents were sold in that year in a private transaction to a gunpowder millionaire, John Farquhar. The following year, Farquhar himself disposed of the contents of the Abbey through Harry Phillips in one of the most famous sales of the nineteenth century; in that sale the baskets are listed as lot 1543 in the Grand Drawing Room at the Abbey, *The Unique and Splendid Effects of Fonthill Abbey*, sale cat., Phillips, Fonthill, September 9–October 29, 1823. The baskets were purchased from the Phillips sale by the dealer Robinson and sold shortly thereafter to the banker Nathan Meyer Rothschild.

11. Michael Snodin and Malcolm Baker, "William Beckford's Silver," pts. 1, 2, *Burlington Magazine* 112 (November–December 1980), 735–48, 820–34. These baskets were identified as Beckford objects by Timothy Schroder in *Gilbert Collection*, 324.

12. Boileau arrived in London about 1787 to work under Henry Holland at Carlton House. He is also recorded as having worked as a ceiling painter at Fonthill Splendens, the house built by Beckford's father. Michael Snodin, "J. J. Boileau: A Forgotten Designer of Silver," *Connoisseur* 198 (June 1978), 133.

13. Snodin and Baker, "William Beckford's Silver," pt. 2, 820.

14. Prominently and skillfully engraved on the Sunnylands tray is the coat of arms of Pelham quartering those of Anderson or Simpson on an escutcheon of pretense as borne by Charles, who was created First Earl of Yarborough and Baron Worsley in 1837. For many years he was Commodore of the Royal Yacht Squadron and was known for hosting magnificent parties aboard his own yacht, *Falcon*. He married Henrietta Anna Maria Charlotte, second daughter of Hon. John Simpson, in 1806. Also in the Sunnylands collection are eight silver-gilt candlesticks stamped by Paul Storr, two dated 1807, six dated 1808, which bear the coat of arms of Pelham.

15. Gentleman Many Years Connected with the Firm, *Memoirs of the Late Philip Rundell, Esq., Goldsmith and Jeweller to His Majesty* (London: J. Fairburn, 1827), 8–9, quoted in John Culme, *English Silver: The Jerome and Rita Gans Collection, Addendum* (Richmond: Virginia Museum of Fine Arts, 1999), 20.

16. The tray is also stamped with the Latin inscription, "Rundell Bridge et Rundell Aurifices Regis Londini Fecerunt," which the firm used to advertise its royal appointment.

17. Each leaf and bunch of grapes is cast separately and soldered to the frame, which has the advantage of making the border more easily adaptable to a variety of shapes.

18. Of these, one of the earliest is a tray dated 1802 and engraved with the arms of William, Viscount Lowther; and one of the latest is a tray dated 1818 and bearing the stamp of Paul Storr.

19. The jars are marked with the cipher "AR" for Augustus Rex.

20. The yellow ground was probably developed in 1725. According to Ingelore Menzehausen, *Early Meissen Porcelain, Dresden* (London: Thames and Hudson, 1990), 203, the yellow ground is first recorded on a Meissen piece dated January 11, 1726.

21. The only recorded instance of Asian porcelain lent from Augustus's collection to the factory took place in 1709: Maureen Cassidy-Geiger, "The Japanese Palace Collections and Their Impact at Meissen," *The International Ceramics Fair and Seminar* (London: International Ceramics Fair and Seminar, 1995), 10.

22. The factory mark—three wavy lines, symbolizing the three waterways of Denmark, the Little Belt, the Great Belt, and the Øresund—was established on May 1, 1775.

23. For a complete history of the service and a full list of the shapes, see Bredo L. Grandjean, *The Flora Danica Service* (Copenhagen: Alfred G. Hassings, 1950).

24. This supposition is based on an entry in the diary of a Dr. F. V. P. Fabricius in which he claimed, with Frantz Müller's son as the source, that the service was "intended for the 'Empress.'" Quoted in Bodil Busk Laursen et al., *Royal Copenhagen Porcelain: 1775–2000* (Copenhagen: NYT Nordisk Forlag Arnold Busck, 2000), 48.

25. The so-called pearl pattern that was chosen for the service at the time of its commission (and seen on the Sunnylands examples) was one that had been recorded at the factory beginning in 1783; the name is based on the row of raised semicircles that forms part of the border. Given the size and complexity of the service, however, many new shapes were required.

26. Quoted in Sir Richard Attenborough and Marilyn McCully, *Original Ceramics by Pablo Picasso*, exh. cat. (London: Nicola Jacobs Gallery, June 6–August 11, 1984), unpaginated.

27. In addition to the unique pieces made by Picasso, which like the Sunnylands plate are dated and on occasion signed, there were two other groups of ceramics associated with him. One group is stamped "Empreinte Originale Picasso." These pieces, which appear in small editions, were produced from moulds especially prepared and carved by Picasso. The second group, stamped "Edition Picasso," are copies or interpretations of original Picasso pieces.

28. Attenborough and McCully, *Original Ceramics by Pablo Picasso*, unpaginated.

29. Georges Ramié, *Céramique de Picasso* (Paris: Éditions Cercle, 1974), 205, 289.

30. See David De Long's essay in this volume for the history of the commission.

31. Charlotte Benton et al., ed., *Art Deco 1910–1939* (London: V&A Publications, 2003), 325.

32. For an example of a Regency chair of this design, see Frances Collard, *Regency Furniture* (Woodbridge: Antique Collectors' Club, 1985), 103.

33. T. H. Robsjohn-Gibbings and Carlton W. Pullin, *Furniture of Classical Greece* (New York: Alfred A. Knopf, 1963), 15–16.

34. Christopher Ogden, *Legacy: A Biography of Moses and Walter Annenberg* (Boston: Little, Brown, 1999), 184.

A MAYA FIGURINE IN JAINA STYLE

1. For further information about Jaina-style figurines, see Christopher Corson, *Maya Anthropomorphic Figurines from Jaina Island, Campeche* (Ramona, Calif.: Ballena Press, 1976); Mary Miller, *Maya Art and Architecture* (New York: Thames and Hudson, 1999); Miller, *Jaina Figurines: A Study of Maya Iconography* (Princeton, N.J.: The Art Museum, Princeton University, 1975); Robert L. Rands and Barbara C. Rands, "Pottery Figurines of the Maya Lowlands," in *Handbook of Middle American Indians*, vol. 2, pt. 1, ed. R. Wauchope and G. Willey (Austin: University of Texas Press, 1965), 535–60; Linda Schele, *Hidden Faces of the Maya* (Poway, Calif.: Alti, 1997); Robert L. Sharer with Loa P. Traxler, *The Ancient Maya*, 6th ed. (Stanford: Stanford University Press, 2005), all of which have provided me with useful data about the figurines.

2. See, e.g., Román Piña Chan, *Breve estudio sobre la funeraria de Jaina, Campeche*, 2nd ed. (Campeche: Gobierno de Estado de Campeche, 2001).

3. This was purchased in 1964 by the Annenbergs before the adoption of the 1970 Unesco antilooting convention and lacks clear provenance.

4. See the references in notes 1 and 2, among others, for further details about Jaina and Jaina-style figurines.

5. Miller, *Jaina Figurines*, 60.

6. Ibid.

7. Hasso Von Winning, *Pre-Columbian Art of Mexico and Central America* (New York: Harry N. Abrams, 1968), 291.

8. Verbal communication of 2006 from Simon Martin, Research Specialist, University of Pennsylvania Museum.

TWO HINDU TEMPLE DOOR PANELS WITH SILVER REPOUSSÉ

1. Nandini Thakur, "The Building of Govindadeva," in *Govindadeva: A Dialogue in Stone*, ed. Margaret H. Case (New Delhi: Indira Gandhi National Centre for Arts, 1996), 11. Other essays in this volume provide a comprehensive description of this temple, its patronage, religious setting, and art.

2. For comparable narrative door panels and ornament, see Case, ed., *Govindadeva*, figs. 3.1–28.

3. For the folklore of Krishna, see John Stratton Hawley, in assoc. with Shrivastava Goswami, *At Play with Krishna: Pilgrimage Dramas from Brindavan* (Princeton, N.J.: Princeton University Press, 1981), passim.

4. On the Amber hall, see special issue entitled "Homage to Jaipur," *Marg* 30, no. 4 (September 1977), 4, 61.

5. Edmund Weber and Tilak Raj Chopra, eds., *Shri Krishna Caitanya and the Bhakti Religion* (Frankfurt: P. Lang, 1988), provides an overview.

6. Pika Ghosh, *Temple to Love: Architecture and Devotion in Seventeenth-Century Bengal* (Bloomington: Indiana University Press, 2005), 185–99, focuses her study on a new temple type developed

for Gaudiya Vaishnavism and on the "hidden Vrindavan" (*gupt Brindavan*), the pilgrimage town of Vishnupur in Bengal. Robert Skelton, *Rajasthani Temple Hangings of the Krishna Cult: From the Collection of Karl Mann, New York* (New York: American Federation of Arts, 1973), 1–110, carefully catalogues and places in their cultural context the painted wall hangings used in Gaudiya Vaishnava temples in Rajasthan.

7. This statement comes from www.shaligram.com/ (accessed March 31, 2007); this is primarily a commercial site catering to Vaishnava households and devotees.

8. Padmanabh Goswami, "Shalagrama-shila—Shastric Evidence": www.bvml.org/contemporary/ssse.htm (accessed March 31, 2007).

9. Ibid.

10. Jayadeva, *Gitagovinda* 1.4, cited in Ghosh, *Temple to Love*, 153, and Barbara Stoller Miller, *The Gitagovinda of Jayadeva: Love Song of the Dark Lord* (Delhi: Motilal Banarsidass, 1984), 69.

CHINESE ART

1. The focus in this essay is on those items listed in the inventory provided to the author by the Annenberg Foundation Trust at Sunnylands. That inventory did not include various lamps made of Chinese ceramics and other materials at Sunnylands. The estate's interior designer William Haines was not alone in his enthusiasm for turning Chinese art works into lamps, even if he was among the more celebrated designers to do so. See David De Long's essay in this volume; and Peter Schifando and Jean H. Mathison, *Class Act: William Haines, Legendary Hollywood Decorator* (New York: Pointed Leaf Press, 2005), 59, 62, 64, 72, 94, 119, 123, 147, 149. For the practice as seen at the Rockefeller family home called Kykuit, Pocantico Hills, New York, see Asia Society, *A Passion for Asia: The Rockefeller Legacy* (New York: Hudson Hills Press, 2006), 72, 73, 76, 77, 95. Nowadays, collectors and curators generally refrain from such adaptations except with artifacts of primarily decorative value (which is the case for most of the lamps at Sunnylands), as it may damage important works of art.

2. The water buffalo is made of jadeite, valued for its sheen and varied colors, a type of jade that became widely available in China only during the Qing dynasty, and the work is attributed to the nineteenth or early twentieth century. Also to be found at Sunnylands are carvings of nephrite, another form of jade, noted for its sensuous texture and subtle colors; this had a multi-thousand-year history in China, and continued to remain popular after the introduction of jadeite. See Roger Keverne, ed., *Jade* (London: Lorenz Books, 1995), 22–27, 170–72.

3. Walter Annenberg's fondness for this work, and its nickname of "Walter" (or possibly "Uncle Walter" in the case of children), was mentioned by both Leonore Annenberg and Linda S. Brooks in interviews, January 27, 2006. Although most sources credit Leonore Annenberg with first dubbing this water buffalo "Walter," John Cooney, in *The Annenbergs* (New York: Simon and Schuster, 1982), 316–17, credited Annenberg's friends. Nonetheless, Grace Glueck, "Portrait of a Collector: Walter Annenberg," originally published April 25, 1990, *New York Times*, obtained from the *New York Times* online archive, specifically credits Leonore Annenberg for this appellation. So, too does Christopher Ogden, *Legacy: A Biography of Moses and Walter Annenberg* (Boston: Little, Brown, 1999), 522.

4. Thomas Hoving, "Inside Sunnylands: A Visit with Ambassador Annenberg," *Connoisseur* 213, no. 855 (May 1983), 78. For other Chinese enameled metalwork at Sunnylands, see the illustrations in Hoving. Annenberg's fondness for this plaque was also noted by Linda S. Brooks, interview with author, January 27, 2006.

5. Interview with Leonore Annenberg, January 27, 2006.

6. Hoving, "Inside Sunnylands," 80. This carving is made of nephrite.

7. Ogden, *Legacy*, 316–19.

8. Held at Christie's, New York, on March 29, 2006, the sale of the collection of Evelyn Annenberg Hall (William Jaffe died in 1972; she subsequently married Melville Hall) was judged very successful; all ninety-four lots sold and the total realized triple the pre-sale estimate. These porcelains were reported to have been purchased primarily from leading dealers from the 1940s through the 1960s, thus coinciding with that period when the Annenbergs and the Haupts, Hazens, and Jaffes were engaged in exploring the New York galleries. See Margaret Tao, "Spring Auctions in New York," *Orientations* 37, no. 5 (June 2006), 82.

9. For more on Cynthia Hazen Polsky, including a mention of "my uncle Walter Annenberg," see the interview with her in *Orientations* 35, no. 8 (November–December 2004), 61–66.

10. Ogden, *Legacy*, 318–19, notes the importance of Knoedler and Wildenstein to the Annenbergs' collecting. A history of the provenance of the Chinese art objects in the Annenberg collection is beyond the scope of this project. A few items still bear visible dealer labels, but many large pieces are permanently affixed to their bases to prevent earthquake damage and thus cannot be examined. Among the Chinese artworks at Sunnylands that passed through the Chait Galleries are Kangxi (1662–1722) ceramics as well as a pair of eighteenth-century painted enamel plates. Labels from dealers based in the United Kingdom were also observed in my study of these artworks, among them Eskenazi (a Tang dynasty tomb sculpture with blue glaze) and Sidney L. Moss (a Tang dynasty tripod).

11. Ogden, *Legacy*, 315–19.

12. Interview with Leonore Annenberg, January 27, 2006.

13. Interview with Linda S. Brooks, January 27, 2006.

14. Hoving, "Inside Sunnylands," 76.

15. The bibliography on the history of the collecting and display of East Asian art in the West is enormous. For material in this essay I am indebted to Julie Emerson, Jennifer Chen, and Mimi Gardner Gates, *Porcelain Stories* (Seattle: Seattle Art Museum in association with University of Washington Press, 2000). See also Alexandra Munroe and Naomi Noble Richard, eds., *The Burghley Porcelains: An Exhibition from The Burghley House Collection Based on the 1688 Inventory and 1690 Devonshire Schedule* (New York: Japan Society, 1986).

16. At the Frick Collection in New York City, one can see Chinese ceramics, primarily from the Qing dynasty, for the most part as they were originally placed, but at the National Gallery of Art, Washington, D.C., for example, the French furniture, Persian and Indian rugs, and Chinese porcelains given by Joseph Widener are shown in separate galleries from his paintings. The best overview of this phenomenon is Josephine Hadley Knapp's essay in Virginia Bower et al., *The Collections of the National Gallery of Art: Systematic Catalogue, Decorative Arts*, pt. 2: *Far Eastern Ceramics and Paintings; Persian and Indian Rugs and Carpets* (New York and Washington, D.C.: Oxford University Press and National Gallery of Art, 1998), 1–3. For an assessment of the Chinese porcelains at the Frick, see John Alexander Pope, *The Frick Collection. An Illustrated Catalogue*, pt. 1 of vol. 7, *Porcelains: Oriental and French* (New York: Princeton University Press, 1974).

17. Here I refer to the "Fonthill vase"; see Margaret Medley, *Yüan Porcelain and Stoneware* (London: Faber and Faber, 1974), 21–22, shown in color in Emerson, Chen, and Gates, *Porcelain Stories*, 25.

18. For an overview of Jingdezhen, see Emerson, Chen, and Gates, *Porcelain Stories*, 269–79. Japan's porcelain trade is discussed ibid., 94–95, 105. Exported Japanese porcelain became rarer as the eighteenth century progressed because it had to compete with the large-scale production once again emerging from China, because of demands in the Japanese domestic market, and also because restrictions upon interactions with foreigners became more severe, allowing only one Western export trading partner, the Dutch.

19. An overview of European aristocratic collections of East Asian porcelain from the late Middle Ages through the eighteenth century may be found in Emerson, Chen, and Gates, *Porcelain Stories*, esp. 24–27, 135–37.

20. See Donna Corbin on the decorative arts at Sunnylands, also in this volume. The best retelling of how porcelain eventually came to be made in Europe is Janet Gleason's acclaimed *The Arcanum: The Extraordinary True Story* (New York: Time Warner, 2000).

21. In Asia Society, *A Passion for Asia*, pp. 70 and 75 show Chinese ceramics in Rockefeller's New York home in 1936 and his office in 1944; pp. 72–73, 76–77 show Kykuit interiors with a variety of Chinese ceramics. A wider array of views of Kykuit and the Chinese ceramics housed there are found in Henry Joyce, *Tour of Kykuit: The House and Gardens of the Rockefeller Family* (New York: Historic Hudson Valley Press, 1994).

22. See De Long, "The Design of Sunnylands."

23. Schifando and Mathison, *Class Act*, passim.

24. The paperback edition of this work is Hugh Honour, *Chinoiserie: The Vision of Cathay* (New York: Harper & Row, Icon Editions, 1973).

25. The best survey of Chinese ceramics remains that by Suzanne G. Valenstein, *A Handbook of Chinese Ceramics* (New York: Metropolitan Museum of Art, 1989). More recent surveys include S. J. Vainker, *Chinese Pottery and Porcelain* (New York: George Braziller, 1991), and He Li, *Chinese Ceramics: A New Comprehensive Survey* (New York: Rizzoli, 1996). For ceramic technology, see Rose Kerr and Nigel Wood, with contributions by Ts'ai Mei-fen and Zhang Fukang, *Science and Civilisation in China*, vol. 5: *Chemistry and Chemical Technology*, pt. 12, *Ceramic Technology*, ed. Rose Kerr (Cambridge: Cambridge University Press, 2004). A brief introduction is that by Stacey Pierson, *Earth, Fire, and Water: Chinese Ceramic Technology: A Handbook for Non-specialists* (London: Percival David Foundation of Chinese Art, 1996).

26. Penelope Mason, *History of Japanese Art*, revd. Donald Dinwiddie (Upper Saddle River, N.J.: Pearson Prentice Hall, 2004), 13–16; Kerr and Wood, *Science and Civilisation*, 1–7, 379–80.

27. Kerr and Wood, *Science and Civilisation*, 115–16, 410, 485–88.

28. Ibid., 135–40.

29. Ibid., 135–46.

30. Among the more noteworthy collection of Chinese ceramics in the Middle East is that in the Topkapi Saray Museum in Istanbul. This has many celadons and porcelains. See Regina Krahl, with Nurdan Ebahar, ed. John Ayers, *Chinese Ceramics in the Topkapi Saray Museum: A Complete Catalogue*, vol. 1, *Yuan and Ming Dynasty Celadon Wares*; vol. 2, *Yuan and Ming Dynasty Porcelains*; vol. 3, *Qing Dynasty Porcelains* (London: Sotheby's Publications in assoc. with the Directorate of the Topkapi Saray Museum, 1986).

31. Kerr and Wood, *Science and Civilisation*, 9–12, 146–47.

32. Ibid., 709–10, 747–63. Because of the difficulty and expense of porcelain manufacture in Europe, imported Chinese porcelain was not displaced from its dominant position until the late eighteenth- or early nineteenth-century invention of "bone china." See Kerr and Wood, *Science and Civilisation*, 763–64, and Emerson, Chen, and Gates, *Porcelain Stories*, 219, 261.

33. China's export of ceramics has been widely studied. Among the more recent sources are Kerr and Wood, *Science and Civilisation*, esp. 709–47, and Emerson, Chen, and Gates, *Porcelain Stories*, 24–25, 71–81, 100. Vainker, *Chinese Pottery and Porcelain*, has a succinct chapter covering the subject (pp. 134–59).

34. Emerson, Chen, and Gates, *Porcelain Stories*, 88–99, 100–108. See also John Carswell, with Edward A. Maser and Jean McClure

Mudge, *Blue and White: Chinese Porcelain and Its Impact on the Western World* (Chicago: University of Chicago, David and Alfred Smart Gallery, 1985).

35. See Carswell, *Blue and White*, passim.

36. Kerr and Wood, *Science and Civilisation*, 443–50, 560–74, 619–707.

37. Valenstein's overview of Ming and Qing ceramics is especially recommended: *A Handbook of Chinese Ceramics*, 151–279.

38. Aside from sources already mentioned, useful texts on later Chinese export porcelain include Michel Beurdeley, *Porcelain of the East India Companies*, trans. Diana Imber (London: Barrie and Rockliff, 1962); Clare Le Corbeiller, *China Trade Porcelain: Patterns of Exchange* (New York: Metropolitan Museum of Art, 1974); Jean McClure Mudge, *Chinese Export Porcelain in North America* (New York: Clarkson N. Potter, 1986). Publications by or co-authored by David Sanctuary Howard deserve special notice: *Chinese Armorial Porcelain* (London: Faber and Faber, 1974); David Howard and John Ayers, *China for the West: Chinese Porcelain & Other Decorative Arts for Export Illustrated from the Mottahedeh Collection*, 2 vols. (London and New York: Sotheby Parke Bernet, 1978); and idem, *Masterpieces of Chinese Export Porcelain from the Mottahedeh Collection in the Virginia Museum* (London: Sotheby Parke Bernet, 1980).

39. The term *Tang sancai* (literally "Tang three colors") for Tang dynasty lead-glazed, low-fired wares does not seem to appear in Tang sources and was perhaps coined by collectors and/or dealers in the early part of the twentieth century. "San" or "three" in Chinese may be used to indicate "many": thus, these wares do not always feature exactly three colors, and they are understood to encompass works with monochrome, bi-chrome, or polychrome glazes, which may occasionally have four or more distinct colors. Nonetheless, as these wares are often seen in green and yellow (or amber) with white, these three colors are understood by many as the "three colors" of Tang three-color ware. Blue is the most frequently encountered other color, but it is not common.

40. See Jan Fontein and Tung Wu, *Unearthing China's Past* (Boston: Museum of Fine Arts, 1973), 14–18.

41. See He Li, *Chinese Ceramics: A New Comprehensive Survey* (New York: Rizzoli, 1996), 296–98, no. 617 for a vessel very similar to this one, there identified as a "water dropper" dated to the Qing dynasty, Kangxi period rather than as a teapot as listed in the inventory provided by the Annenberg Foundation Trust at Sunnylands.

42. Here I follow the description in the inventory provided by the Annenberg Foundation Trust at Sunnylands. Despite the prevalence of green, varieties such as "eggs and spinach," with enamels used as glazes are not generally referred to as *famille verte*, a category usually reserved for wares with intricately painted designs.

43. See Bower et al., *Collections of the National Gallery of Art*, 14–23. Other terms credited to Albert Jacquemart such as *famille jaune* and *famille noire* do not seem to appear in his writings, and were most likely coined by others by analogy. See Albert Jacquemart, *Les Merveilles de la Céramique* (Paris: Librairie Hachette, 1874), and idem, *History of the Ceramic Art*, trans. Mrs. Bury Palliser (London: Sampson Low, Marston, Searle and Rivington, 1877).

44. Bower et al., *Collections of the National Gallery of Art*, 14–23. See also Wang Qingzheng, *A Dictionary of Chinese Ceramics*, 231–33.

45. In the inventory provided to the author, this vessel is referred to as a chocolate pot, but comparable published works are usually called coffee pots.

46. See Howard and Ayers, *China for the West*, 1: 280, no. 278, for a color reproduction of a plate with a design related to that found on the Annenberg pot, and references to two coffee pots sold at Sotheby's with a very similar pattern to that seen on this pot. See idem, *Masterpieces of Chinese Export*, 51–52, no. 278, for a color reproduction of one of these two coffee pots sold at Sotheby's. For help in obtaining the text and illustration of the first coffee pot sold at Sotheby's, one that looks especially like the one at Sunnylands, I thank Suzanne G. Valenstein; see Sotheby & Co., London, *Catalogue of Fine Chinese Ceramics, The Property of W. W. Winkworth, Esq.*, December 12, 1972, 50–51, lot 173. For help in obtaining the text and illustration of the second coffee pot (which looks slightly less like the one at Sunnylands), I thank Elizabeth Naccarato, Sotheby's, New York; see Sotheby & Co., London, *Catalogue of Oriental Export Porcelain Jades and Works of Art*, Thursday, June 27, 1974, 132–33, lot 266.

47. Eighteenth-century Chinese art, including ceramics, includes work with Western subjects intended for the appreciation of an imperial Chinese audience, but these are generally much more refined than that seen here. See, e.g., Rosemary Scott, *Elegant Form and Harmonious Decoration: Four Dynasties of Jingdezhen Porcelain* (Singapore: Percival David Foundation and Sun Tree Publishing, 1992), 162, no. 187.

48. Le Corbeiller, *China Trade Porcelain*, 36–37; Jessie McNab, "The Legacy of a Fantastical Scot," *Metropolitan Museum of Art Bulletin* 19, no. 6 (February 1961), 172–80, and idem, "Monteiths: English, American, Continental," *The Magazine Antiques* 82 no. 2 (August 1962), 156–60. In the latter article, 157, fig. 7, a silver, oval-shaped vessel on four legs dated to 1710 may presage the form seen here at Sunnylands on ball and claw feet.

Regarding the sweetmeat set (*cuan pan*), see Wang Qingzheng, *A Dictionary of Chinese Ceramics*, ed. Chen Kelun et al., trans. Lillian Chin and Jay Xu (Singapore: Sun Tree Publishing and Oriental Art Publications, 2002), 20.

49. See Metropolitan Museum of Art, *Oriental Ceramics, the World's Great Collections*: vol. 11, *The Metropolitan Museum of Art* (Tokyo and New York: Kodansha International, 1980–82), color pl. no. 26, 163–64, where mention is made of the possible inspiration of mahogany straight-rimmed wine coolers of the early eighteenth century. Another *famille verte* example of this type may be found in Beurdeley, *Porcelains*, 160, no. 52.

50. Emberson, Chen, and Gates, *Porcelain Stories*, 106–7, pls. 9.4, 9.5; Mudge, *Chinese Export Porcelain*, 139–40, fig. 205; Valenstein, *Handbook of Chinese Ceramics*, 257.

51. Valenstein, *Handbook of Chinese Ceramics*, 257, nos. 271–75. Similar but not identical to the Annenberg and Metropolitan Museum covered jars is one from a garniture of five beakers and jars illustrated in R. L. Hobson, *Chinese Pottery and Porcelain* (1915; repr. New York: Dover, 1976), color pl. 120.

52. Interview with Leonore Annenberg, January 27, 2006.

53. Mudge, *Chinese Export Porcelain*, 193; 194 fig. 305.

54. For these observations I am indebted to Amanda Lange's essay accompanying a "peacock pattern" dish, no. 57, in *Chinese Export Art at Historic Deerfield* (Deerfield, Mass.: Historic Deerfield, 2005), 174–75.

55. These platters were so identified in the inventory provided to me, an identification confirmed by Howard, *Chinese Armorial Porcelain*, 320.

56. Beurdeley, *Porcelains*, 69–135, discusses and illustrates a large number of Chinese export services created for individuals in Europe, Russia, and the Americas, many of armorial type.

57. Kerr and Wood, *Science and Civilisation*, 1–6, 280, 379–80. Kerr and Wood note that evidence is thus far lacking that in China fired and unfired clay figures were created earlier than fired or unfired clay vessels.

58. Kerr and Wood, *Science and Civilisation*, 1–6, 280, 379–80; for more on the Hongshan, see Yang Xiaoneng, *The Golden Age of Chinese Archaeology: Celebrated Discoveries from the People's Republic of China* (Washington, D.C.: National Gallery of Art, 1999), 78–81, 96–97; and Jessica Rawson, ed., *Mysteries of Ancient China* (London: British Museum, 1996), 44; and for the Shijiahe culture, 46–47.

59. Overviews of the development and history of Chinese mortuary ceramics may be found in Virginia L. Bower, *From Court to Caravan: Chinese Tomb Sculptures from the Collection of Anthony M. Solomon*, ed. Robert D. Mowry (Cambridge, Mass.: Harvard University Art Museums and Yale University Press, 2002); and in Los Angeles County Museum of Art and Overseas Archaeological Exhibition Corporation, *The Quest for Eternity: Chinese Ceramic Sculptures from The People's Republic of China* (Los Angeles: Los Angeles County Museum of Art, 1987). For more detail and the most up-to-date information, consult Wu Hung, "From Neolithic to the Han," 17–103, and Yang Hong, "From the Han to the Qing," 105–97, in Angela Falco Howard, et al., *Chinese Sculpture* (New Haven: Yale University Press and Foreign Languages Press, 2006). The general comments that follow here, e.g., on Tang mortuary styles, are based on the material in these sources.

60. The "Terra-cotta army" is discussed with more references in all the sources above. Archaeological discoveries now include figures of acrobats and civil officials. For an illustration of acrobats see Wu Hung, "From Neolithic to the Han," 55, fig. 1.31.

61. Asia Society, *A Passion for Asia*, 74–76.

62. William Haines commonly used what appear to be Chinese mortuary figures (perhaps not all authentic) in interiors; see Schifando and Mathison, *Class Act*, 94, 106, 113, 119, 121, 137, 147–49, 151, 180, and Sunnylands, 184–85.

63. Kerr and Wood, *Science and Civilisation*, 499–503. See also Nigel Wood, *Chinese Glazes: Their Origins, Chemistry and Recreation* (Philadelphia: University of Pennsylvania Press, 1999), 189–206.

64. For Tang burial regulations, essentially a type of sumptuary law, see Bower, *From Court to Caravan*, 48, which includes further references.

65. With regard to core groups of ceramic tomb guardian figures, see Robert D. Jacobsen, "Ceramic Tomb Sets of Early T'ang," *Minneapolis Institute of Arts Bulletin* 64 (1978–80; Minneapolis: Minneapolis Institute of Arts, 1981), 4–23, which may have been the first to enunciate this concept explicitly, although the germ of the idea is found in earlier sources.

66. This conclusion is based on a review of many excavated and dated tombs with works of similar size and appearance, including works in tombs of imperial family members published in Chinese and other languages. See Los Angeles County Museum of Art, *The Quest for Eternity*, esp. 131–13. The 42-inch (107-cm) military figure at Sunnylands is remarkably similar to a 103-cm work in an unidentified private collection: Adrian M. Joseph, Hugh M. Moss, and S. J. Fleming, *Chinese Pottery Burial Objects of the Sui and T'ang Dynasties* (London: Hugh M. Moss, 1970), no. 70.

67. An inventory label from Eskenazi, London, was noted on the side of the blue-glazed official figure, and it was confirmed by representatives of that firm that this work was published in Eskenazi, *Ancient Chinese Bronze Vessels, Gilt Bronzes, and Early Ceramics, 13 June–14 July 1973* (London: Kegan Paul, Trench, Trubner, 1973), 62–63, no. 35. For a summary of recent research on blue glazes during the Tang, see Virginia L. Bower, "Cobalt Blue: Perfecting Tang *Sancai*," in *Blue Glaze of Tang* (New York: Berwald Oriental Art, 2006), 4–9.

68. Anthony M. Solomon, who gave his collection to the Harvard University Museums, focused his attention on unglazed mortuary

ceramics dating from the Han through Tang dynasties. See Bower, *From Court to Caravan*, 21–22 for collection overview, 48–54 for Tang references.

69. Interview with Leonore Annenberg, January 27, 2006; interview with Linda S. Brooks, January 27, 2006. Ms. Brooks noted the great care with which they had been crated, and how carefully they were unpacked upon arrival at Sunnylands.

70. Bower, *From Court to Caravan*, 50–51. "Heavenly King" tomb guardians fall into two types: those standing on placid beasts, of which at least one is a bull, and those shown stamping on one or more demons. Buddhist iconography influenced both.

71. Kerr and Wood, *Science and Civilisation*, 509–22.

72. Grace Glueck, "Portrait of a Collector." Walter Annenberg's role in placing these rabbit tiles in front of this painting was also noted by Linda S. Brooks, interview, January 27, 2006.

73. For the Annenbergs' affection for this Picasso, see Ogden, *Legacy*, 521. Film- and theater-goers may recognize the name of the bar, Le Lapin Agile or "Nimble Rabbit," from the Steve Martin play, *Picasso at the Lapin Agile*, 1993.

74. See Honour, *Chinoiserie*, passim. See Ogden, *Legacy*, 399, 450, for Annenberg's delight in bird-watching and his interest in collecting images of birds.

75. Sources on this ware include John Ayers, *Blanc de Chine: Divine Images in Porcelain* (New York: China Institute Press, 2002); Robert H. Blumenfield, *Blanc de Chine: The Great Porcelain of Dehua* (Berkeley and Toronto: Ten Speed Press, 2002); P. J. Donnelly, *Blanc de Chine: The Porcelain of Têhua in Fukien* (New York: Frederick A. Praeger, 1969).

76. Albert Jacquemart used the term "Blanc de Chine" in reference to an illustration of a *Guanyin* of a type connected to Dehua in his *Les Merveilles*, 61, coining this term as he did others. But Mrs. Bury Palliser, *History of the Ceramic Art*, does not use the term in her translation of the discussion of this illustration, 27.

77. See Chün-fang Yü, *Kuan-yin: The Chinese Transformation of Avalokitesvara* (New York: Columbia University Press, 2001), for the Indian background of this Bodhisattva, as well as for this figure's history in China.

78. The inventory provided to the author dated this work to about 1800 C.E. Dating *Blanc de Chine* or Dehua ware remains difficult. In some sources massive figures a bit like this, though not identical to it, are dated to the seventeenth century: see Donnelly, *Blanc de Chine*, pls. 81a and b. In other sources, massive figures somewhat like this are assigned to the nineteenth century: see Blumenfield, *Blanc de Chine*, 96.

79. Ayers, *Blanc de Chine*, 28–32. *Guanyin* figures described as "crude" by Ayers were already being mass-produced for European markets by the seventeenth century: 29, fig. 5. Other figures seem less easily distinguished as domestic or for export.

80. Important collectors of Chinese enameled ware in North America and Europe include Samuel P. Avery, Jr., Robert and Marian Clague, and Pierre Uldry. See John Getz, *Catalogue of the Avery Collection of Ancient Chinese Cloisonnés* (Brooklyn: Museum of the Brooklyn Institute of Arts and Sciences, 1912), and Lin Xiaoping, "The Blue of Jingtai: The Samuel P. Avery, Jr. Collection of Chinese Cloisonné in the Brooklyn Museum," *Orientations* 21, no. 7 (July 1990), 30–38. I thank Frances Z. Yuan for bringing the latter article to my attention. See Claudia Brown, *Chinese Cloisonné: The Clague Collection* (Phoenix, Ariz.: Phoenix Art Museum, 1980); idem, "Chinese Cloisonné: The Clague Collection," *Orientations* 11, no. 9 (September 1980), 37–42; "Collector" [anon. author], "Chinese Cloisonné: The Robert and Marian Clague Collection," *Arts of Asia* 5, no. 1 (January–February 1975), 25–34. See Helmut Brinker and Albert Lutz, *Chinese Cloisonné: The Pierre Uldry Collection*, trans. Susanna Swoboda (New York: Asia Society Galleries, in association with Bamboo Publishing, London, 1989).

81. This sentence occurs in a letter from William Haines to the Hon. and Mrs. Walter H. Annenberg, February 29, 1972, correspondence files, Sunnylands Trust. Also in the Sunnylands Trust correspondence file associated with this item is a February 25, 1972 letter from a New York art dealer offering these tables to William Haines. There they are described as dating to ca. 1640, which would place them at the end of the Ming dynasty (1368–1644), the period to which they are now attributed according to the Sunnylands inventory provided to the author. However, the dealer oddly characterized them as "Kang Hs'i"—this would be the Qing dynasty emperor whose name is now Romanized as "Kangxi," and who reigned from 1662–1722, the Qing dynasty being established in 1644. In any case, they were reported to have been obtained "quite recently" from the collection of Lord Loch of Drylaw, who would have been an heir of Henry Brougham Loch [Baron Loch] (1827–1900), once resident in China. Judging from the 1972 date of the proposed acquisition, this would have been George Henry Compton Loch, Third Baron Loch (1916–1982), whose predecessor died in 1942.

82. Much of the *cloisonné* enamelware was acquired in London; interview with Leonore Annenberg, January 27, 2006. A small, square, covered *cloisonné* box, dating to the eighteenth century, still bears a label from Spink, a London dealer in Asian art until 2000–2001; Spink now deals primarily in medals and coins.

83. See Erika Speel, *Dictionary of Enamelling* (Brookfield, Vt.: Ashgate, 1998), 46. This work is especially useful in dealing with the non-Chinese history of enamel.

84. Besides the sources already noted, other important sources discussing the history of *cloisonné* and *champlevé* in China include Gunhild Gabbert Avitabile, *Die Ware aus dem Teufelsland: Chinesische*

und japanische Cloisonné- und Champlevé-Arbeiten von 1400 bis 1900 [Ware of the Devil's Country: Chinese and Japanese Cloisonné and Champlevé from 1400–1900] (Hanover: Verlag Kunst & Antiquitäten, 1981), and Chen Hsia-sheng, *Ming Qing falangqi zhanlan tulu* [Enamel Ware in the Ming and Ch'ing (Qing) Dynasties] (Taipei, Taiwan: National Palace Museum, 1999).

85. Kerr and Wood, *Science and Civilisation*, 618–19.

86. Ibid., 619–22.

87. The origins and development of the *famille rose* palette remain controversial, as some contend the foreign contribution to this is questionable. See Kerr and Wood, *Science and Civilisation*, 634–51.

88. Los Angeles County Museum of Art, *The Painted Enamels of Limoges: A Catalogue of the Collection of the Los Angeles County Museum of Art* (Los Angeles, 1993), 21–24; Speel, *Dictionary of Enamelling*, 90–92, 108.

89. A good overview of Chinese painted enamels is in Michael Gillingham, "Chinese Painted Enamels: An Historical Overview," *Chinese Painted Enamels of the Eighteenth Century* (New York: Chinese Porcelain Company, 1993), iv–viii.

90. Large quantities of *cloisonné* were made in China from the Ming dynasty on, but relatively little *champlevé* can be dated to the Ming, and it is sometimes combined with *cloisonné*; see Gabbert-Avitabile, *Die Ware aus dem Teufelsland*, 16, 18. Significant quantities of high-quality *champlevé* survive mainly from the eighteenth century.

91. See Gillingham, "Chinese Painted Enamels," iv–v, who claims that the ground layer of enamel is first fired at a low temperature; and Speel, *Dictionary of Enamelling*, 71, 90–92, who emphasizes the difference in fusibility of the enamels used for the grounding layer and the décor.

92. Brinker and Lutz, *Chinese Cloisonné*, 23–45; Brown, *Chinese Cloisonné*, 5–7.

93. Still adhering to the bases of these dishes are labels from the Chait Galleries, a still-prominent New York dealer in East Asian art. Enamels with European subjects were also created for the imperial court, but are of generally even more refined appearance than those presented here; see Chen Hsia-sheng, *Ming Qing falangqi zhanlan tulu*, 236–37, nos. 121–22.

94. The inventory provided to the author dated these to 1745. My thanks to Margaret Gristina for her insight that these colors indicated an earlier date for these works.

95. See Gillingham, "Chinese Painted Enamels," viii, a description of Kangxi wares. I thank Margaret Gristina for pointing this out.

96. Judging from its illustration and further description, the closest analogy for the dishes is in Stephen W. Bushell, *Chinese Art*, vol. 2 (London: Board of Education, 1924), 85, fig. 101. See also The Chinese Porcelain Company, *Chinese Painted Enamels of the 18th Century* (New York: Chinese Porcelain Company, 1993), 44–45,

no. 41, for a work with an elaborately painted base, but one that is otherwise not so similar.

97. See Hoving, "Inside Sunnylands," 78, for an illustration of this plaque *in situ*.

98. Brinker and Lutz, *Chinese Cloisonné*, 120–22; Brown, *Chinese Cloisonné*, 10.

99. Brinker and Lutz, *Chinese Cloisonné*, 120–22, note the usage in table screens and metal stands; an example of a framed *cloisonné* landscape panel may be found in Chen Hsia-sheng, *Ming Qing falangqi zhanlan tulu*, 123, no. 45.

100. See Tian Jiaqing, *Classic Chinese Furniture of the Qing Dynasty* (Hong Kong: Philip Wilson and Joint Publishing, 1996), 38, 129, no. 50, for the throne in the "New Summer Palace" that is, the late nineteenth-century/early twentieth-century Yiheyuan in Beijing. Wan Yi, Wang Shuqing, and Lu Yanzhen, compilers, *Daily Life in the Forbidden City* (New York: Viking, 1988), 252, show a pair of barrel-shaped stools in a room within this imperial palace. No date is provided, and the picture is dark, but they appear to be of the eighteenth or nineteenth century.

101. As noted above, the attribution to the late Ming or first part of the seventeenth century is made in the inventory provided to the author. The enamel décor relates to that on a low square table attributed to the second half of the seventeenth century in the Pierre Uldry collection; see Brinker and Lutz, *Chinese Cloisonné*, 123, no. 182. However, this décor is simpler, with colors and flowers more closely identified with Ming styles. With regard to the rarity of Ming dynasty furniture with enamel, see Tian Jiaqing, *Classic Chinese Furniture*, 38: "As far as is known no example of Ming furniture with cloisonné inlay has ever been recorded." For an overview of Chinese stools, see Sarah Handler, *Austere Luminosity of Chinese Classical Furniture* (Berkeley: University of California Press, 2001), 82–102. My thanks go to Sarah Handler for her advice on this subject.

102. Julian Henderson, Mary Tregear, and Nigel Wood, "The Technology of Sixteenth- and Seventeenth-Century Chinese Cloisonné Enamels, pt. 2," *Archaeometry* 31 (August 1989), 133, speculate that enamelers and potters, brought together for the first time in imperial workshops during this reign, may have influenced each other in new ways, ways uncommon before because most ceramic kilns were rarely near glass enamel workshops.

103. The attribution of this vase to the Kangxi reign was made in the inventory provided to the author.

104. Chen Hsia-sheng, *Ming Qing falangqi zhanlan tulu*, 153, no. 68.

105. For an overview of reign marks, and other marks and inscriptions found on Chinese ceramics, much of which is applicable to other such marked wares, see Wang Qingzheng, *A Dictionary of Chinese Ceramics*, 294–320.

106. As the use of incense has increased in recent years, the once some-

what esoteric term "joss-stick" is more frequently recognized as a term for the incense sticks much used in China and other parts of the Far East. The Sunnyland holders are similar, although not identical to, a joss-stick holder, also with Qianlong mark, in the Clague collection; see Brown, *Chinese Cloisonné*, 116, no. 51.

107. Berthold Laufer, *The Bird-Chariot in China and Europe* (New York, 1906, reprinted and excerpted from Berthold Laufer, ed., *The Boas Anniversary Volume, Anthropological Papers Written in Honor of Franz Boas* [New York: G. E. Stechert & Co., 1906]), 409–24.

108. Brinker and Lutz, *Chinese Cloisonné*, 137, nos. 257–58, 258 with Qianlong mark; Chen Hsia-sheng, *Ming Qing falangqi zhanlan tulu*, 156–57, no. 70; Getz, *Catalogue of the Avery Collection*, 26–27, no. 46.

109. Works attributed to the Qianlong era with somewhat similar décor may be found in Brinker and Lutz, *Chinese Cloisonné*, no. 270, and Gabbert-Avitabile, *Die Ware aus dem Teufelsland*, 151, no. 81.

110. See Ogden, *Legacy*, 450, noting Annenberg's complete edition of porcelain birds by Dorothy Doughty.

111. Evelyn Rawski and Jessica Rawson, eds., *China: The Three Emperors* (London: Royal Academy of Arts, 2005), 360, 391, no. 21: a pair of *cloisonné* cranes from a throne room in the Forbidden City, ht. 53.74 inches (136 cm); Robert L. Thorp, *Son of Heaven: Imperial Arts of China* (Seattle: Son of Heaven Press, 1988), 98, nos. 35–36: a pair of *cloisonné* cranes from the Shenyang Palace throne room, ht. 52 inches (133 cm). The cranes at Sunnylands have a height of 55 inches (139.7 cm), and are visible in Hoving, "Inside Sunnylands," 78, lower illustration.

CONTRIBUTORS

Virginia Bower, Adjunct Associate Professor at the University of the Arts, Philadelphia, is a frequent visiting lecturer at other institutions, including Rutgers University. She has published widely in the field of Chinese art.

Donna Corbin is the Associate Curator of European Decorative Arts at the Philadelphia Museum of Art. She has published widely on European decorative arts and is currently working on catalogues of the French porcelain at both the Cleveland Museum of Art and the Philadelphia Museum of Art.

David G. De Long is Professor Emeritus of Architecture at the University of Pennsylvania, where he chaired the Graduate Program in Historic Preservation from 1984 to 1996. An architect and architectural historian, he has published widely on American architecture.

Anne d'Harnoncourt (1943–2008) was the George D. Widener Director and Chief Executive Officer of the Philadelphia Museum of Art from 1982 until her death in 2008. She received her bachelor's degree from Harvard University and her master's degree from the Courtauld Institute of Art in London. A specialist in twentieth-century art, d'Harnoncourt was internationally respected both as an art historian and as an administrator.

Kathleen Hall Jamieson is Professor of Communications at the Annenberg School for Communication, University of Pennsylvania, Director of its Policy Center and Program Director of the Annenberg Foundation Trust at Sunnylands.

Suzanne Glover Lindsay is Adjunct Associate Professor in the History of Art at the University of Pennsylvania and has held various curatorial positions, notably Acting Head of the Sculpture Department, National Gallery of Art. She has produced major publications and museum exhibitions on modern French sculpture and painting.

Mary Jean Smith (M. J.) Madigan was Curator of American History and Decorative Arts at the Hudson River Museum and later served as editor-in-chief of the magazines *Art & Antiques, Hospitality Design*, and *Interiors*. She has written extensively on American decorative arts and design.

Michael W. Meister holds the W. Norman Brown Professorship in South Asian Studies at the University of Pennsylvania. He has chaired both the History of Art and South Asia Studies Departments and been Director of the South Asia Center. An art historian, he has published widely on South Asian art and culture.

Jeremy A. Sabloff, formerly the Christopher H. Browne Distinguished Professor of Anthropology at the University of

Pennsylvania and the Curator of Mesoamerican Archaeology at the University of Pennsylvania Museum, is president of the Santa Fe Institute in Santa Fe, New Mexico. Among his many books are *A History of American Archaeology* (with Gordon R. Willey), *Cities of Ancient Mexico*, and *The New Archaeology and the Ancient Maya*.

Gwendolyn DuBois Shaw is Associate Professor of History of Art at the University of Pennsylvania where she also serves as Director of the Program in Visual Studies and is Faculty Master of Gregory College House. A historian of American art and culture, she has published widely on art from the colonial period through to the present day.

INDEX

Page numbers in italics indicate illustrations.

A

A. Quincy Jones and Associates, 5
Abstract Composition (1) (Agam), 80
Abstract Composition (2) (Agam), 80
Adam, Robert, 30
Africa (Bearden), 83, *89*, 89–90
Agam, Yaacov, 67, 70, 79–81
Aiken, Conrad, 101
Albert Edward, Prince of Wales, 113
The Album (Vuillard), 71
Alexandre, Arsène, 73
All This You Must Imitate (Rossi), 68, *70*
Altman, Benjamin, 142
Amor and Psyche (Rodin), 73–74
anamorphoses, Renaissance, 81
Anderson, David, 13, 15, 18, 28
Andrew, Prince, 61
Annenberg, Leonore (Lee) Cohn, 1–4, 71; art
    collection and, 70, 83; building process and,
    22; Chinese art and, 129, 143; collections and,
    38, 40; designers and, 5; design of Sunnylands
    and, 8, 18, 19; dining room and, 39; guests at
    Sunnylands and, 60–61, *63*, 158, 159; Haines
    and, 6, 12; interior design and, 30; on land-
    scaping, 15; main living area and, 50; serv-
    ing staff and, 60; as U.S. Chief of Protocol,
    60–61, 97; Wyeth portrait of Walter and, 57;
    Wynnewood home and, 131
Annenberg, Moses, 87, 115
Annenberg, Sadie, 71
Annenberg, Walter, 1, 4; ambassadorial career,
    38, 60, 96–97, 105; art collection, 70, 71,
    77, 83; Chinese art and, 129, 146, 155; death

of, 65, 158, 159; designers and, 5; design of
    Sunnylands and, 7; as guest of Hearst, 41;
    guests at Sunnylands and, 60–61, *63*, 158–59;
    Haines and, 12; Jensen silverwork and, 115,
    118; landscaping and, 15, 28; on Maya col-
    umns, 38; private study, 57; Steuben glass
    collection and, 96, 97, 101, 103; Wyeth por-
    trait of, 57, 79–87, *86*, *87*; Wynnewood home
    and, 131
Annenberg family, 62, 65, 87; English royalty
    and, 57
antiques, 30, 38, 50
architects, 4, 15, 38, 59, 65
architecture, 1, 4, 6, 8, 59
Arcimboldo, Giuseppe, 81
Arp, Jean, 40, 50, 67, 71, 74–75, 77
arrival court, 42, 44, *44*
Art Deco, 95, 118
Art Nouveau, 95, 113–15
Arts and Crafts movement, 107
Arts & Architecture magazine, 6
Atkins, Lloyd, 99, 101
atrium, central, 8, 18, 38; in plan of main house,
    20–21; Rodin sculpture, 46, *46–49*, *82–83*;
    view across, 45–46, *46–49*
Auden, W. H., 101
Auguste, Henri, 108
Augustus II, king of Poland, 110, 132
Au Lapin Agile (Picasso), 146
aviary, 8
Ayers, John, 142

B

Balinese Funeral (Atkins and Djate), *99*
Ball, Lucille, 4

Ballin, Mogens, 107
Barker Brothers, 118
Barrias, Louis-Ernest, 72
basket (1797–98), 100, 108, *108*
Bayer, Johan Christoph, 113
Bearden, Romare, 83, 89–91
Beckford, William, 100, 108
bedrooms: guest, 15, 40, 41; master, 12, 29, 57,
    58–59, 143; staff, 8, 19, 59
Belle de nuit (Hajdu), 77, *78*
Bennett, Constance, 6
Bennett, Joan, 6
Benny, Jack, 4
Bertoia, Harry, 40, 53, 67, 68, 71; bird theme
    in sculpture and, 70; kinetic sculpture and,
    79–80
Bicycle Wheel (Duchamp), 79
billiard room, 8, 38
Birds and Fishes (Pollard and Vickrey), 101
Birds of Welcome (Price), 67, *156*
Blanc de Chine, 143–44, *149*
Bloomingdale, Alfred, 5
Bloomingdale, Betsy, 5, 6
Bloomingdale house, 18
Bodhisattva (Pollard and Saito), *94*
Boileau, Jean-Jacques, 108
Böttger, Johann Frederick, 132
Boulton, Matthew, 110
boxes (*cloisonné*, Ming dynasty), 154, *154*
Brancusi, Constantin, 68, 75
Brandt, Edgar, 118
Brewer, Rachel, 84
Bridge, John, 110
Brody, Sidney, 5
Brody house, 5, 6
Bruggen, Coosje van, 79
Bullock, George, 118

Bush, Barbara, 60
Bush, George H. W., 60
Bust of Diego (Giacometti), 77–79, *78*

C

cabinets, *30*, 40, 57
Calder, Alexander, 79
candelabra (Jensen), 113–15, *114*
candlesticks, figural (Qing dynasty), 146, *147–48*
Capote, Truman, 61
Carder, Frederick, 95
Carter, Rosalynn, 60
Cartier, Louis-François, 105
Case Study House, 6, 21, 41
Castle Howard (Yorkshire, England), 65
Catherine II, empress of Russia, 113
Cellini, Benvenuto, 93
Chaitanya, 126
champlevé enamels, 152
Chapeau Forêt (Arp), 75, 77
chargers (Qing dynasty), *135*, 143, 149
Charles, Prince, 61, 97
Charlotte, queen of England, 105
Cheyenne people, 68
Chinese art, *128*, 129–31, *130*, *131*; architectural, decorative, and religious sculpture, *144*, 146, *147–48*, 149; ceramics, 133, *133–39*, 135, *140*, 140–41; collection in context, 131–33; earthenware and stoneware vessels, *141*, 141–42; enameled metalware, 149, *150–51*, *152*, 152–54, *153*, *154*; mortuary sculpture, 144–46, *145*; porcelain vessels, *134–35*, 142; sculpture in ceramic, 143–44, *144*
Chinese pavilion, 40, *41*
"Chinoiserie," 90, 97, 110–11, *111*, 133, 146
Chinoiserie: The Vision of Cathay (Honour), 133
Cho Chung-Yung, 94
chocolate or coffee pot (Qing dynasty), *134*, 142
Christian VII, king of Denmark, 112, 113
Class Act (Schifando), 6
Clinton, Bill, 60
Clinton, Hillary, 60
cloakrooms, guest, 46
cloisonné, 149, 152–54
Cohn, Harry, 1,4
Cohn, Rose, 4
Colbert, Claudette, 6
Colonial revival style, 11
Conference Chair, *117*, 118–19
Cook, Allen, 65
Le Coq (Gilioli), *68*, 77
Corning Glass (company and museum), 38, 95, 99, 101
Crane, Melville, 101
Crawford, Joan, 6

Crosby, Bing, 4
Cubism, 90
Cukor, George, 6

D

Dalí, Salvador, 95, 98
Daum, R. J., 21
Davis, William, 143
decorative arts, 105; basket (1797–98), 100, 108, *108*; candelabra and tureen (Jensen), 113–15, *114*; epergne (1761–62), 100, *107*; Flora Danica china, *112*, 112–13; furniture, Haines/Graber designed, 115, *116–17*, 118–19; Meissen covered jars, 110–11, *111*; plate, decorated by Picasso, 115, *115*; tray (1807–8), *104–5*, *109*, 109–10
Delaunay, Nicolas, 100
De Long, David, 67, 71, 131, 158
Demeter (Arp), 75, *76*
department stores, 118
Derain, André, 95
design, of Sunnylands, 1, 7–8, 11–15, 18–19; Letter of Agreement, 8; main house, views of, 8, *8*, *9*, *14–19*
Deutsch, Armand, 5
d'Harnoncourt, Anne, 61
Diana (Saint-Gaudens), 79
dining room, 38–39, 46, 50, *52*; night view from terrace, *51*; service wing and, 59; table settings, *62*
Djate, Made, 99
Dogwood VII (Bertoia), 80
Doheny, Edward L., 28
Domínguín, Luis-Miguel, 88–89
Douglas, Kirk, 4
dressing rooms, 11, 15, 40, 57
Duchamp, Marcel, 79, 90, 91
Duchamp, Suzanne, 90
Duhem, Henri, 73
Dulles, John Foster, 99

E

Eakins, Thomas, 158
Edward, Prince, 61
Eichler, Joseph, 5
Eichler Homes, 5, 21, 41
Eisenhower, Dwight D., 57, 60, 99–100, 158–65
Eisenhower, Mamie, 60
"Eisenhower palms," *61*, 61
Elizabeth II, queen of England, 41–42, 61
Emmons, Frederick Earl, 5
L'Enfant au Biberon (Villon), 83, 90–91, *91*
English Regency style, 30

Entenza, John, 6
entrance, main, 18, 34, 40, *44–45*
epergne (1761–62), 100, *107*
Erlacher, Roland, 103
Ernest Augustus, duke of Cumberland, 105
Eternal Spring (Rodin), 67, *69*, 73–74, 79
Eve (Rodin), 45–46, *46–49*, *66*, 67, *72*; Arp's *Torso* and, 75; base for, 71; detail of founder's inscription, *72*, *73*; Guanyin figure contrasted with, 149; historical background of, 72–73; turning movement on base, 79; Woman as theme of art collection and, 70–71

F

Fabergé, Carl, 93
Fallingwater, 65
famille rose ("rose family"), 142–43, 146, 149
famille verte ("green family"), 111, 142
Fantin-Latour, Henri, 77
Fareed (Omar) house, 5
fence, at entrance gate, 40–41
Feron, Louis, 103
Finley, David E., 99
fireplace, 46, *48–49*
Flora Danica china, 61, *112*, 112–13
flower arranging/pressing rooms, 11
Fonthill Abbey, 100, 108
Ford, Betty, 60
Ford, Gerald, 60, 85
Francesca da Rimini (Rodin), 73
Frey, Albert, 4
Frick, Henry Clay, 132, 144
furniture, 30, 38, 42, 65, 132; Chinese, *cloisonné*-embellished, 38, 129; dining table, *32–33*; of Haines and Graber design, 115, *116–17*, 118–19; hexagonal table, *31*; in main living area, 50

G

Gable, Clark, 4
game room, 8, 18, 38, 53–55; artwork in, 68; entrance to, *53*; interior views, *54*
gardens, 19, 28, 29, 44
garniture de cheminée, 143
Garvey, Marcus, 90
Gates of Hell (Rodin), 72
George III, King, 105
George Washington (Peale), 83–85, *84*
Giacometti, Alberto, 67, 70, 77–79
Gilioli, Émile, 67, 70, 77, 79
Gilot, Françoise, 115
Goetz, Edie Mayer, 6
Goetz, William, 6

golf course, 11, 12–13, 19, 64; Chinese pavilion, 40, *41*; construction of, 22, 24, *26*; as country's "best-maintained" golf course, 64; "Delos" bench, 40, *41*; layout, *15*; Northwest Coast totem pole, 67, 68
Gopis in the Grove of Vrindavana (Thompson and Roy), 99
Goya y Lucientes, Francisco, 88
Graber, Ted, 5, 6, 38; furniture designed by, 115, *116–17*, 118–19; as guest of Annenbergs, 62; interiors and, 30; Steuben glass collection and, 93, 96
Grand Hotel (movie), 118
Grant, Cary, 4
Greenberg, Clement, 79
Gropius, Walter, 59
Gross Clinic (Eakins), 158
Grosz, George, 90
Guanyin (Goddess of Mercy) figure (porcelain, Qing dynasty), *144*, 149
guest rooms, 7–8, 54–55, *55*

H

Haines, William S., 5, 6–8, 34–35, 38, 50; Bloomingdale house and, 18; building process and, 21; Chinese art and, 129–31, 133, 149; furniture designed by, 115, *116–17*, 118–19, 132; as guest of Annenbergs, 62; as guest of Hearst, 41; Hollywood Regency style of, 6–7, 118; interiors and, 30; painting collections in design plans, 40; Steuben glass collection and, 93, 96
Hajdu, Étienne, 67, 70, 77
Haley, Alex, 89
Hamilton, Lady Emma, 100
Hamilton, Sir William, 100
Hammarskjöld, Dag, 94
Harvey, Joseph, 22, 28
Haupt, Enid A., 40, 64, 130
Haupt, Ira, 130
Havlik, Ladislav, 103
Hawkes, Thomas, 95
Hawksmoor, Nicholas, 65
Hazen, Lita, 130
Hazen, Joseph, 130
Hearst, William Randolph, 1, 41, 115
Heath, Edward, 97
Hemingway, Ernest, 88–89
Hepworth, Barbara, 75
Hindu temple door panels, *124–25*, 125–27, *126*, *127*
Hirshhorn, Joseph, 68
Hirzel, Georg, 74
Holden, William, 4
Hollywood movie industry, 4, 6, 118

Hollywood Regency style, 6–7, 30, 118
Honour, Hugh, 133
Hope, Bob, 4, 61, 157, 158
Höroldt, Johann Gregorius, 111
Hostess Chair, 119
Houghton, Arthur Amory, Jr., 95, 96, 98, 101, 102
Hoving, Thomas, 60, 131
Howard, David, 142
Humes, John, 96

I

Impressionist paintings, 40, 50, 71, 129; given to Metropolitan Museum, 83; interior décor and, 132; moved from Inwood to Sunnylands, 131
interiors, 30, *31–33*
Inwood house, 4, 11
Inwood Room, in plan of main house, *42*
irrigation system, 21, *21*

J

jade carvings, *128*, 129, 130
Jaffe, Evelyn and William, 130
Jaina style figurine, *120–21*, 121–22, *123*
jar, ovoid (celadon, Ming dynasty), 140, *140*
Jensen, Georg, 113–15, 118
Johnson, Lady Bird, 60
Jones, Archibald Quincy, 5, 6, 8, 34–35; central atrium design, 18; commissions sponsored by Annenbergs and, 65; interiors and, 30; landscaping and, 28, 29; Maya theme and, 7–8, 11, 38; modernist design and, 41; Rodin sculpture and, 46, 71; windows and, 24; Wright and, 60
Jones, Elaine K., 65
Jones, Frances, 5
Journal du Garde-meuble, 100

K

Kangxi emperor (China), 132, 142, 153, 154
Kaufmann, Edgar, 4, 65
Kent, William, 100
Kermesse (Rubens), 74
King, Susan B., 97–98
The Kiss (Rodin), 74
kitchen, 40, 59
klismos chair, 119
Knoedler Gallery (New York), 130
Kup, Karl, 98–99

L

lakes, interconnecting, 11, 28
landscape (*cloisonné*, Ming dynasty), *130*
La Quinta Hotel, 4
Large Glass, or, The Bride Stripped Bare by Her Bachelors, Even (Duchamp), 91
laundry, 59
Leaf on Crystal (Arp), 68, *71*, 75
Le Corbusier (Charles Edouard Jeanneret-Gris), 4, 59
Léger, Fernand, 98
Levertov, Denise, 101
library, 40
Liets, Louis I. (Bud), 34
living area, main: changes to, 38; fireplace, 46, *48–49*; furnishing plan, *31*; interior décor, 30; paintings in, 40; size (square feet), *41*; spaces leading to guest pavilion, 55
Lock, Matthias, 100
Lock and Copeland, 100
Lokapalas ("Heavenly Kings"), figures of, 146
Lord & Taylor, 118
Los Angeles, city of, 4, 5, 6

M

Madoura pottery, 115
Maillard, Léon, 74
main house: approach to, 42, *43*, 44; construction of, *26–27*; courtyards and, 40; elevation, 8, 19, *20–21*; exterior views, *34–36*; model, 22; plan, *9*, *13–19*, 35, *42*; prospective view, *7*; serving area, 15, *18*
Martin, Mary, 158
Martin, Simon, 122
Marx, Harpo, 4
Mary II, queen of England, 132
Mather, Louis, 74
Mathison, Jean Hayden, 6, 30
Matisse, Henri, 67, 95, 98
Maya theme, 8, 11, 34; columns in arrival court, 38, *39*, 42, 44, 67, *69*; Jaina style figurine, *120–21*, 121–22, *123*
Mayer, Louis B., 6
McCoy, Esther, 7
Meissen covered jars, 110–11, *111*
Las Meninas (Velázquez), 88
metalware, enameled, 149, *150–52*, 152–55, *153*, *154*
Metropolitan Museum of Art (New York), 40, 60, 61, 146; Annenbergs' donations of art to, 83; Chinese ceramics in, 133, 142; Steuben glass and, 98, 99
Mies van der Rohe, 59
The Mill (Wyeth), 85

Miller, Mary, 122
modernism, 4, 8, 68, 69, 81; furniture design, 118; Steuben glass and, 95
Monet, Claude, 83
Montebello, Philippe de, 61
monteith (Qing dynasty), *135*, 142
Moore, Marianne, 101
Morgan, J. Pierpont, 132–33, 144
Morrison, Michael, 6, 30
Müller, Frantz Heinrich, 112

N

National Gallery of Art (Washington), 99
Native Americans, 68
Nelson, Lord, 100
Neoclassical style, French, 108
Neutra, Richard, 4
New Year's Eve parties, 61, *63*, 165
New York Public Library, 98, 99
Nixon, Patricia, 60
Nixon, Richard, 60
Noguchi, Isamu, 95

O

officials, figures of (Tang dynasty), *136, 139, 145*, 145–46
O'Keeffe, Georgia, 95, 98
Oldenburg, Claes, 79
Ordóñez, Antonio, 88–89
Owl Friend, 69

P

Palm Beach, Fla., 1, 4
Palm Springs, Calif., 4, 5
Palm Springs Desert Museum, 81
Paris Exposition (1925), 118, 119
Parker, John, 100
pavilion, guest, 11, 13, 18, 22, 53, 55; artwork in game room, 68; dining room linked to, 39; furnishing plan, *19*
Peacock (Bertoia), 40, 53, 67, 71, 80, *80*
Peale, Rembrandt, 83–85
Philadelphia, city of: Annenbergs' home near, 4, 11, 38, 71, 105, 145; *Philadelphia Inquirer*, 1, 115; Philadelphia Museum of Art, 61
Picador on Horseback (Picasso), 83, 87–89, *88*
Picasso, Pablo, 83, 90, 105, 146; bullfighting and, 88–89; plate decorated by, 115, *115*
Picasso: Toros y Toreros (Picasso and Dominguín), 88
Pittendrigh, Ann, 96, 97

Pitts, William, 105
plate, decorated by Picasso, 115, *115*
Plohn, Mrs. Jay, 105
Poetry Society of America, 101
Pollard, Don, 99–101
Polsky, Cynthia Hazen, 130
porcelain, Chinese, 129, 132, *134–35*, 141–43
Portrait of Walter Annenberg (Wyeth), 85–87, *86, 87*
Post-Impressionist paintings, 40, 50, 71, 129; given to Metropolitan Museum, 83; interior décor and, 132; moved from Inwood to Sunnylands, 131
Powell, Colin, 158
Powell, William, 4
Pre-Columbian architecture, 8, 11
Pre-Columbian Art of Mexico and Central America (Von Winning), 122
Preedy, Joseph, 105
Price, Art, 67, 68, 70

Q

Qianlong emperor (China), 153–60
qing (celadon) glaze, on ceramics, 140
Queen Mother, 57, *57*

R

Rafn, Aage, 119
Ralph M. Chait Galleries (New York), 130
Ramié, Georges and Suzanne, 115
Rancho Mirage, Calif., 4, 35, 71, 145
Reagan, Nancy, 60, 62, 85
Reagan, Ronald, 60–62, *63*, 70, 85
Reflecting Space (Agam), 80
Renoir, Pierre-Auguste, 83
Reynolds, Joshua, 79
Ridinger, Johan Elias, 142
Rilke, Rainer Maria, 74
Rishel, Joseph J., 61
Robinson-Jeffers, John, 101
Robsjohn-Gibbings, T. H., 119
Rockefeller, John D., Jr., 135
Rockefeller, Nelson, 144
Rococo style, 100
Rodin, Auguste, 45, 50, 67, 78, 79
roofs, 8, 18; of atrium, 46; in model, 22, *22*
roof tiles, rabbit-form (Ming dynasty), *137*
Room of Memories, 40, 68, 95; inscribed photographs in, *56, 57, 57*; paintings in, 83–87; Steuben glass in, 78
Roots (Haley), 89
Roots Odyssey (Bearden), 90
Rorimer, James J., 99

Rossi, Paul, 68, 70, 71
Roto-Reliefs (Duchamp), 79
Roy, Jamini, 99
royalty, English, 50, 57, *57*, 61, 113; decorative arts and, 9; Steuben glass collection and, 97
Rubens, Peter Paul, 74
Rudier, François, 72
Ruhlmann, Jacques-Émile, 118
Rundell, Bridge & Rundell, 110
Rundell, Edmond Walker, 110
Rundell, Philip, 111

S

Saint-Gaudens, Augustus, 79
Saito, Kiyoshi, 94
sancai ceramics (Tang dynasty), 141, *141*, 145, 146
San Simeon (Hearst Castle), 41
Saunders, Harry, 5, 11, 60; building costs and, 21; dining room changes and, 39–40; mausoleum pavilion and, 65
Sayings of Confucius (Pollard and Cho), *94*
Schelling, Peter, 103
Schifando, Peter, 6, 38
Scott, Randolph, 4
Screen Guide, 4
sculpture, Chinese: architectural, decorative, and religious, 146, *147–48*, 149; ceramic, 135, *136–41*, 143–44, *144*; mortuary, 144–46, *145*
sculpture, Western modernist, 40, 50, 67–68, *68–71, 70–71*; kinetic (moving), 79–81, *80, 81*; Parisian (twentieth-century), 74; Rodin, *72, 72–74, 73*
Sculpture Classique (Arp), *68*, 75, 77
seating alcove, 46, *47*, 50, *50*
Seidel, Alexander, 103
service à la française, 100, 109
service wing, 59
Shore, Dinah, 4
Shou (longevity) characters, *153*, 154, *154*
Simon, Harriet, 5
Simplicité Sinueuse (Arp), 75, 77
Sinatra, Frank, 4, 61, 157, 165
site plan, *9, 10*, 11, *13*
Situations (Agam), 80, 81, *81*
Skelton, Red, 4
skylights, 41, 46, 50, 57
Smith II, Benjamin, 109, 110
Souvenir d'Athènes (Arp), 71, *71*, 75, 77
Spanish colonial style, 4
Spencer, Lady Diana, 97
Square Wave (Agam), 67, *69*, 71, 80, 81
staff, serving, 8, 11, 18–19, *24–25*, 41, 60
Stassen, Harold, 98
Stele III (Giacometti), 79

Steuben glass collection, 38, 46, 50, *50*; Annenbergs and Steuben, 95–98; *Asian Artists in Crystal* series, *92–94*, 93, 96–101, *99–100*; *Belted Kingfisher*, 97; brief history of Steuben glass, 95; "British Artists in Crystal" exhibition, 98; *Carrousel of the Sea* (Thompson), 93, 96, 97, 103; *Chinese Pavilion* (Pollard, Seidel, Erlacher, Feron), 93, *94*, 97, 103, *103*; *The Crusaders*, 97; *Eagle*, 93; *Excalibur*, 93; *Great Explorers* series, 93, 95, 102; *Hernando Cortes*, 102; *Islands in Crystal* series, 93, 95, 102; *Masterworks* series, 93, 97, 102–3, *103*; *Poetry in Crystal* series, 93, 95, *101*, 101; *Romance of the Rose* (Pollard), 93, *94*, 97, 103; *Thousand and One Nights*, 97; *The Unicorn and the Maiden* (Pollard, Seidel, Havlik, Schelling), 93, *94*, 96, 97, 103, *103*
stools, Ming dynasty, *152*
Storr, Paul, 108, 110
Stuart, Gilbert, 84
Sunnylands: aerial view, *2–3*; building process, 22, *22–23*, 34–35; changes (after 1966), 38–41; descriptions of, 60; designs and designers of, 1, 5–7; guests, 60–62, 157–65; landscaping, 8, 11, 13, 15, 28, 28–29, *29*, 158; naming of, 34–35; Venetian quality of, 157–65. *See also specific rooms, features, and collections*
Sunnylands (Agam), 80
swimming pool, 8, 18, 28, *28*, 54, *55*

T

Tamarisk Country Club, 4
teapot/water dropper (Qing dynasty), *133*

tennis courts, 28
terrace, *52*, *53*, 67
Thatcher, Denis, 61
Thatcher, Margaret, 61
Thompson, George, 99, 103
Three by Six Double Frame Interplay (Agam), 80
Toddy jugs, 143
tomb guardians (earthenware, Tang dynasty), 131, *131*, *136*, *138*, 145, 146
Tor de Schiavi (Rome), 65
Torso (Arp), 74, 75, *75*, 77, 79
tray (1807–8), *104–5*, *109*, 109–10
trellises, 8, 19, 46
Truman, Harry, 95
tureen (Jensen), 113–15, *114*
TV Guide, 89
Twentieth Century-Fox, 6

U

University of Southern California, 6, 15, 65
Untitled (Agam), 80

V

Vanbrugh, John, 59
Velázquez, Diego, 88
Vickrey, Robert, 101
Vietor, Alexander D., 102
Villon, Jacques (Gaston Duchamp), 83, 90–91
Von Winning, Hasso, 123
Vrindavan (India), "Mughal temple" at, 125, 126
Vuillard, Édouard, 71

W

Wakelin, Edward, 106
walls, 8, *8*, 41; planting areas along, 40; revised plans, 18; Room of Memories, 57
"Walter," *128*, 129, 131
Warner, Jack, 4, 6
Warner Brothers, 6
Washington, George, 83–85, *84*, 87
water buffalo ["Walter"] (jadeite carving), *128*, 129, 131
Waugh, Sidney, 95
Wemple, Emmet, 15
Whistler, James McNeill, 132
Whitehouse, David, 96–97
Widener, Joseph, 133
Wildenstein Gallery (New York), 130
Wilhite, Rolla J., 15, 28–30, 64
William Haines Inc., 6
Williams, E. Stewart, 4, 81
Williams and Williams, 37
Wilson, Dick, 8, 11, 15, 28, 64
windows, 11, 24, 57. *See also* skylights
Winfield House (London), 65, 96, 105
Wolf Soldier Band, 68
Wright, Frank Lloyd, 8, 59, 60, 65
Wyeth, Andrew, 57, 83, 85
Wynnewood neighborhood (Philadelphia), 4, 131, 145

Y

Ying Zheng, first emperor of China, 144
Yongzheng, emperor of China, 142, 153

ACKNOWLEDGMENTS

On behalf of the scholars represented here, I would like to express our deep appreciation to Leonore Annenberg for her kind and generous assistance. Over an extended period of many months she graciously allowed us to visit Sunnylands so that we might conduct the most important aspects of our research at the estate itself, and she shared memories and experiences with us that greatly enriched our narratives.

We are grateful to the many members of the Sunnylands staff who assisted with our visits and with our work, in particular Linda S. Brooks, Estate Manager; Kenneth Brooks, Grounds Manager; and Michael Comerford, Head Butler. We also wish to acknowledge staff members who provided assistance at Inwood, the Annenberg home in Wynnewood, Pennsylvania, especially Mary Baffa, Estate Manager.

Kathleen Hall Jamieson, Program and Center Director, the Annenberg Foundation Trust at Sunnylands, initiated this project; we thank her for her enthusiastic support and caring attention, as well as her enlightening foreword. In consultation with Peter Conn, Andrea Mitchell Term Professor of English (and at the time Acting Provost at the University of Pennsylvania), and Professor David B. Brownlee, Shapiro-Weitzenhoffer Chair of the History of Art at the University of Pennsylvania, Professor Jamieson determined the contents of this book and selected its contributors. We thank Professors Conn and Brownlee for their early involvement and ongoing advice as the project developed.

Staff members of the Annenberg Public Policy Center at the University of Pennsylvania have assisted in major ways with the development and coordination of this project. In particular, we wish to thank Joyce Garczynski, Project Coordinator, and her successor, Cheryl Pauley. Thanks are also due Joshua Gesell, Coordinator of Operations; Deborah G. Stinnett, Staff Director and Chief Budget Officer; Annette Price, Events Planner; Reza Cuffey and Annie Burridge, assistants to the director; Lena Wetherbee, Financial Coordinator; and Laura Jane Kordiak. Their contributions were facilitated by Kathleen Hall Jamieson in her second role, as Director of the Annenberg Public Policy Center.

During the course of my writing, I benefited greatly from information and insights provided by those involved with the original design and construction of Sunnylands. I thank Elaine K. Jones and Harry W. Saunders, AIA, from the office of A. Quincy Jones; Jean Hayden Mathison, from the office of William Haines and Ted Graber; Peter Schifando, whose firm is the successor to the office of Haines and Graber; and Rolla J. Wilhite, ASLA, who implemented the landscape design and provided valuable documentation of its extensive layout. Special thanks are due Harry Saunders, who with long and painstaking effort re-created the plan of Sunnylands as originally built and depicted for the first time a complete plan of Sunnylands as it presently exists. He donated these plans for our publication in honor of Leonore Annenberg.

Among the many archival sources the eight of us examined as part of our research, those maintained by the Annenberg Foundation Trust offices in Radnor, Pennsylvania, provided key information; we thank Dianne Lomonaco, Megan O'Hare, Danielle Khordi, and other staff members for their help. Staff members at many other archives and organizations have also earned our special thanks; these include Simon Elliott, Department of Special Collections, Charles E. Young Research Library, University of California at Los Angeles, and his co-workers who facilitated access to the A. Quincy Jones archive; Janice Lyle, then Director of the Palm Springs Art Museum (now Center Director, Annenberg Foundation Trust at Sunnylands), and Sidney Williams, Associate Curator of Architecture, Palm Springs Art Museum; Joseph Baillio, Wildenstein & Co., New York; Antoinette Le Normand-Romain and Virginie Delaforge, Musée-Rodin, Paris; in Corning, New York, Peter Drobny, designer, Steuben Glass; Michelle Cotton, Director, and Kris Gable, Research Consultant, Corning Incorporated Department of Archives and Records Management

(CIDARM); Gail Bardhan, Reference Librarian, Rakow Library of The Corning Museum of Glass; and Marie McKee, President and CEO, Steuben Glass. We also thank Jason Sun, Associate Curator, Department of Asian Art, and Suzanne G. Valenstein, Research Scholar, both at The Metropolitan Museum of Art, New York; Florence Chan and Elizabeth Naccarato, both at Sotheby's, New York; the staff of Eskenazi Ltd., London; and Margaret Kaelin Gristina, formerly of The Chinese Porcelain Company, New York; and Frances Z. Yuan, Princeton University.

We also wish to convey our gratitude to many other individuals who have provided much appreciated assistance and support, especially Cynthia Hazen Polsky, Walter Annenberg's niece. At the University of Pennsylvania, we are indebted to Nancy S. Steinhardt, Professor of East Asian Studies and Curator of Chinese Art; Professor Michael Leja, Department of Art History; Simon Martin, research specialist, University of Pennsylvania Museum; Robert D. Jamieson, P.E.; and Suzanne M. Hyndman, Maureen Anne McDougall, and Bruce Campbell of the University of Pennsylvania. In addition, we thank R. Craig Miller, Curator of Design Arts, Indianapolis Museum of Art; Florence R. Rossi, wife of sculptor Paul Rossi; Professor Pika Ghosh, University of North Carolina, Chapel Hill; Benjamin B. Bolger, Miguel de Baca, and John Vick, research assistants for Gwendolyn DuBois Shaw; and Sarah Handler, independent scholar of Chinese art.

The University of Pennsylvania Press has been involved with this project from its inception; for encouragement and welcome advice, we acknowledge in particular Eric F. Halpern, Director; Jo Joslyn, Art and Architecture Editor; and Mariana Martinez, her assistant, for their dedicated efforts. We owe particular thanks to Graydon Wood, photographer for the Philadelphia Museum of Art, whose long hours at Sunnylands led to the handsome images in this book. We also thank Ned Redway for his supplemental photography and David Glomb, Palm Springs photographer, for his consultation. For her remarkable patience and understanding assistance we give special thanks to Anne Hoy, our first editor; Noreen O'Connor-Abel, the Penn Press project editor; and Judith Stagnitto Abbate, the designer of this book.

The late Anne d'Harnoncourt (1943–2008), George D. Widener Director of the Philadelphia Museum of Art, and Joseph J. Rishel, Gisela and Dennis Alter Senior Curator of European Painting at that same institution, give special meaning to this book through their contribution, and we thank them for their generosity. Everyone associated with this project and with the Annenberg Foundation Trust at Sunnylands mourns the loss of Anne d'Harnoncourt. Finally, we wish to thank the Trustees of the Annenberg Foundation Trust at Sunnylands who commissioned this book, gave the project their unwavering support, and provided valued editorial contributions.

DAVID G. DE LONG, *on behalf of*
Suzanne Glover Lindsay
Gwendolyn DuBois Shaw
M. J. Madigan
Donna Corbin
Jeremy A. Sabloff
Michael W. Meister
Virginia Bower